ADVANCE PRAISE FOR

Food Stories:

Navigating the Academy with Cultural Lessons from the Kitchen

"Food is so critical to our cultural survival. In the most deliciously powerful ways, *Food Stories* illustrates how food - as an expression of community practice - helps us battle alienation and fight for justice in higher education. A refreshing and delightfully different flavor of academic writing, *Food Stories* serves up wonderful examples of how we can love ourselves and each other within institutions that won't love us back."

—Wayne Au, Dean and Professor in the University of Washington Bothell School of Educational Studies and longtime *Rethinking Schools* author and editor

"*Food Stories* is a thoughtful anthology that uses food as a powerful metaphor for connection, reflection, and justice. The book interweaves memories, cultural traditions, and teaching practices, revealing how food nourishes not only the body but also the mind and soul. This collection shares ancestral recipes and heartfelt stories, offering lessons in building kinship, living authentically, and creating spaces of equity through the shared language of food."

—Yolanda Sealey-Ruiz, Ph.D.
Professor, Teachers College, Columbia University
Author of *Love from the Vortex & Other Poems* and *The Peace Chronicles*

"This volume offers readers a beautiful invitation to the risks and creativity of scholarly and pedagogical work in education through the common lens of food. The parallels these chapters offer between foodways, stories of family and culture, and pedagogical and scholarly practices in the academy, remind us all that at its best, education is a human and humanizing practice that can foster welcoming, mutual understanding, and dignity. I highly recommend this volume, particularly for those who are feeling disaffected from academe. These lovely stories remind readers that we can create hospitality through our creative offerings of food and our professional work."

—Sue Ellen Henry, Ph.D.
Professor at Bucknell University and Immediate Past-President, American Educational Studies Association

"*Food Stories: Navigating the Academy with Cultural Lessons from the Kitchen* is a compelling anthology that beautifully intertwines the art of cooking with the journey through academia. Edited by T. Jameson Brewer and Cleveland Hayes II, this book offers a rich tapestry of narratives from diverse scholars who share how culinary traditions have shaped their academic paths. Each chapter is a testament to the power of food as a source of resilience, community, and cultural identity. A must-read for anyone seeking to understand the profound connections between food, culture, and education. This book is both heartwarming and intellectually nourishing."

—John P. Broome, Ph.D.
Clinical Associate Professor at Purdue University

"As someone who considers themselves a true "foodie," always seeking vegan restaurants with my friend and colleague Dr. Kofi Lomotey during conferences like AERA and UCEA, endorsing this book feels natural. Cooking has been a part of my life since I was very young, and despite being a vegetarian, I take pride in being quite handy in the kitchen. Preparing meals often serves as a form of stress relief, a way to center myself amidst the complexities and demands of my role as Provost. After challenging days, I often find solace in a Kalamazoo eatery, savoring the connection between food and community.

Food Stories weaves together narratives that resonate deeply with these experiences. For example, "The Academic Buffet" explores balancing the complexity of academic life with the lessons learned through cooking, such as portioning and creating meaningful connections, much like perfecting an empanada. Similarly, "Soul/le Credentials" reflects on the power of collard greens as a symbol of cultural resistance and academic participation, a theme that resonates with the intersection of food, identity, and resilience. Another chapter, "Critical Lessons Learned While Making Cinnamon Rolls with My Son," underscores how cooking fosters patience and builds relationships, lessons that extend to both life and academia.

Traveling the world has given me the chance to explore diverse culinary traditions, trying new restaurants and dishes that inspire both my palate and my perspective. This book, with its focus on navigating academia through cultural lessons from the kitchen, resonates deeply with my belief that food is not just sustenance—it's a bridge to culture, creativity, and resilience. For all these reasons, I wholeheartedly recommend this insightful and deliciously reflective work."

—Julian Vasquez Heilig, Ph.D.
Provost, Western Michigan University

Food Stories

Culinary Canvas: A Series on Integrating the Arts and Food into Higher Education

T. Jameson Brewer and Cleveland Hayes, Editors

Culinary Canvas: A Series on Integrating the Arts and Food into Higher Education is a book series that explores the innovative integration of arts and food into higher education. This series aims to inspire a paradigm shift in academia, advocating for a more holistic, creative, and inclusive approach to learning, teaching, researching, serving, and existing in the academy. The **Culinary Canvas** series will serve as a guide for educators, administrators, and policymakers in higher education, providing them with the inspiration and practical tools to transform their institutions into more vibrant, engaging, and inclusive spaces for learning. It will argue that by embracing the arts and food, higher education can become a more enriching and fulfilling experience for all students.

Titles in the Series

Food Stories: Navigating the Academy with Cultural Lessons from the Kitchen
edited by T. Jameson Brewer and Cleveland Hayes (2025)

Edible Tales: Folklore, Myths, and Food Narratives in Higher Learning
edited by Mila Zhu and Sarah Morrison (2026)

Recipes of Motherhood: Cultural Narratives in Academia
edited by Mila Zhu and Sarah Morrison (2026)

Tasting Education: Theoretical Considerations of Taste Across Discourses
edited by Laura M. Jewett and Zulitazhira Hinojosa

Authors and collection editors who wish to have their projects considered for publication in the series are encouraged to submit a prospectus (https://zfrmz.com/rmlvGq7xgL2RTgPkByk9) to the series editors, T. Jameson Brewer (Jameson.Brewer@ung.edu) or Cleveland Hayes (clehayes@iu.edu).

Food Stories

Navigating the Academy with Cultural Lessons from the Kitchen

EDITED BY T. Jameson Brewer
and Cleveland Hayes II

Myers Education Press

Gorham, Maine

Myers Education Press

Published by Myers Education Press, LLC
P.O. Box 424
Gorham, ME 04038

Myers Education Press is an academic publisher specializing in books, e-books, and digital content in the field of education. All of our books are subjected to a rigorous peer review process and produced in compliance with the standards of the Council on Library and Information Resources.

Library of Congress Cataloging-in-Publication Data available from Library of Congress.

13-digit ISBN 978-1-9755-0698-8 (paperback)
13-digit ISBN 978-1-9755-0699-5 (library networkable e-edition)
13-digit ISBN 978-1-9755-0700-8 (consumer e-edition)

Printed in the United States of America.

All first editions printed on acid-free paper that meets the American National Standards Institute Z39-48 standard.

Books published by Myers Education Press may be purchased at special quantity discount rates for groups, workshops, training organizations, and classroom usage. Please call our customer service department at 1-800-232-0223 for details.

Cover design by Teresa Lagrange.

Visit us on the web at **www.myersedpress.com** to browse our complete list of titles.

DEDICATION

TJB: For Mamma, who fed my childhood and my life . . . and who also happened to cook for me.

CH: For the women in my life who not only taught me how to cook but also feed my hunger and my soul. My grandmothers Carnell Jones Brown and Olivia Durr Hayes Smith and my mother Charlie Ann Hayes, these three were also teachers who also helped to frame my pedagogy as a classroom teacher.

CONTENTS

INTRODUCTION

T. JAMESON BREWER & CLEVELAND HAYES

Jameson

For me, like most of us, food and cooking has always been a staple conception in my life but not in the same way throughout the years. While food was, at times, a gut-wrenching reminder of the abject poverty of my childhood, some food during that time served as a symbolic moment of peace and safety from the extreme physical abuse I suffered at the hands of my stepfather. While I am fortunate to have survived (though I often struggle with survivor's guilt), I have a lifelong neurological speech disorder that manifests as a strained voice—spasmodic dysphonia—as a result of that abuse. While "struggle food" is a concept that is both cherished and spoken of tongue-in-cheek by many, it has a unique ability to ground me in the experiences that culminated into who I am today. A soft taco from Taco Bell has the power to transport me back to a time of painful memories where my mother, half-brother, half-sister, and I would scour the car for just enough loose change to buy a soft taco and then split it four ways. At the same time, saltine crackers and milk (eaten like cereal—don't knock it until you try it) immediately transport me to my grandmother's house, which was my eternal place of safety.

The very best memories of my childhood revolve around my grandmother's kitchen. Without a doubt, this was a result of the respite from the abuse I experienced from my stepfather but it also arises from the mouth-watering Southern comfort food she made every single day, from fried rabbit and collard greens to a vast array of sweets. In my grandmother's kitchen I was not only nourished and safe but I experienced what it meant to provide comfort and care for others through food. While I took an interest in cooking a short time before her passing, I find that I now spend more time in the kitchen preparing meals for others than I did before. In some ways, I imagine that I am living out her memory through my actions in ways that may not be fully understood yet by myself or those for whom I prepare a meal.

What does it mean to think intentionally about exploring the academy through the lens of cooking and food? There are some fairly straightforward ways to consider the lessons that can be gleaned from the kitchen and the academy. Of course, a recipe helps a cook break down the steps and tasks associated with cooking a meal in the way that a scholar should approach a project by breaking it down into portions and timelines, relying on collaborators to work on their portions in the way a sous chef relies on the saucier or the poissonnier to each do their respective jobs to bring a dish together. For me, I have worked very hard at developing the skills associated with mise-en-place in both my work in the kitchen and the work I do as an academic. The French chef's disposition of "everything in its place" has been one of the "secrets" of my work to this point in my career—a clean workspace, everything laid out and in order before the work begins, as well as a detailed plan of accomplishing the task at hand. It is easy to know where you stand with a recipe or a paper at any given point if you have a clear roadmap and all of the materials you need for the job. Without such an approach, most dishes and papers are doomed to starts and stops, unimportant garnishes and tangents, and a debilitating sense of being overwhelmed. Cooking and writing can both be messy endeavors and it is okay to get some flour on the floor or have a sentence in a published piece that causes you to cringe years later. What matters most is that the cake, and the paper, get done and done with the highest fidelity you have to offer at that time. We are all evolving as cooks, writers, and educators and we get better by doing the work that offers us insights into how we could—or should—improve. My approach to smoking a brisket for 17 hours is very different from my approach to a highly technical French cooking method. In the same way, my approach to varied academic projects varies to meet the demands of skill, focus, and output expected by the aims of the project. But across all types of cooking and writing I never begin without a detailed plan, clear expectations for myself and any collaborators, I take notes during and after projects so that I can understand what worked and what requires improvement. Perhaps most importantly, I am patient with myself and I give myself not only the space to understand where improvement is warranted but the permission to improve. I do not consider myself to be a pitmaster or a Michelin star chef, nor do I consider myself to be the best educator or author. On the flip side, I think it is important to work through and throw off as much of the imposter syndrome as you can. While I may not be a pitmaster, I know that my BBQ is better than (fill-in-the-blank BBQ chain) and I know that my writing, while never perfect, is better than allowing a project to go unwritten.

Cleveland

My childhood was deeply rooted in the warmth of my grandmother's and mother's kitchens, where I spent countless hours watching them cook. These kitchens were the heart of our home, places where love, tradition, and life lessons were kneaded into every dish. I remember the rhythmic sounds of chopping, the sizzle of ingredients meeting the pan, and the comforting aromas that filled the air, signaling that something special was being prepared.

As a child, I was captivated by the way my grandmother and mother moved with such confidence and grace, their hands expertly measuring, mixing, and molding ingredients into meals that brought our family together. They taught me that cooking was more than just a task—it was a form of expression, a way to show love and care for others.

I learned the importance of patience as I waited for dough to rise or a stew to simmer. I understood the value of precision and the beauty of improvisation when a recipe called for it. These moments in the kitchen were my first lessons in creativity, resilience, and the importance of tradition, laying the foundation for the person I would become.

The culinary wisdom imparted by the women in my life has deeply influenced my journey as an educator. Eating homemade biscuits, molasses, and bacon at breakfast during my weekend stay at Big Mama's was more than just sustenance—it was a lesson in patience, creativity, and care. This grandmother taught me that food is a medium through which love is expressed and cultures are preserved. This understanding of food as a conduit for connection has translated directly into my teaching philosophy.

During Christmas dinner in Holly Springs, Mississippi at the grandmother's house I called Mommie, where she would prepare probably the best chocolate cake, cornbread dressing, and macaroni and cheese, is where I connect my approaches to education and teaching like a cherished recipe, which by the way we never followed but still didn't stop the careful preparation, adaptability, and an understanding of the diverse tastes and needs of my students. Just as a recipe is adjusted to suit the ingredients at hand or the preferences of those at the table, I tailor my teaching methods to meet my students where they are, recognizing that each student brings their unique flavor to the learning environment.

I had never been able to cook cornbread dressing until this past Thanksgiving when my mom walked me through over the phone how to cook it. She showed the patience required to perfect a dish that has mirrored the patience I practice with my students. The creativity involved in making a meal from whatever is available has inspired me to be resourceful and innovative in my teaching methods. The communal aspect of food—where stories, traditions, and values are shared—has influenced my commitment to creating a classroom environment that fosters collaboration, respect, and mutual learning.

Ultimately, the food traditions shaped by the women in my life have not only nourished my body but have also fed my soul, guiding me to be an educator who values connection, creativity, and the continuous sharing of knowledge.

About This Book

You hold in your hands an intentionally curated selection of narratives from folk across the varied levels of the academy that lay bare for you, dear reader, deeply personal explorations of the intersection of food, culture, and the academy. The aim of this project was twofold. First, we wanted to provide a space for scholars at different levels of the career to think reflectively, intentionally, and with respect toward their own personal, and familial, practices and culture sur rounding food. As the academy becomes increasingly siloed, and that is saying something given its long history of siloing, and evermore competitive for jobs, publications, grants, teaching schedules, etc., we often find that discussions of the thing that connects us all—food—provides not only an opportunity to find common ground as well as an opportunity to share differences in food and culture but a respite from the "grind" of what it means to be in the academy as a student and faculty member. The connecting thread for many families centers around meals, and many of the most important, difficult, happy, and sad conversations often find the kitchen table as the stage. Food as a centering aspect of culture and our humanity provides nourishment for our bodies as well as an opportunity for creative expression, joy, learning, and growth. It is on these lines that the second focus of the project took aim. In what ways can we think about what it means to do the work in academia *through* the lens of food and cooking? What lessons can we translate from cooking a recipe into navigating what it means to be a graduate student? A new faculty member on the tenure track? Or just simply maintaining our humanity and culture in an environment that often works to dehumanize us?

This project has been a project of joy and meaningful reflection for all of us that have been involved. A fun project that does not foray into deep data analysis and program evaluation but, rather, holds space for the authors to share deeply personal insights into their childhoods, family and culture, and what it means to them as a scholar but, more importantly, as a human. We received far more submissions than we could reasonably include here as well as notes of thanks from many others who simply expressed gratitude for the concept of, and the space given to, this project. We trust that your reading of these chapters will not only bring you joy but that you will find connection with many of the experiences shared within and a deep reverence for the experiences and cultures in which you do not have knowledge. That, in our view, properly satisfies the first aim we set out to achieve. Further, we do hope that you are able to consider, and implement, some of the pragmatic insights shared about navigating the academy through this unique lens of food. As the first book in the Culinary Canvas series, we are eager to continue this conversation of reflective practice and the intersection of new ways of exploring what it means to do the work that we do in higher education. From the Editors, Jameson and Cleveland, we wish you happy cooking and bon appétit.

So that our readers can experience photos that accompany the chapters and recipes in their fullness and complexity, please visit https://tjamesonbrewer.com/food-stories to view photos from the chapters as well as view additional recipes and resources that the editors and authors hope you will try.

CHAPTER 1

The Academic Buffet: Navigating the Balance Between Education and Empanadas

MIA FURMAN, ANDREA ARCE-TRIGATTI,
AND DOROTA SILBER-FURMAN

Introduction

In the fast pace of the 21st century, everybody puts too much on their plate—pun intended! We all want to eat healthy: Calories in and calories out, as they say. You also need to eat your vegetables, but not potatoes, because you should watch out for carbs. Wait, do not forget to eat enough protein. Also, do not eat too much fat, but you can have the good kind. Oh! And remember again, watch your calories. Healthy eating and diet culture has thrown society for a loop, and this is not to mean throwing health out the window and eating whatever, but how do we know what is healthy with such conflicting information?

To this end, there is a common theme between healthy eating and academic learning, which clarifies why there is a disconnect between the individual and the goal, be it healthy eating or proficient learning. Personal differences cause varying diets and learning styles to give different results. Similarly, different genetic factors impact which diet is healthy, and various learning abilities influence the best learning methods for the individual. Some will eat meat and feel energized, while others will feel better on a more plant-based diet (Bojarczuk et al., 2024). Some individuals learn through note-taking, others through videos. At times kinesthetic learning is the goal and in other instances auditory or visual approaches are the most valuable ways of instruction. In the way people do not eat sugar or processed foods to be healthy, students should not put off their homework or be bombarded with busy work if they want to learn. Overall, there must be a balance for personal health and personal learning. While we do not all eat and learn the same way for positive outcomes, we have a good idea of what not to do—overfill a plate, crash diet, or always eat the same old, same old.

In this chapter we look at examples from our relationship with food that can offer insight into how to navigate the open buffet of academia in a way that is healthy, and ultimately, balanced. Specifically, this chapter presents our stories and continuous attempts for a more well-balanced plate both regarding food and education. These stories start in childhood and are rooted in our backgrounds and revolve around lessons learned with respect to putting too much literally on a plate. In the first story, we take a faculty perspective, and we look at the role of empanadas in balancing potentially full plates and how a lot of flavor can be packed into a small package, similar to educational lesson plans and content design. In the second story, we continue with the faculty perspective and reminisce how our grandmothers' full plates of familiar foods can often drag us away from trying other flavors; this is similar to academia wherein we tend to stay in our silos and limit venturing outside into other areas. In the concluding story, we take a student perspective and explore how alternating from overloading your plate and crash dieting is an unhealthy and unproductive habit that is reflective of workload balance and burnout in academia.

Background and Context

Postsecondary education is a nuanced context that can be a difficult terrain to navigate if you are unfamiliar with how to balance opportunities. For first-year students, and more profoundly for first-generation students, the college experience can pose varying challenges that shift based on the context of the institution, the region in which it is located (urban and rural), and the financial situation of the student (Kelley et al., 2023). Moreover, the cultural and social connections that the faculty or student bring may implicate the work ethic, expectations, and load that each individual takes on as part of the postsecondary experience.

For example, we all manage numerous responsibilities simultaneously as we navigate through personal and professional lives and, very often, each of us needs to focus on mental health, education, employment, childcare, self-care, nutrition, finances, and various other commitments. For educators, specifically, our roles encompass teaching students, evaluating assignments, attending meetings, conducting observations, participating in training sessions, providing mentorship, and much more (Arce-Trigatti & Silber-Furman, 2021). This is further exacerbated by ever increasing expectations to perform required duties related to teaching, service, and research, which lead to a publish-or-perish race between peers in the same field (Aliukonis et al., 2020). Opportunities in academia are endless, including those to collaborate, contribute, partner, or share your expertise as a faculty in a given area. With limited guide rails and encouragement from administrators trying to get everyone to help move a needle on a strategic plan, navigating academic expectations can truly become an endless buffet of options in which faculty can indulge.

Also, students traverse an unknown terrain of college and higher education with multiple responsibilities such as reading and writing, class attendance, and homework submission (Silber-Furman & Arce-Trigatti, 2021). When postsecondary life introduces students to a fast-paced, potentially competitive atmosphere that may be unfamiliar to them, students may begin to feel isolated or alienated in their experiences; this, in turn, could lead to low self-efficacy and increased anxiety as part of the postsecondary experience (Kelley et al., 2023; Salis Reyes & Nora, 2012; Soria & Roberts, 2021).

To effectively handle these obligations, it is crucial that we prioritize maintaining our physical health by ensuring our diet includes nutritious food and good hydration. Balancing our plate and a healthy diet can be essential in performing the day-to-day work responsibilities of teaching and studying. Just like enriching academic opportunities can fulfill and enhance the learning experience, we acknowledge the value that food plays in sustaining the energy to engage in these experiences and root our lives in the present. As postsecondary educators and students, we offer insight into our own experiences in academia and how we have connected our lessons learned through food stories that have helped us to better cope with this unique environment.

Story 1—Education and Empanadas

Empanadas typically contain a variety of culinary combinations, changes that reflect local culture, produce, and preference. The Argentine empanada, for example, can be either sweet or salty, with beef, chopped eggs, onions, and chimichurri mixed together as the filling. They can be fried or baked and are encompassed in a white flour dough filling. The Colombian empanadas, in turn, are usually smaller, made with chicken, potatoes, and sometimes red sauce filling contained within a fried yellow corn flour disc.

Privileged to have learned both traditions through family lessons and gatherings, one of the major takeaways was always to make sure to get the filling just right. This includes an understanding of the flavor, quantity of meat and vegetable fillings, and measurement of portion. Too much meat and you are basically eating a steak, too much sauce and you are eating a soggy disc soup, and too much filling and you will be left with an open, hard disc with no filling. There were several ways to gauge if ever any of these items were unproportional, including an inherent "*a ojo*" method only perfected by the most practiced *abuelas, mamás*, and *tías* in the business.

Perhaps the other lesson learned in making empanadas is how to close them. The *repulgue*, or the wonderfully intricate closures that become crispy dough delights after cooking, also determine whether your empanadas survive. In asking how to make these once, my grandmother simply said "tight, you make it tight" and then went on to visually demonstrate the technique. Leaving the borders without a *repulgue* is not an option, as the filling will slip out in the process of cooking. Simple techniques can be used, but, whatever method you use, as *abuela* said, it must be tight.

For both faculty and students, the lessons learned in cooking empanadas hold implications for designing lesson plans (faculty) and engaging with complex content (students). For one, portions, flavoring, and measurement matter. Like an empanada, semesters are encompassed in a designated number of weeks. So, for faculty—yes, the entirety of your content matter could fit into that timespan, but what does that do to the flavor of your lesson plans? Are you filling it with too much of one content? Is there a balance of spice or are you overpowering the content to your taste? Instead of overwhelming your students' palate with the variety of topics that a rich content area could offer, consider leveraging specific angles or perspectives of that content that can enhance the flavor of the overall experience for students. Think about the takeaways, the lingering flavors of the content, that will have students coming back for seconds of your bite-sized, full-impact lessons.

As for the second lesson, the idea of tightness matters here in designing content. Are there natural pauses in the semester where you can reinforce points from the content that are important? Are the pieces of the content you design fitting nicely into the space allotted in the semester? Or is it spilling over because the connections made are not holding? In deciding what stays in or is left out of the content for your semester or lesson plan, think about the connections that can be made within that experience. If you are having students stretch their cognitive processes too thin, then the *repulgue* of your lessons may not be tight enough to make the point clear. If content can be rearranged to help tighten that *repulgue*, consider moving chapters around, or making connections in class that help make your lesson plan compact and deliciously designed.

For students, the same lessons apply. In engaging with college courses, faculty may not necessarily be organizing their lessons into empanada-sized content; however, this does not mean you cannot consider how to reorganize your thoughts into measurement proportions that make sense. Perhaps a professor's recipe for connections and organization are not aligned with your preference. Consider assessing your own flavor profile and collecting your thoughts in a way that makes sense for the design of your empanada. A few other reflection questions from these lessons learned to consider with respect to studying include: when you have the choice to select your courses, are you meshing everything into a disc, or measuring and tasting for an overbalance of spices that may overextend even the strongest disc? When you are called to make connections in class, or find ways to interpret new material, are your thoughts tight? Or are you letting the filling spill out?

Leveraging skills from empanada making are useful for content design at the postsecondary level. Most content shared in this environment is meant to be complex and engaging; however, scaffolding may or may not be an implicit part of the teaching and learning process at this level. In turn, making lessons that are bite sized, appealing, and tight, like empanadas, helps. The best empanadas are preferably bite-sized samples of culinary majesty: balanced, satisfying, and digestible. Faculty and students—can the same be said of your lesson plans or course engagement? If not, consider fixing the portions and closing the dough tighter.

Story 2—Home Cooking and Silos

Imagine the smell of your grandmother's kitchen when she just finished cooking your favorite snack or meal or your mother's dinner that she used to serve on special occasions prepared and cooked just for you. For me, that experience was the smell of freshly baked *karpatka* filling up the small kitchen of my childhood home or the bite of mushroom and cabbage *pierogi* right out of the pan topped with melting, hot butter. The family recipes are often treasured in homemade cookbooks made out of notebooks that are being passed from generation to generation with utmost care and love so future loved ones have an opportunity to partake in family traditions and have a bite of a familiar, generational meal.

Often, the familiarity provides comfort as comfort foods are the go-to guilty pleasure that offer warmth and hassle-free acceptance in a world that demands so much. We reach for comfort foods, we are drawn to them as they trigger our brain's response of feeling good and welcomed. Especially now, in our modern age, when there is never enough time in the day and 24 hours never seem enough, preparing that go-to meal can be a lifesaver and an often awaited prize.

Although the tenderness of comfort food is tempting, trying new foods can be exciting, providing a sense of adventure and exploration. After a few initial weeks or months, college could feel like eating familiar foods; students decide about their major, they take the classes that go along with the program of study, and often hang out with peers already familiar to them. However, academia should also be about taking risks. Very often students have those predetermined preferences and 10-year plans that help them on the educational path; but, while it is good to experience academia in a guided manner, it is also valuable to explore other experiences that allow for growth. Maybe a student has a program of study set for a certain major, but it is that extra endorsement or that unexpected minor that excites them the most or gets them to finish their degree on time or even pursue a different career path altogether. Or maybe it is that extra course that gets them to go for the master's degree or even the doctoral degree.

We love eating familiar foods over and over again, but eating other foods can be rewarding as well. College can offer a plethora of education opportunities: diverse courses, different student organizations, university events. It is important for students to be open minded and try what *tastes* right or maybe even try out and decide that a certain opportunity is not the one. Overall, college is the time for exploration and discovery.

In terms of faculty experience, this can mean going to that conference in another area or pursuing another research topic. Interdisciplinary collaborations, although different at times, are valuable to understanding what the food is like in other departments and what condiments may complement your own teaching or research. This type of academic exploration not only assures collaboration and collegiality but also provides insights into other research fields and fosters faculty professional development.

To sum up, we all appreciate our grandmother's and mother's cooking recipes, but venturing past their kitchen walls can bring the feeling of exploration and maybe, just maybe, we discover that we opt for anew creating our own menus of food and academia altogether.

Story 3—Crash Dieting and All-You-Can-Eat

There is an ideal of the individual who has both a "hot" body and academic success. In today's fast-paced world, we all want both, and we want it now. With the rise of diet culture coexisting with academic culture, there are parallels between the two. From crash dieting and cram studying, overeating and procrastination, and extrinsic pressure but conflicting information on both, health and student struggles have more in common than first meets the eye.

The current influx of undergraduate students who have grown up with social media at their fingertips is greatly impacted by its influence. Social media has glamorized health, fitness, and academics with ideals: Every new "it girl" trend involves a healthy, successful individual, and the rise of the term "academic weapon" idealizes the person with only A's on their transcript. Diet culture, perpetuated by social media, has led many to seek their own health journeys, and as students, many of us strive towards the 4.0. However, the methods brought to us for health and academic success are convoluted with conflicting diet information and academic burnout-inducing mindsets. Many diets, like keto, vegan, paleo, carnivore, low-fat, and calories in–calories out, are preached about and scrutinized, making people believe that they are either health saviors or killers. Restrictive diets, social media, and inconsistent health advice lead to common crash dieting and overeating cycles. For a student, this noticeably parallels the academic lifestyle as there is often pressure to cram for exams or in times of high workload, only to end up with mental burnout when procrastination kicks in. Social pressure to look and do well in school leads to these normalized, unsustainable cycles.

Maybe this is why work–life balance is such a hot topic and a conundrum for many. The one-size-fits-all approach facilitates the disconnect between students with academic and health goals. Unfortunately, there is no perfect diet for everyone, but there is a perfect diet for you. Lifestyle, genetic, and even geographical factors impact what diet suits a person best. The link between an individual's genetics and nutritional needs creates a subfield of nutritional science called genomic nutrition or nutritional genomics, which analyzes genetic influences on how the body responds to nutrients and the following health outcomes. Prescribing a perfect diet ignores cultural, lifestyle, and geographic differences, which can optimize a person's health and satisfaction (Roman, Campos-Medina, & Leal-Mercado, 2024). Asking someone who is not a big meat eater to follow a carnivore diet, someone to leave behind their cultural comfort food, or someone who lives in the South to skip out on local produce in favor of a crash diet is unsustainable. Ultimately, the standardization of food is leading us down an unhealthy route where we should instead strive to use our differences to maximize health.

We all do not need to eat the same and we all do not need to learn the same either. There must be a balance when it comes to studying and workload. The academic cycle of cramming information to burnout is detrimental to student mental health and success. Similar to individualized diets, individualized learning styles can be used to maximize academic success. Like health, background factors influence how we think and learn. Furthermore, attention should be brought to the standardization of learning and the idea of busy work. Students need the space to find unique and different ways to absorb knowledge in order to augment their potential and foster growth.

To suggest an idea considered out of this world, but more like out of this time, we should slow down and take a step back, giving ourselves the space and compassion to find what works for us and not to chase an ideal, but to be our own.

Lessons Learned

Such lessons are valuable not only in dietary measures, but they are also transferable lessons that hold weight in academia. In the first story, we were introduced to empanadas and what it means to pack a punch in a doughy, crispy, mini bite. In terms of academia, for faculty, this means to reflect on your own lesson plans and how content is served to the students, making sure that it is neither soggy nor overfilled. For students, this could mean reframing how they engage in difficult topics, reorganizing ideas into palatable bites instead of confronting big ideas or challenging topics head on. In the second story we learned that familiarity with food can bring comfort, but the exploration of new foods, or new experiences in academia, can bring rewarding opportunities that can be valuable to personal and professional growth for both students and faculty alike. In our third story, we were presented with a student perspective wherein crash dieting or overeating were unhealthy and unproductive habits that are reflective of workload balance and burnout in academia. For students, it is paramount that, just as they try to keep a healthy balance with their actual diet, they engage in academic opportunities in a way that also helps them to balance their plates.

Conclusions

Although we have all presumably heard of a mystic work–life balance that needs to be worked towards as academics, it can be difficult to do so when the buffet of options offered by academia, and the pressure to consume the all-you-can-eat option, remains open in the face of a dearth of resources, a lack of certainty, and a continual push for survival (Kelley et al., 2023; Silber-Furman & Arce-Trigatti, 2021). More so than not, dietary parameters, in terms of what is consumed related to work stress, what is put on your plate in terms of work responsibilities, and what we put on others' plates in terms of student expectations and university administrative guidelines, impact how healthy one can be with respect to their academic lifestyle. We all try to find the holy grail of nutrition that would fuel not only the physical aspects to our being but also the mental and emotional dimensions needed for lifelong learning. By keeping curricula as tight as an empanada, by recognizing the equilibrium between familiarity and taking a risk, and by harmonizing one's plate, so it is neither full nor scarce, the buffet of academia can be strategically managed, and enjoyed, by both faculty and students alike. Bon appétit!

References

Aliukonis, V., Poškutė, M., & Gefenas, E. (2020). Perish or publish dilemma: Challenges to responsible authorship. *Medicina (Kaunas, Lithuania), 56*(3), 123. https://doi.org/10.3390/medicina56030123.

Arce-Trigatti, A., & Silber-Furman, D. (2021). Riding the pan(aca)demic waves: A one year portrait of two educator's experiences teaching in higher education through the 21st century pandemic. In S. McCarther (Ed.), *Snapshots of History Portraits of the 21st Century Pandemic* (pp. 1–15). Special Edition of the American Educational History Journal.

Bojarczuk, A., Egorova, E.S., Dzitkowska-Zabielska, M., & Ahmetov, I. I.(2024). Genetics of exercise and diet-induced fat loss efficiency: A systematic review. *Journal of Sports Science & Medicine, 23*(1), 236–257. doi:10.52082/jssm.2024.236.

Kelley, J., Arce-Trigatti, A., & Haynes, A. (2023). A road less traveled: Possible selves as a theory for mentoring first-generation students in postsecondary education. *Journal of First-generation Student Success, 3*(3), 193–206. https://doi.org/10.1080/26906015.2023.2210774.

Roman S, Campos-Medina L, Leal-Mercado L. Personalized nutrition: the end of the one-diet-fits-all era. *Frontiers in Nutrition, 11*(1370595). doi: 10.3389/fnut.2024.1370595.

Salis Reyes, N., & Nora, A. (2012). *Lost among the data: A review of Latino first generation college students* [White paper]. Hispanic Association of Colleges and Universities. https://vtechworks.lib.vt.edu/bitstream/handle/10919/83075/LostAmongtheData.pdf?sequence=1.

Soria, K., & Roberts, B. (2021). The benefits of living on campus for low-income, first-generation students' belonging, perceptions of campus climate, and resilience. *Journal of First-generation Student Success, 1*(2), 111–126. https://doi.org/10.1080/26906015.2021.1926373.

Silber-Furman, D. & Arce-Trigatti A. (2021) Empathy and flexibility in teaching in the era of COVID-19. *Kappa Delta Pi, Teacher Advocate*, The Quarterly Magazine for Professional Teachers. http://digital.watkinsprinting.com/publication/?i=706621&p=10.

CHAPTER 2

Ordinary Ingredients: Hosting as a Pedagogical Practice

MARK STERN

The Visit

What a lark! What a plunge!

— Virginia Woolf, *Mrs. Dalloway*

While not the first words of the novel (those are also quite good: "Mrs. Dalloway said she would buy the flowers herself" (Woolf, 1925/1981, p. 3)), I always think of them as such (they are, in fact, like the fourth line). Mrs. Dalloway—Clarissa—the central character in Woolf's postwar tome about, among other things, empire, gender, capital, biopolitics, and the new world order, is stepping out into a London morning on the day of a party she is hosting for the city's bourgeoisie (she refers to the party later as "an offering" (p. 121)). Mr. Dalloway—Richard—is a member of Parliament and not only will his colleagues be there, but so will members of the aristocracy and monied class, some of whom Clarissa has deep and intimate ties with (romantic, nostalgic, and otherwise). She is giddy: to bring people together, for there to be conversations of great import, and for the presiding sensation that she has been the convener. She *is* the host. They *are* the guests. One welcomes. Others are welcomed. There is something to that. An offering.

And yet. Hosting is never fully an exercise in control; or, it needn't be. It can also be an object lesson in the anxiety of losing control and the unknowable possibilities of an emergent situation. Clarissa finds herself in a hosting tizzy when, a bit later in the evening, a Dr. and Mrs. Bradshaw arrive and, in the middle of discussing pleasantries with the hosts (*How is your kid at Eton?*, etc.), Mrs. Bradshaw notes that their tardiness was due to a sad emergency that Dr. Bradshaw had to attend to: the suicide of one Septimus Smith, a former British soldier who suffered from posttraumatic stress disorder (another term, in this space, for empire and its machinations in the post-World War I context). This news was not on the original invite list and Clarissa doesn't know how to incorporate the spectral presence within the context of her party. "What business had the Bradshaws to talk of death at her party? A young man had killed himself. And they talked of it at her party—the Bradshaws talked of death" (p. 184). Consumed, Clarissa retreats to a quiet place in the house to consider what it means and how one might, or ought, respond.

Heeding to linguistic resonance, one might suggest here that there are, at least, two kinds of responses. In the first, what we might call the *What a Lark!* option, Clarissa regains control of the party—its ambiance, its vibe, its timbre and tone—by disciplining the Other (here, the specter of Septimus and the affect it presides over) through a variety of means that incorporate it into the structure itself. The goal of this is for nothing to change. If the eerie affect wants to stay, it's on Clarissa's terms and what is best for the sovereign hosts who let it in the door (regardless of their relational responsibility to the situation). The ghostly presence of Septimus can stay, but on the condition that it disrupts neither Pimm's nor tea sandwiches. The night will unfold exactly the way Clarissa had hoped. Those who benefit from empire are not going to be asked to face any ghosts under her watch. It is just a lark, after all.

The second response, what we might call the *What a Plunge!* option, would allow for the presence and will of the specter/affect/stranger to disrupt, overtake, challenge, and transform any and everything in the space it found itself into. What might it mean to be response-able to Septimus, his death, his ghost, and experiences? The spectral presence is the proverbial record scratch. Crudités might fall by the wayside. Drinks might not get refreshed. There is that saying about best-laid plans. The future, which too often follows a telos, here presents as unknown. If larks are conditional to guests behaving the way they should and actions reifying positions, plunges, then, happen with a certain kind of abandonment to the present and its centripetal forces. To plunge is to have some fidelity to openness (one takes a plunge on the precipice of risk). In larks, the host remains the host. In plunges, the host, actually, becomes the guest. To use Derridean (2002) language, the host is taken hostage by the guest. In a lark, you put the home back together exactly how it was after the party. In a plunge, there is no going back. Not an odyssey. Not a return. But an openness to being adrift and on unsteady ground. The future. Excitement. The ethical question, it seems, turns on the kind of offering one is making by hosting. A lark or a plunge? Or, as Mrs. Dalloway might portend, both?

What's the Use?

I remember my dad sitting at the wooden kitchen table every night tallying numbers on his electric calculator keeping the books on the discount shoe stores my parents owned (he sometimes did this in his tan bathrobe). I remember my sister talking on the canary yellow phone that hung from the floral wallpapered wall when talking on the phone was a different kind of public act/performance. I remember my mom's girlfriends (my "aunts") popping in on their way home from work and sitting around the kitchen table talking, as Paul Simon (1980) sang, *the way some ladies do*. I remember Harry Kalas' voice coming from the radio that hung under the cabinet with the mugs during Phillies games; Merril Reese's during Eagles games; and Sid Marx's hosting *Fridays with Frank* and *Sundays with Sinatra*. There were metal tins of Charles Chips (one for chips (ridges); one for pretzels) that Sam delivered around dinnertime in the small pantry. Jello molds with fruit swimming around in the fridge. Two bottles of Wishbone salad dressings in the door (whatever happened to Catalina flavor!?!), a head of iceberg lettuce, a plastic pitcher of tap water, and a random bottle of Kelchner's cocktail sauce. The Sunday edition of the *Philadelphia Inquirer*, replete with coupons (ice cream, peanut butter crackers) sat on the shelf next to the table. And I remember my mom, leaning over the sink, gazing out the back window holding a piece of matzah with yellow mustard and a couple slices of turkey breast in her hand, thinking about something. The lighting was fluorescent, the floor linoleum.

While we lived in a home with different rooms, basically any memory I have from growing up happened in that kitchen. The weird thing is that I have few, if any, memories that actually involve eating or cooking in that kitchen. Like, we did both of those things—we ate dinner together most nights as a family, and, while perhaps not aspirational gastronomy, foods were defrosted or emptied from a can and put into a pot and warmed up to eat (love you moms!). There was no fuss, no talk of organic, nothing bespoke, no one cared about antioxidants (likely would have sounded vaguely threatening), and it was generally assumed that if something food-wise was local it was worse than if it was from elsewhere (save for Tastykakes). And so, in a space that was, ostensibly, designed for a particular kind of utility, it was never the reason why the kitchen was the most memorable backdrop in the house. While there was rarely any actual fire in the kitchen, it was most certainly the hearth that kept us warm, oriented, and grounded. Nutrition was not a huge concern. Nourishment, in all its material and immaterial permutations, was. It was bland and ordinary. And yet . . .

I'm going to skip over the couple decades in which I get obsessed with cooking shows, take home economics in school, start cooking for myself, get a job for a catering company, get a job at a fancy lunch spot, work as a waiter, as a cook, and do the early shift at the food coop in college. I'll also skip over the number of times I've found myself (crying while) watching *Tampopo, Ratatouille, Julie and Julia, Chef*, and, maybe most pathetically, *Burnt*. I'll also gloss over the overwhelming sense of problematic nostalgia I feel watching *Diners, Drive-Ins, and Dives* (Contois, 2020), the stint at King Arthur Bread School, the class I started teaching last year about fermentation, bacteria, and pedagogy, and the one this past term about the history of home economics. What would be important in terms of narrative is to note that eating and cooking, those things that aren't really in the cupboard of my memory warehouse, but were supposed to take place in the space that held all of my most special memories, became a central object in my life. A lay psychoanalytic reading here isn't all that mysterious: I was chasing food as a kind of phantasmic fetish object as my own life moved away from that kitchen and all it held. Food, the thing that wasn't there, became the thing I was trying to find.

While I had considered going into the culinary arts professionally (my biggest daydream remains a small breakfast and lunch spot with a long counter, free refills of coffee, and Gillian Welch's voice on the radio), I was also spending lots of time in classrooms as a student and, eventually, as a professor. Again, for the sake of space, I won't rehearse the ways in which many classrooms I was lucky enough to be in cultivated processes of conscientization and self-actualization. While some classes maybe seemed like more traditional teaching and learning spaces, many tarried with other forms of collective knowledge making and interrogation. I remember one class in college where I had to build something in a forest that was never seen by the professor who assigned it. Another started with there being an altar (candles, flowers, incense) at the front of the classroom and us sitting (on benches we made) in quiet meditation until the professor appeared. I remember being a teaching assistant in a sociology class about race relations and saying something in our peer section that was a result of my own socializations in whiteness, which led to an impassioned dialogue where I came to understand things I hadn't before (it was the first, but not the last, time the phrase "fucking white people" was catalyzed by something I said). I read lots. I was intentional about unlearning. I wrote things. Made stuff. Spent countless hours in used bookstores and the library. Cigarettes. Bourbon. Weed. Derrida (last time!). Etc. I was nourished in these spaces in ways that, I think, exceeded their intention and purpose as classrooms. They were classrooms, but they were somehow something completely otherwise. And yet . . .

The classroom and the kitchen. The kitchen and the classroom. Places that are designed to do one thing (cooking/eating or teaching/learning), yet host things that exceed their utility. What do we learn about nourishment when we find ourselves satiated in ways that are surprising and emergent?

Alterity

At some point I started fermenting things. I know that, post pandemic, that sounds blasé, maybe even #basic. And I know that if I say I was fermenting things back before white and vaguely politically progressive people were fermenting, that would sound defensive. But I was. I swear (on Bernie and AOC!). The seeds were sown early in life as, and as I've written about elsewhere, I grew up going to Jewish delis and loved nothing more than the pickle bar (Stern, 2024). I knew not that the bar was hosting fermented delicacies. I knew not about probiotics and bacteria. I knew not about Sandor Katz (more on him later). What I knew is that you got a bowl and could put as much green stuff in it as possible and the taste was, like, tilted (what I now would call funkadelic). I think, often, places where one learns about what community is often is a place that has food. This could be the kitchen. This could be the church basement. This could be the backyard barbeque. Spaces that hold community ferment relationships. In my case, the deli was the vessel that taught me things. Pickles, which were hosting communities of bacteria, also became associated with hosting communities of warmth and belonging.

Fermentation 2.0 happened in college. While I was studying to become a school counselor, I was also befriending hippie-types who said words like tempeh, tofu, miso, and kefir. As one might remember from above, I grew up in a house where Campbell's Chunky Sirloin Burger was lingua franca. I actually don't know if I knew lettuce other than iceberg existed, what a mango was, or who avocados were. Added to the particular kind of bildungsroman that is, at its best, a thing of parody (white kid goes to college, takes yoga, reads *Zen and the Art of Motorcycle Maintenance* and Noam Chomsky, decides to "turn on, tune in, and drop out," then goes to graduate school), my interests in these new foods resonated sharply with what Heldke (2001) calls *food adventuring*: the constellation of colonial forces that use things like experience, authenticity, and exoticness as criteria for virtue and taste. It was kind of like my *Eat Pray Love* arc. I traveled through new and colorful foods in order to find myself. I started making my own sauerkraut, kimchi, beer, and pickles. I didn't have a philosophy about what I was doing outside of frugality, dumpster diving, experimentation, and newness. No relation. No hosting. Nothing more than itself. All in the present tense.

As this story goes, at some point years later I came across Sandor Katz's (2012) *The Art of Fermentation*. Not dissimilar to other texts that radically changed the way I thought about relationality as a political and ethical project, the book completely reimagined being-as-such (see also Butler [2004], Delany [1999], and Glissant [1990]). The book was not just a how-to fermentation, but a philosophical and historical text that, with humility and acknowledgement, offered readers a means of being—with bacteria as a means of being—in the world in an age of climate change, neoliberal capital, orientalism, and, among other things, a certain strand of pharmacological-forward biopolitics. Less *add two cups of rice and one cup of starter culture* and more, "Just as microbial cultures exist only as communities, so too do our broader human cultures. Food is the greatest community builder there is [. . . and] fermented foods–especially beverages–play a significant role in community building" (p. xix). Not how to, but how one can. Microbes exist in communities. People exist in communities. Microbes need places where their communities can live and thrive and do their magic. People need places where their communities can live and thrive and do their magic. There needs to be an offering of space and, likely, the space itself needs to be open to transformative things. In its domesticated permutations, the human in the fermentation process makes an offering by way of a space for certain strains of bacteria—the yummy kind—to thrive. Clarissa likely thought about things like lighting and temperature and noise during her party. Fermenters do the same. We talk to our ferments. Sing to our ferments. Smell our ferments. Taste our ferments. And make changes to the environment based on these check-ins. But fermentation also goes a step (or two) further in the hosting process. Fermentation also begins to peel away at the layers of difference between organisms and species, between people and microbes, between Clarissa and Septimus, hosts and guests. In this sense, and as the brilliant Maya Hey (2021) writes in considering that the human body is made up of as many bacterial cells as human ones, ". . . the notion of *we* already encompasses multiple species. So, *how do we practice being humans*, let alone healthy and sustainable ones, given that our ontological status is, and *has never been*, solely human" (pp. 1–2; emphasis original)? What does it mean to host something that is not sovereign and different, but something that, from genesis, was already and always in relation? What does it mean that that which one believes is coming as a guest, is actually part of the host? Rhizomes, not roots. If Clarissa's relationship (lark) to hosting is Host & Guest as two distinct entities, fermentation takes a plunge by changing difference into relation. What we might write as host/guest (a set of relations that contain the potentiality for both and otherwise) is a reorientation that defers the categories in a shifting set of emergent moments. *And yet*: meaning is neither static nor derivative. The journey is errant and indeterminate (I know, more Derrida). Sometimes wine, sometimes vinegar. And, but yet . . .

Vessels

When I was invited to Sandor's Residency Program a couple years ago, it felt like I had found one of the Golden Tickets á la Willy Wonka. Twice a year he invites people to apply for a residency program at his home in the mountains of Tennessee where he's lived in an off-grid queer community for 30-ish years. There is an application process and a sliding scale. During the term I attended, there were maybe 10 of us from across the globe and across personal and professional metaverses and levels of fermenting experience. We showed up. On a mountain. In the middle of the woods. And for 5 days, we learned. Together.

And, yes, when I say we learned, I do mean new things about fermentation (which was amazing). But, and to my surprise, what I think I really came away with was this idea that hosting is pedagogical: that how one welcomes people into space determines the possibility of what can be learned and experienced. And I don't know how to really explain what this looked like or how it felt, but he *really* invited us into his home. People were sleeping in the backyard or on the floor in the house. There was a shared outhouse and shower. Nothing felt proprietary. Not even the knowledge, which is something Sandor hammers on in all of his work about fermentation:

"People largely assume," he writes, "that for microbial transformations [ferments] to be safe, they require extensive knowledge and control and are therefore a specialized domain best left to experts" (2012, p. xvii). Not the case. This is key as it is about control and hosting. We were not invited there to be in awe. We were not there to watch and learn. We were not there to sit and take notes. We were invited to be a part of a process of emergence. "I am on a mission," Sandor continues in *The Art of Fermentation*, "of sharing skills, resources, and information related to this important art, in the hope that these long-standing coevolutionary relationships, embedded in cultural practices, are not lost but rather spread, cross-pollinated, and adapted" (p. xviii). In this articulation, and in the experience, the invitation was to come as we were, add what we could, and learn from each other.

The Set Up

Until very recently, I've kept two loves of my life separate—cooking and teaching. There were times when I would cook with my students under the guise of "community building," but never the two shall meet at the level of content. Historically, my scholarship and teaching had focused on the neoliberal present and its relation to policies, privatization, and affect. I wrote about charter schools, Teach for America, and gentrification. I tried to document why particular (white) feelings about education, democracy, and justice were happening in our current historical moment. As might sometimes be the case, when one starts writing about something, or a constellation of things, it becomes clear that what one is actually interested in wasn't quite the thing one was writing about directly. In my case, I think what I came to realize is that the work that I did was mostly interested in how something called *community* was being reterritorialized in ways that were, I think I indirectly argued, antithetical to ideals that could be described as democratic or aspirational or just plain good. This came out thinking about parents who had all but no choice but to send their kids to a newer and sometimes better funded charter school in different neighborhoods, which meant people who lived next to each other on the same block sent their kids to different schools. About shuttered porn theaters that once served as sanctuaries for those who could only find it there. About diners across the country that have closed down due to rising rents and changing eating habits. I'm reminded of a quote by the owner of a diner in Reading, PA, Elsayed "Steve" Emourzouky. Talking about the role of diners in the social fabric of communities, he said: "It's not just about coming to eat . . . It's to come and have a good time while you eat. That was my goal: a family atmosphere and warmth, and *that* feeling (qtd. in Diener-Stokes, 2016, para. 4; emphasis added; see also Stern 2019).

***That* Feeling**

I think that's what I was talking about above in the kitchen in the house I grew up in, in some classrooms I was a part of, in delis, and in Sandor's kitchen (def. not at Clarissa's party). *That* feeling is not that of an overly cautious guest tiptoeing on eggshells so as not to mess anything up. It is not one of an overbearing host who is trying to keep order at all costs. It's also not all acceptance and affirmation. You know the way a waitress at a diner is about one second away from being like, "Are you fucking kidding me? Let's go already"? That's also part of it. It is a feeling of acknowledgement and admission of relation: I and thou.

While I have always been conscious of the kinds of spaces I've tried to create in the classroom, the past year teaching about food has been the most interesting. In the early parts of *Teaching to Transgress*, and in speaking against the necrophilia of hierarchical traditional classrooms, hooks (1994) argues that the classroom should always be exciting, and never boring (p. 7). Thinking about her time in higher education, hooks writes that

> *Excitement* in higher education was viewed as potentially disruptive of the atmosphere of seriousness assumed to be essential in the learning process. To enter classroom settings in colleges and universities with the will to share the desire to encourage excitement, was to transgress. Not only did it require movement beyond

> accepted boundaries, but excitement could not be generated without a full recognition of the fact that there could never be an absolute set agenda governing teaching practices. Agendas had to be flexible, had to allow for spontaneous shifts in direction. (pg. 7; emphasis original)

Which is what happened to Clarissa. At her party, there was no space for excitement. No space for spontaneity. If hosts are pedagogues of a certain kind, then what are the possibilities for education when structures or identities are predetermined, teleological, and predictable? What does one actually learn in a space that is a hermetic seal?

It's notable that, as Katz (2020) writes in *Fermentation as Metaphor*, "The English language uses the word *fermentation* to describe not only the literal phenomenon of cellular metabolism that it is [. . .] but also much more broadly to indicate a state of *agitation, excitement, and bubbliness*" (p. 9; my emphasis). If education needs to be exciting, and fermentation is exciting, then there might be something to be said about teaching fermentation as a kind of transgressive and biophilic praxis. While not a replacement for reading texts and talking about their visions and possibilities, there is something to be said for actually engaging in the act of excited transformation—for being response-able to bringing something into being. I remember a conversation we had once during the residency at Sandor's house about the deferred nature of fermentation—some ferments can take weeks, months, or even years to be ready, and I responded that it seems like fermentation is a hopeful kind of making. It assumes there will be someone there to accept it. That there will be a future. Making something as a kind of unguaranteed hope.

In what I can only call a simple twist of fate, Sandor and all my students were at some point in my kitchen. And during that weekend, and after a long day of making many messes and mistakes in the kitchen, Sandor said to me something like: *there are two kinds of people: ones who can let other people make a mess in their kitchen and those who can't.* The classroom, like the kitchen, is a place where, if you're interested in your students and their lives and invite them as they are to participate, things are going to get messy, things are going to get put back the wrong way, things will get burnt, and things will break. I've known this intellectually and experientially for a long time, but working with food has given it new meaning and caloric delight. The question, as a pedagogue, is about what kinds of nourishment this kind of excitement might offer that differs from other critical kinds of classrooms and what does it offer our historical moment. What does it mean to prepare for not being ready? To teach with the tensions of hosting and being overtaken? What a lark! What a plunge!

References

Butler, J. (2004). *Precarious life*. Verso.

Contois, E. J. H. (2020). *Diners, dudes, and diets: How gender and power collide in food media and culture*. UNC Press.

Delany, S. (1999). *Times Square red, Times Square blue*. NYU Press.

Derrida, J. (2002). *Acts of religion*. (G. Andijar, Ed.). Routledge.

Diener-Stokes, C. H. (2016, April 16). The conversation: Elsayed "Steve" Elmarzouky. *Reading Eagle*. Retrieved from https://www.readingeagle.com/business-weekly/article/the-conversation-elsayed-steve-elmarzouky.

Glissant, É. (1990). *Poetics of relation* [Trans. B. Wing]. University of Michigan Press.

Heldke, L. (2001). "Let's eat Chinese!": Reflections on cultural food colonialism. *Gastronomica: The Journal for Food Studies 1*(2), 67–69.

Hey, M. (2021). Attunement and multispecies communication in fermentation. *Feminist Philosophy Quarterly, 7*(3), Article 4. S197–S206.

hooks, b. (1994). *Teaching to transgress: Education and the pursuit of freedom*. Routledge.

Katz, S. (2012). *The art of fermentation*. Chelsea Green.

Katz, S. (2020). *Fermentation as metaphor*. Chelsea Green.

Simon, P. (1980). Late in the evening [Song]. On *One-trick pony*. Warner Bros. Records.

Stern, M. (2019). On closings: Diners, porn theaters, and schools. *Review of Education, Pedagogy, and Cultural Studies, 41*(2), 69–98.

Stern, M. (2024). In a pickle: The pedagogical possibility of fermentation. *Food, Culture & Society*. https://doi.org/10.1080/15528014.2024.2426837.

Woolf, V. (1981). *Mrs. Dalloway*. Harcourt. (Original work published in 1925).

CHAPTER 3

"Stand There and Watch": Witnessing Cooking Methods in Black Studies

BONNIE SAMANTHA MALDONADO

There are no written recipes in my family. There is no book passed down through generations. No scraps of paper or index cards living scattered in an old box. There are recipes that are creations from the matriarchs' hearts and minds in my family. When I would ask my mother how to make something, rather than giving me a step by step process, she would say, "Parate ahi y mira/Stand there and watch." I have spent three decades watching, observing, and learning, gathering information on how much salt is too much for making rice, or when to hear for the sizzle of the stewed meat and the almost charred smell to know it needed another splash of water to continue cooking. This knowledge acquired through the senses—taste, smell, sight, feel, and sound—becomes intergenerational, embodied knowledge of countless people standing and observing how something is made, gathering information orally or through experience. The common denominators in this gathering are proximity in space, intimacy within a place, and the ability to spend time in order to witness from up close. Three years ago, I did just that. I stood there and witnessed my mother make *Habichuelas con dulce* (a typical Good Friday dessert of sweet beans) and translated my mother's movements in the kitchen to a recipe. When people ask me how something is made, it is my job to translate words from Spanish to English, eyeballed measurements to metric and imperial systems, and performances into the written form. The ephemerality of cooking without recipes in my mother's kitchen was my first lesson in research methodologies, lessons that exist both within and outside academia.

As a Black Studies scholar with a specific focus on affect, Black Feminist theory and epistemologies, and Caribbean Theory and History, translation is necessary. Food and food-making practices through a Dominican cultural lens feed my own ethnographic and archival research as they both require prescriptive practices and individual and collective experimentation informed by deep feeling and embodied knowledge. In this chapter, I outline how the act of witnessing 2.0, "an embodied practice" as defined by Deborah Thomas (Thomas, 2019, pp. 2), necessitates a transformation through a practice of doing, a practice of *researching* and *cooking* in the field of Black Studies that is an inherent part of what D. Soyini Madison defines as critical ethnography (Madison, 2019). I introduce the research method of "comiendo boca" to demonstrate that this transformation necessitates a different relationship to time, so that we may slow down, stand there and listen, feel, and taste Black aliveness (Quashie, 2021; Wright, 2019). These practices exist outside of academia, a performance that Sylvia Wynter heeds is necessary in remembering the plurality and opacity of Black Studies as a field that seeks to tell the truth of Black life. Cooking, I argue, teaches me that to exist in the academy as a Black Studies scholar is to remember that like the practice of cooking, one's research and selfhood does not always belong within the kitchen and does not always require a recipe. As an embodied researcher, there is space for evolution of affect, transformation, and truth telling that refuses to exist within academia.

Black Studies is transdisciplinary. It refuses to be held into a prescriptive recipe but rather is in constant experimentation through embodied knowledge, repetition, and both objective and subjective truth. College institutions incorporated the Black arts and Black aesthetics movements to create Black Studies in the late 1960s. Sylvia Wynter, however, urges us to return to the spirit of arts and aesthetics and the multiplicity of definitions of Blackness (Wynter, 2003). Rather than favor the rigidity of the academic superstructure, Wynter (2005) calls us to consider the genealogy of the corrective intervention of Black Studies as a territory rather than a map. The function of a territory as a metaphor implies ownership, a perceived capturing of an entity with defined borders. Existing beyond said borders, the origins of Black Studies—Black aesthetics and Black arts movements—were diasporic and invested in ways of being that existed outside of an essentialized version of Blackness. Wynter invites us to consider "epistemology as a terrain" as a map that can be turned into a territory and calls the audience of Black Studies scholars to consider the labor they will take up within the academy (Wynter, 2016). Mapping the borders of Black Studies through interventions, keywords, and methods (whether that is through discipline, geographic, or language), can take the form of descriptive, prescriptive, and corrective means.

Scholars intervened in the field of Black Studies to correct the ways in which the truth about Black life was told (Du Bois, 1899). Others describe Black life in its full texture and prescribe methods for how to do Black Studies ethically (Hurston, 1990). Black feminist scholars continued to return to the importance of subjectivity, holding the experiences of Black women equally as important as objective truths (Hill Collins, 2000). As a Food Studies scholar that pays attention to Blackness in the Dominican Republic, my dissertation relies on qualitative research that consists of analyzing primary and secondary historical documents and texts, art and literary analysis, and ethnographic research methods that include oral history interviews using co-performance and participant observant strategies. The combination of these methodological practices is a Black feminist practice that suspends prescriptive methods and facilitates telling the truth of Black life through both objective and subjective data.

Black feminist scholars and Black women admonish us to view and experience the kitchen is a space of translation, experimentation, remembering, (re)membering, worldmaking, and care (Danticat, 1994; Hill Collins, 2000; Lorde, 1982; Morrison, 1995). The kitchen is a space where objectivity and subjectivity meet to create places rendered on maps as places that exist beyond the territorial grasp of the colonial nation state (Wynter, 2003). And yet, in the Caribbean, and specifically the Dominican Republic, it is laden with coloniality, marked by cooking tools, eating times, ingredients, and the very hands that make it (Lowe, 2015; Mignolo, 2011). Like the kitchen, Black Studies exists in the liminal space of capture and liberation. The intellectual labor of Black Studies thinkers and scholars is to translate while acknowledging that some things may not be easily translated (Edwards, 2003). The act of cooking Dominican meals reminds me that learning and translating the truth of Black life requires witnessing, patience, a suspension of objective truth and time, and collaboration between interlocutors and researchers to honor one's right to opacity and demonstrate reciprocal care.

Epiphenomenal time offers a way to suspend time and view its dimensions to reconsider how we think about Blackness. Using epiphenomenal time, Wright critiques a middle passage epistemology that is grounded within modern Western conceptions of time that moves in one direction (Wright, 2015). More specifically, a linear telling of history that relies on the colonizer's interpretation of events rather than highlighting paradigms of power that repeat through euro patriarchal definitions of man (Benitez-Rojo, 1989; Wynter, 2003). Instead, epiphenomenal time exists in the now, while also recognizing history as an assemblage of rhizomic moments that redistributes power through the ability to locate utterances of Blackness across relational spacetime (Glissant, 1999; Wright, 2015). Like Wright, Christina Sharpe (2016) takes on the Middle Passage to imagine metaphors of the crossing of a ship to invoke the wake and wake work as method to apply to Wright's epiphenomenal time. The wake can mean the mark left on the water as the ship crosses, a coming into being and consciousness, and finally, a tending to the dead to make Black life visible through relation and care. Living in the wake through epiphenomenal time opens the possibility of making Black life visible through memory and (re)membering. History and memory, however, are distinct; the former is a site of intellectual production that no one can claim as their own while the latter is multiplicitous and ephemeral (Nora, 1989). Sites of memory are created with intention and are anchored in a collective memory that questions history. This memory is fluid and always returns to the point of creation (Morrison, 1984, 1995). In this sense, a recollection of the past that moves away from linear time creates the possibility to feel, taste, and care for resonances of Black life, in the past, present, and future through food and food-making practices.

To return to the space of the kitchen, Elizabeth Pérez turns us to the intimate points of relation with the spiritual world that are created in the kitchen. Her ethnographic monograph centers the Afro-Cuban spiritual tradition of Lucumí. Lucumí practitioners are attuned to gods' tastes and feed them as a form of worship. Food acts as both an offering and a way to communicate with spirits; however, the practitioner must be ready to both receive and serve the spirit through learning by doing. This learning by doing is created through a set of micropractices, "routine and intimate sequences of operations that can be broken down into more minute units of activity" (Pérez, 2016, pp. 9). Pérez's ethnographic accounts demonstrate that choreography that is performed, taught, and learned in the kitchen creates food that fuels memory that looks to the past to inform the future. To Pérez, food and consumption allows us to understand how Black diasporic traditions have been sustained through micropractices and acts of cooking, talking, and future-oriented memory. These acts then become embodied and emblazoned in the memory of the practitioners, memories that they translate through food.

Cooking with my mother in her kitchen has offered the foundation to how I approach my current research alongside research methods and theory. We both learned to cook by watching and by listening, watching our family members' micropractices while cooking and listening to their instruction, and the sounds of the food, hands, and feet movement harkening to transgenerational practices before experimenting. Oral tradition, communication, and knowledge becomes embodied, as we commit the recipe to flesh memory through repetition in our own kitchens (de Certeau et al., 1998). As I conduct ethnographic and autoethnographic research in the Dominican Republic, I am reminded these embodied practices are central acts of care that sustain us within violent and colonial institutions to produce research ethically outside of the kitchen. A combination of oral history and critical, co-performance ethnography is necessary as I consider food-making practices as everyday acts and performances that highlight embodied knowledge (Madison, 2019). Co-performance demands an ethics of care in how my presence is impacting how participants interact with myself and each other. As a native ethnographer, my own connection and identification as a Black Dominican person necessitates autoethnography as method as I consider the afterlives of collective care between my interlocutors, collaborators, and myself (Hurston, 1990).

This care is aligned both within the service and research components within academia. For example, while living in my family's home, my aunts would regularly send me a voice note on WhatsApp stating, "Baja a buscar algo que te tengo aqui/Come down to get something I have for you here." The act of care is consistent, soothing the experience and processing of overwhelm from first- and secondhand violence in everyday life and traditional and nontraditional archives (Hurston, 1990). The nourishment my aunts give that begins in the kitchen extends beyond the physical space and nourishes the community. In exchange, we nourished each other. Through explicit asks and spending deep time with them, I learned that one of my aunts enjoyed chicken feet soup, so I made sure to pass her a bowl of soup whenever I made it. Another aunt cooked for her children and grandchildren to support them while the parents were away at work. Instead of passing her a plate, I would purchase the ingredients she needed to create the seasoning base of her meals. Alexander (2005) documents the process of an academic institution watering down care through the creation of task forces, when in fact, research is a form of looking after and tending to Black life, in the past, present, and future (Sharpe, 2016). In this sense, my aunts and I were tending to Black life in the present with resonances of how we have previously learned to care for one another from our ancestors while ensuring that our future generations would be taken care of as well. A prescriptive recipe of how to care for one another denies us from recognizing that the knowledge that exists in the flesh and nurtured through collective responsibility requires a patient, intuitive practice that fully listens to the assemblage of archives converging into what can present itself through ethnographic research.

The archives of how to care for one another not only exist in academic spaces, but through oral tradition and embodied movement, liminal spaces that Thomas calls archives of affect. Taking heed from Gayle Wald, Deborah Thomas identifies archives of affect as technologies and documentation that are not bound to time and open the possibilities to feel sovereignty, violence, and everyday life (Thomas, 2019, pp. 6, 20). This documentation can take the form of images, videos, music, and other modes of documenting popular culture, including food. In the Dominican Republic, food-making practices and recipes are difficult to locate within traditional archives. Food investigations determine contemporary Dominican cuisine as an amalgamation of Indigenous, African, and Spanish influences, strengthened by enslaved Africans' creativity based on their knowledge of how to transform ingredients in Ayiti that they found similar to those on the continent of Africa (Veloz Maggiolo, 2007, pp. 90). Dominican scholars attribute certain dishes as those that belong to the national identity, bolstering the narrative of the Dominican cultural identity to be based within the Dominican nation state.

The oral tradition of Dominican criollo recipes creates a space of refusal against the nation state. Criollo in this sense is a compilation of various cultural practices and traditions to make one of the place (Veloz Maggiolo, 2007). In her monograph, Lara (2020) argues that criollo traditions (including rituals, ceremonies, and performances that celebrates Blackness, indigeneity, and Spanish ancestry in the Americas) offer a way of being that remembers embodied practices of freedom. Her desire for a decolonial future is one that is only possible if freedom and sovereignty are imagined outside of the parameters of the oppressive Christian colonial state of the Dominican Republic. This Christian coloniality is one that erases, defines, and disciplines the ways queer, Black, and indigenous bodies and practices move in the island, demanding that people, politically, socially, and culturally, adhere to biblical notions of womanhood, manhood, marriage, family, and worship.

If Dominican recipes are criollo, they do not belong to the state nor can be cited as the intellectual property of one person. Each can be transformed and innovated on by individuals and collectives, an archive of affect that can signal towards everyday life. For example, Dominican anthropologist Juan B. Nina investigates the cultural traditions of meals cooked during the Catholic liturgical period of lent. His research resulted into a recipe book acquired through ethnographic methods. In his discussion of the cultural tradition of making Habichuelas con Dulce (sweet beans), Nina calls the dish one of the most exchanged dishes in Dominican cuisine. On Good Friday, Dominicans in the countryside, the city, and across the diaspora cook this creamy, sweet, slow dessert and exchange dishes with their neighbors and visitors. While, Nina notes, this may be a way to showcase Dominicans' own cooking styles, he highlights that it is a way to circumvent the rising economic costs of food in the country (Nina, 2015). Nina's book holds the recipes for many Good Friday meals, traditional and new, so that readers may follow a prescriptive way to celebrate the holiday. However, cooking, like researching in the academy, does not always have a methodological process for completing a meal. Cooking Dominican meals then coincides with the aesthetics of Black Studies, difficult to maintain within a discipline and borne of creativity.

Ironically, a primary intervention in my research is to create a digital cookbook, with recipes collected through cooking labs and oral history interviews with interlocutors. Dominicans across the diaspora have expressed to me a difficulty in connecting with Dominican culture without knowing how to make foods we grew up with. Both the cooking labs and oral history interviews are recorded by audio and visually. This, as Thomas argues, allows for a witnessing that can attend to what cooking, and furthermore, home feels like. The first of these recipes came from a project I collaborated with my mom in, titled "Se Puede Casar: Cooking a Good Friday Meal." I stood there, watched, and video recorded my mother cook a typical Dominican Good Friday meal of rice and pigeon peas, fried red snapper, and habichuelas con dulce. While she cooked, I recorded her hand and feet movements, paying special attention to how much milk she added, how her wrists flicked in a particular way while squeezing the blended beans through the sieve. While she cooked, we talked, exchanging tips as I listened to family secrets I did not expect to receive. I transcribed the recipe and replicated her movements the following week. I sought to answer, what is she doing when she is cooking? The transcribed recipe exists as a map, a straightforward description of what to do and how to do it. The recipes and reflections offered are my attempt in offering a tour, signaling the gestures and movements around our specific kitchens and how we make meaning of them (de

Certeau, 1980). The Habichuelas con dulce recipe is a combination of both of our dishes, in hopes that readers may take the best iteration of my mother's dishes and my own as a guide to create their own. There were multiple moving parts as I observed my mom: (1) the sharing of family recipes through oral tradition; (2) the necessity of paying full attention with all of my senses to be able to transcribe the recipe to written form; and (3) how deep attention and time can create safer environments for interlocutors to share more of themselves. I learned how to transcribe recipes through oral and visual learning. However, I was reminded of the importance of the right to opacity by maintaining Black feminist ethics of withholding information shared during the project. Conflicted with what to share and what to hold dear, the act of cooking felt tight, restricted, and sad. My hands were not able to replicate the meal for 3 years.

Growing up, I commonly heard that the seasoning is in someone's hands. This Black femme practice of opacity led me to develop my own method so that my cooking and writing may be unique to my own seasonings and attunement to the world. In my own research, I call the practice of standing there, watching, and gathering information through participant observation and living daily life as "comiendo boca." Directly translated, comiendo boca literally means eating the mouth. In colloquial Dominican terms it means minding the business that is not yours. As an anthropologist, I have found myself going about my daily life gathering information as I go along my day, paying attention to moments that may not seem directly related to food but offer insight on food acquisition and food-making practices. This has looked like listening to the time of day food trucks pass by my parents' home and listening to what is being sold. It has also looked like listening to three elder women on the bus discuss the best way to cook strong and sustaining meals for their aging husbands. These moments illuminate the attention required to listen to how Dominicans acquire and prepare food, a listening that does not always happen in the kitchen and can illuminate food access, gender roles, local economic structures, and dispersal of knowledge of food-making practices. This method, like witnessing 2.0, can destabilize what we think we know or aim to complete as scholars and invites speculation, ambiguity, and an openness to outcome that is intertwined with the lived realities of our collaborators. Comiendo boca invites questions that consider what can and cannot be shared to academic audiences and trust that my interlocutors are also mindful of what they choose to hold dear and keep within their own archives.

Three years after recording my mother making Habichuelas con Dulce, I found myself in an apartment in Santo Domingo, 33 kilometers from my aunts in San Cristobal and 2471 kilometers from my mother in New York. My neighbors were now my friends and academic peers. Packets of ingredients with beans, Carnation milk, cinnamon, raisins, vanilla, and sugar lined the aisles in major supermarkets. Holy Week was only a week away and Dominicans were preparing Habichuelas con Dulce during the entire season of Lent. Missing was the sweet potato. I listened to shopgoers comment on the missing ingredients and their own special recipes. Finally, I asked an elder how to pick the best sweet potato. The sadness, the tightness, and restriction around making this meal finally lifted. My hands felt free to replicate what I remembered, with the assistance of the written recipe deep in my computer files. I invited my friends and colleagues over for dinner and shared the dessert. I saved a tub of beans for my aunts and one for my parents who were arriving to the country in a week. Here, my methods became my own comiendo boca so that the seasoning would be my own. My aunt received them with glee, recognizing the hidden citations of my mother's own cooking style in the light sweetness of my Habichuelas con dulce.

Cooking reminds me that research takes different forms. It sometimes requires slowness, sometimes requires thinking quickly on our feet, sometimes requires comiendo boca. Each cook and scholar has their unique seasoning, concocted through their methodological training, experience, and ethics. Cooking is not confined to enclosed walls or modern structures of kitchen spaces. It spills where one thirsts for care. The act of cooking reminds us to witness the assemblage of tastes, violences, histories, and performances required to sustain our lives outside and within academia. There are recipes I can follow, but sometimes I have to stand there and watch, taste, experiment, listen, and adjust to what is required, trusting the final product tells the truth about Black life.

References

Alexander, M. J. (2005). *Pedagogies of crossing: Meditations on feminism, sexual politics, memory, and the sacred*. Duke University Press.

Benítez Rojo, Antonio. (1989). *La Isla Que Se Repite: El Caríbe y La Perspectiva Posmoderna*. Ediciones del Norte.

Danticat, E. (1994). *Breath, eyes, memory*. Soho Press.

de Certeau, M. (1980). *The practice of everyday life*. University of California Press.

de Certeau, M., Giard, L., & Mayol, P. (1998) *The practice of everyday life volume 2: Living and cooking*. University of Minnesota Press.

Du Bois, W.E.B. (1899). *The Philadelphia Negro: A social study*. University of Pennsylvania.

Edwards, B. H. (2003). *The practice of diaspora: Literature, translation, and the rise of Black internationalism*. Harvard University Press.

Glissant, Édouard and J. Michael Dash (1999). *Caribbean Discourse*: Selected Essays. 3. paperback printing. Univ. Press of Virginia.

Hill Collins, P. (2000). *Black feminist thought: Knowledge, consciousness, and the politics of empowerment*. 2nd edition. Routledge.

Hurston, Z. N. (1990). *Mules and men*. First Perennial Library edition. Perennial Library.

Lara, A. M. (2020). *Queer freedom: Black sovereignty*. State University of New York Press.

Lorde, A. (1982). *Zami, a new spelling of my name*. Persephone Press.

Lowe, L. (2015). *The intimacies of four continents*. Duke University Press.

Madison, D. S. (2019). *Critical ethnography: Method, ethics, and performance*. 3rd edition. SAGE Publications, Inc.

Mignolo, W. (2011). *The darker side of Western modernity : Global futures, decolonial options*. Duke University Press.

Morrison, T. (1995). The site of memory. In R. Baker & W. Knowlton Zinsser (Eds.), *Inventing the truth: The art and craft of memoir* (pp. 84–102). Houghton Mifflin.

Morrison, T. (1984). "Memory, Creation, and Writing." *Thought* 59, no. 4: 385–90. https://doi.org/10.5840/thought198459430.

Nina, J. B. (2015). *Gastronomia de cuaresma: Historia y recetas*. Talleres Gráficos Dalis: Moca, República Dominicana.

Nora, P. (1989). "Between Memory and History: Les Lieux De Mémoire." *Representations*, no. 26: 7–24. doi:10.2307/2928520.

Pérez, E. (2016.) *Religion in the kitchen: Cooking, talking, and the making of Black Atlantic traditions*. New York University Press.

Quashie, K.E. (2021). *Black Aliveness, Or a Poetics of Being*. Duke University Press.

Sharpe, C. E. (2016). *In the wake: On Blackness and being*. Duke University Press.

Thomas, D. A. (2019). *Political life in the wake of the plantation: Sovereignty, witnessing, repair*. Duke University Press.

Veloz Maggiolo, M., Tolentino Dipp, Hugo. (2007). *Gastronomia dominicana: Historia del Sabor Criollo*. CODETEL.

Wright, M. (2015). *Physics of Blackness: Beyond the Middle Passage Epistemology*. University of Minnesota Press.

Wynter, S. (2003). "Unsettling the coloniality of being/power/truth/freedom: Towards the human, after man, its overrepresentation—An argument." *CR: The New Centennial Review, 3*(3), 257–337. https://doi.org/10.1353/ncr.2004.0015.

Wynter, S. (2016). "On how we mistook the map for the territory, and reimprisoned ourselves in our unbearable wrongness of being," Of Desêtre: Black studies toward the human project (2005). In F. L. Hord, Mzee Lasana Okpara, & J. S. Lee (Eds.), *I am because we are: Readings in Africana philosophy* (REV-Revised, 2, pp. 267–280). University of Massachusetts Press.

CHAPTER 4

Soul/le Credentials: Collards as Resources for Academic Participation

MARIA JOSÉ BOTELHO AND R. JAMAAL DOWNEY

You know who used to wear a collard in his lapel just like a proud carnation?

Thelonious Sphere Monk from North Carolina is who.

I like to imagine some hotstuff jazz critic

-maybe Leonard Feather or another jiveass-Asking, Say monk, what is *that thing you've got on?*

And Thelonious replies: You looking at my sole credentials.

— Fred Chappell

Foodways are a product of history, culture, and power. In reading *Leon's Story*, the memoir of a sharecropper's son told in vignettes, we were brought up close to a U.S. socio-economic system that echoed slavery. While Leon's family struggled to meet their basic needs, one food item sustained them: collard greens. When Leon's mother prepared dinner for the white landowner's family, they would send her home with the broth from dishes with collard greens. She would turn the broth or "pot-likker" into soup, which nourished the children and adults. The white family couldn't understand why the Black children were healthier than their own. Leon insists: ". . . we found out later on in life, when you boil the greens and cook the greens, the vitamins went down into the juice, so we got the best part" (Tillage, 1997, p. 15). This text reminded us of the sole presence and qualities of collard greens in our disparate but also shared lived experiences.

In this chapter, we assemble vignettes to understand how a white European American woman and a biracial man connected over a leafy green. Putting the theory of practice to work centers the collard green in the analysis of our vignettes as we make sense of the details of everyday foodways against histories and societies (Pink, 2012). We gain insights into the presence of collard greens in our cultural communities and their import for participating in academia. The chapter challenges the traditional understanding of academic rigor while also providing insights that only the liminal spaces among these processes and practices can produce.

We use vignette writing to assemble our stories. These short storying-rememberings lend themselves to analyze what is said and how it is said. We write these interlocking texts to represent the similarities and differences in our lived experiences. Vignettes are useful in examining unexpected emergences as they "intensify unpredictable but relatable disruptions . . . as connections are produced in the mind[s] of the researcher[s], creating concepts and provoking questions" (Masny, 2013, p. 343). These questions lead to more inquiry. The writing held still diverse and dynamic lived moments and memories (Davies, 2000), allowing us to make and engage with these data (Ellingson & Sotirin, 2020), and offering a method of inquiry and analysis (Richardson & St. Pierre, 2005). The iterative processes and practices of talking and writing and reading, rereading, and rewriting the vignettes helped to reveal our shared experiences and deepen our understanding of collard greens and its many lessons.

Sampling the Literature: Health Benefits and Origins

The humble collard green, or collards, are part of the cruciferous family (*Brassica oleracea*), which includes cabbage, brussel sprouts, broccoli, and kale. Collards are similar to kale nutritionally but some claim that they are the most nutrient-rich vegetable in the world. The flavor of collards can range from a slightly bitter and earthy flavor to a sweeter taste. This flavor variance depends on their growing conditions, how fresh they are, and when they were harvested. They possess powerful health-promoting qualities like protein, fat, carbohydrates, and fiber and nutrients like calcium and iron. Thirty percent of their calories come from protein. Studies show that they have anti-cancer properties and support heart and brain health as well as support blood glucose control and eye health.

The origin story of collards, or formerly known as colewort, has not been definitively located. The *Brassica oleracea* has been thought to grow wild on the shores of western France, southern coast of Britain, and northern shores of Spain. In roughly 1820, the collard green began thriving in the American South. How the collard green was transplanted to the Americas is mysterious but four possible paths exist: Africa via the Middle Passage, Portugal and/or Brazil, Spain, and Britain. Three of these countries share common colonial pasts.

Jamaal's Vignettes

Being biracial and living with my white mom in mostly white spaces has created a divide between myself and my Blackness. I have often felt that, while I know I'm not white, I've never felt Black enough to be accepted within the Black community. Admittedly, these are my own feelings, not always attributed to the way the Black community has treated me. The same can be said for my feelings towards academia.

I remember walking into my Great-Grandmama Terethia's kitchen. She was one generation removed from slavery. I remember seeing this physically frail, but emotionally and mentally strong, Black woman sitting on a makeshift stool as she was cleaning out chitterlings. The rank and pungent smell smacked you in the nose. Watching the care she took in cleaning out those pig intestines cued me into the importance of our culture being passed on through food. I would sit with Grandmama T for hours (albeit the only thing I had to do as I was new to the area). My time in Memphis was the only time in my life that I was part of a strong Black community. Since, I have struggled to feel my Blackness internally although I am reminded daily how Black I am, externally.

When my sister, 4 years my elder, was around age 16, she began making collards. I was weary at first. But after a healthy dose of pepper sauce, I chowed down and continued to ask for more. It took a while before I began to cook my own collards. But when I did, I felt an unearthly connection to something larger than myself—I felt I belonged. It was something I couldn't explain, I just felt deep in my bones. Whenever I was in doubt, whenever I questioned myself, if I felt untethered or that I didn't belong, a batch of collards was surely to follow.

When I'm rinsing those collards—the way the water beads on the topside and slides off similar to the way we let those hurtful words and water cannons slide away, the stiffness of the spine of the collards like the backbone of my resilient ancestors, while also having the tenderness of those baby leaves at the bottom—this ritual calls on all of those before me to come through me and nourish my mind, body, and soul. Cooking and subsequently eating collards is no simple physical process. For me, it's existential. When I'm standing at the sink, it's as if I am watching my own hands as though they aren't mine. This ritual is written in my DNA; it's instinctual.

Cooking collards for me is a ritual that ties me to my peoples. It reminds me that despite what the world has to say, who they think I am, question what I do, that I am part of a much larger community that has survived and persisted throughout time. My past people have endured slavery—my current people enduring the weight of systemic and institutional oppression that bars them from fulfilling their extreme potential. In the present and seemingly future, I'm feeling the weight of not belonging in academia and therefore undeserving of my place in life and all that follows.

Maria José's Vignettes

Gardening practices are one way immigrants recreate the landscapes they left behind. I remember the community garden in East Cambridge that many immigrants from the Azores cultivated alongside immigrants from Italy. (The Azores are a nine-island archipelago in the middle of the North Atlantic that are part of Portugal.) The small tracts of land were rationed among the gardeners. The plots tended by the Azorean gardeners had rows and rows of collards alongside rows and rows of tomatoes grown by the Italian gardeners. The chain-link fence that contained the garden from the sidewalk and the main street was typically covered with creeping green bean plants.

My parents, two brothers, and I were fortunate to rent an apartment in my sister's two-family house that had a backyard. While mostly cemented over, the yard had enough earth exposed to grow a grapevine, hydrangeas, dahlias, day lilies, and other flowers. The small garden was located on the left side of the backyard. This is where my father made the earth say collards.

My father used to say that "*Os Portugueses são nada sem sopa*" (The Portuguese are nothing without soup). He meant the Portuguese, who left the Azores for economic reasons and immigrated to Massachusetts, were sustained by the soups they made. Collards were implicated. Immigrants grew and reached for this simple vegetable and turned it into a meal with small amounts of cabbage, carrots, potatoes, and/or a bit of *chouriço*, a smoked pork sausage. These ingredients turned little into abundance.

Collards figure largely in my family's foodways. They were a prominent vegetable in our garden in the Azores and in the small urban garden patch in Massachusetts. The collard greens flourished in the plot of earth overshadowed by two- and three-family houses in Cambridge as they did in the mineral-rich volcanic soil and semi-temperate climate in São Miguel, Azores. They grew year-round in the Azores and, in Massachusetts, from summer into winter. They became sweeter with the cold months but sometimes paler in color in the city environment. My parents harvested these greens with care and then washed the leaves, trimmed off the spines, and rolled up the broad leaves like newspapers and sliced them into ringlets. These prepared collard greens became a central ingredient in soups.

We made *sopa de vegetais*/vegetable soup (with collards, cabbage, carrots, sweet potato, beans), *sopa de couves*/collards soup (with collards, potatoes, carrots, meat), and *caldo verde* (with collards, potatoes, and *chouriço*). All these soup recipes begin with the key ingredients in Portuguese cuisine: onion, garlic, ground and fermented red pepper, and olive oil. These soups nourished us and were extended with slices of bread, a small bit of cheese, and/or *chouriço* throughout the week. As leftovers, sometimes these soups became breakfast and lunch.

The grocery store's produce section is one space that reflects my family's foodways. The other day I stood in front of a beautiful display of organic collard greens that were on sale because they are in season in California. These greens traveled a long way, over 2300 miles, much like we did when we left my home island. I checked the leaves for their tenderness and firmness and evenness of color.

Lessons From the Garden and Kitchen

Our ways of knowing and doing and analyzing produced liminal spaces, inbetweenness, to help us to take notice of these life lessons. We invite readers to shuttle back and forth among the informational literature, vignettes, and the three lessons and consider how they might be resources for their academic identity making and participation. Let the reading be slow so as to take notice of the details of our lives and learning, and consider what those details offer. Here are the insights that we gained in doing this slow research: cultivation of self and home, resourcefulness as creativity and resilience, and embodied memories as wellsprings. Let's begin with our past because, as Karen Barad (2007) maintains: "The past is never finished. . . . we never leave it and it never leaves us behind" (p. ix).

Embodied Memories as Wellspring

The academy wants us to live in our heads, to logically reason everything. We need more. We need to *feel*, not just think. We need to understand the world through our bodies, minds, and souls. We also accept that all things can't be known. This part of our lived experience is the soul, "the mysterious energy that gives meaning and purpose to [our lives]" (Miller, 2014, p. 2). Some claim that the soul resides in the heart and that it is the cumulation of emotions, thinking, and memories.

Collards heighten all of our senses—their depth of color, the feeling of holding freshly harvested bouquets, the crunch of the leaves, their intense fresh smell during rinsing and preparation, their taste, and not to forget *the process*. Collards engage your senses along with the most important entity of our entire being: our hearts, our thinking hearts. In remembering, reading, and writing together, our senses were awakened and memories came tumbling that intensified our multisensory memories of this green. Some memories were small but consequential; some were expansive and detailed; and all were embodied.

These memories reminded us of how our inner knowing has guided us. Dissociating the mind from the heart severs us from our intuitive thinking—our inner voice. This academic severing is dehumanizing. Not engaging our whole body in academia is limiting our potential as human beings. Our embodied participation can be resources for academic learning and engagement.

Resourcefulness as Resilience

One thing that stood out to us as we engaged in this process was the multiple truths that exist for the word "resilience." While it regularly brings up the idea of sturdiness, perseverance, persistent, withstandness, and tough stock, resourcefulness is one way resilience is not often talked about. By considering collards through the theory of practice, we were able to articulate how important resourcefulness is to the concept of resilience. Not that one definition is more important than the other but rather that they hold each other up.

Collards and their permanence in our lives as the ability to tap into our whole embodied experiences with different ways of being, seeing, and moving, inspire us to hold tight to those cultural practices. We make choices as to what to carry forward, both in our lives as an immigrant or as one perpetually feeling on the outside and not authentic. Collards are a resource for us to cultivate who we are—an iterative process of becoming and re/becoming. Learning about collards and their omnipresence across different cultures with the throughline of resourcefulness, that is, collards used in different dishes across different contexts and climates, heightened the importance and emphasis we put on the way we view our own use of collards. This rethinking allowed us to think about the importance of resourcefulness, especially shared resourcefulness.

Resourcefulness is the soft underbelly of resilience. It is the making something out of nothing, of stretching your means to satisfy. Resourcefulness is the ability to find comfort in uncomfortable spaces knowing that you have what it takes to do, provide, and be well. These traits are pillars of resilience, and we wish to include collards in this softer manner rather than the rugged and individualistic understandings of resilience (though they are tough little plants, indeed!). Learning, thinking, and remembering about collards allowed us to reenvision, recast, redefine. Resourcefulness, generating resources from what is available, are familial and community practices that fortify and generate resilience and cultural making.

Cultivation of Self and Home

Collards amplify the importance of the cultivation of self and home. The imposter syndrome is pervasive in academia because many of us feel like we shouldn't be where we are. Considering collards through our thinking tool of practice and our ways of knowing and doing, we realized that these greens allowed us to change our internal mantra to "We should be here." Something about the process of calling on our ancestors and all those before us brings a deep calm, a shift that allows cultivating our home and selves to inform and enrich our academic identities and work.

As a society, we are consumed with moving away and moving up. The cultures of first-generation students are fertile ground. We invite, beg, wistfully hope to not lose the old for the new. For Jamaal, collards are a connection to his past and culture as a biracial person. Collard greens, for Maria José, take her back to her childhood insular and urban landscapes and the cooking her mother and father produced from small living wages. Through a process of remembering, re/remembering through writing, analyzing, and welcoming possibility, we are cultivating the new soil of our lives with our old ways, knowing something new will grow but housed in and from our deep layered selves, pasts, presents, and gesturing to futures. Our cultures are an inner knowing that guides and gives us courage, direction, and steadfastness.

Closing Comments

For Leon's family, the collard green was a sole ingredient that provided great nutrition. For Thelonious Monk, the collard was his "sole credential" that connected him to a long history of resourcefulness and resilience. These connections contributed to his jazz improvisations of dissonances and melodious twists. Contemplating collards has allowed us to reassemble ourselves through our ethnicities, social classes, biculturality, languages, senses, memories, minds, and hearts. *This sole credential is also soulful.*

This project fed our souls. Collards, for Jamaal, serves as a link between his ancestors and current evolving self. Being biracial means straddling two distinct cultures while not fully feeling at home in either. While feeling untethered, collards remind Jamaal of who he is and his place in this layered and nuanced world as he feels the weight of not belonging in academia.

For Maria José, a white Portuguese American woman of peasant-working-class background, collards were a staple. The ability to prepare hearty meals on a meager budget and her connection to a North Atlantic island were the beginning of her relationship with collard greens. Collards have been a resource for engaging in academic spaces that her parents dreamed of but never had the opportunity to participate in.

These lessons are not isolated from each other. We assemble them for different academic purposes. Making use of what is available and trusting what we have experienced and known can be resources for our teaching, research, and service. Conversely, this academic work, informed by these assemblages (Deleuze & Guattari, 1987), has the potential to produce unexpected disruptions, questions, and possibilities.

Recipes as Mentoring

Jamaal's Recipe: Collards

- Procure two bunches of collards with a dark-green complexion and a milky white stalk. Grab some blackeye peas too. The stock is made of onions (way more onions than you think you'll need), smoked ham hocks, and bay leaves. As for onions, I use a variety of yellow and Vidalia onions (sweet onions will suffice; however, don't tell any native Georgian I said that). Dice up those onions, get some butter melted and olive oil in a large stock pot (large enough to host stock for both the collards and peas). Sweat the onions with a bit of salt. The sweating of the onion brings out the sweetness rather than the bitterness that regular sautéing can bring. Once your onions are translucent, add the ham hocks. I usually put four to six for a large batch of stock. Add water. Start by covering everything by about double. You'll be adding water as the process continues.

- You want your stock to be on a low boil. You're going to cook that stock down and refill a few times throughout the day. If you start it in the morning, the stock should be done by dinner. Turn it off and set it aside. Before bed, soak your peas in cold water on the counter.
- Prepping your collards is an act of love. It's a bit reminiscent of that which I never experienced in this world but intrinsic to my identity as a Black person in America. Unbinding those collards opens my soul to receive all of the gifts, thoughts, and other-worldly knowledge that my ancestors wish to bestow upon me. Gently run cold water on the front and backs of those greens. I generally cut the stem up to the first small leaves. I used to cut the spine up well into the leaf. However, I like a bit of a bite to my collards so I leave them in now. Do you. Once you've rinsed your collards, stack them on top of each other. Peel off about an inch or so of leaves, set them on the bench, and roll them up like a newspaper. Start at the opposite side of the stem, and cut the collards into ribbons as wide as you like. Your collards are ready for the stock.
- Take the large pot of stock and split it in half. I then take the ham hocks out and pull off the meat. I evenly separate the meat into the pots. In one pot, add your black-eyed peas, bring to a boil, and then back off to low rumble. In the other pot, add your collards while also adding a healthy glug of apple cider vinegar. While that comes up to a boil, cut your head of cabbage in half, and then quarters. Cut the core out and slice the quarter head of

cabbage into thin ribbons. Once you've cut the cabbage into thin ribbons (think: coleslaw), add it to the pot. I shoot for a 70/30ish ratio (collards/cabbage, respectfully). Check back in about an hour. Cook the collards and peas to your preferred texture. We like our collard cooked but not killed. We like our peas a bit al dente.

- Here comes another controversial topic: hot sauces. The traditional topper for your collards is pepper vinegar (the clear jar with small green peppers and filled with vinegar). However, I prefer something with a bit more kick like Louisiana hot sauce. Whatever your spice preference is, this is where you add it. I start off my bowl with an even split of peas and collards on their separate side. But shortly thereafter, it all gets mixed together.
- If your ham hocks didn't have enough meat, you'll want to brown it in the pot before you add your onions. If you forgot, you can just brown it on the side, cut up the meat, and add accordingly. My ancestors would renounce my Black card if I didn't suggest making a cast iron pan of cornbread to sop up all that pot likker.

Maria José's Recipe: Portuguese Vegetable Soup

Collards are an essential ingredient in soup making in my cultural community. They are the ingredient that is added last, though, because they are tender and cook quickly. Enjoy their deep green color, freshness, tenderness, and handle them with care.

- Begin by filling a stock pot halfway with water. Add a peeled whole onion. My father claimed that it is important to remove the onion after cooking, otherwise it can sour the soup. So I remove the whole onion with a ladle before I store leftovers in the refrigerator. I store the soup in large mason jars. Make sure to take notice of the ring of oil left behind by the collards in the pot. Sometimes I use a bit of bread to trace the circle to collect the nutritious oil.
- Peel 8 to 10 garlic cloves (I'm told that it is always good to deal with uneven amounts of garlic; it brings great fortune—seven or nine cloves) and then smash them with the palm heel of your hand or a wide knife. (This way of preparing garlic seems to

release its full flavor.) Add the garlic to the water. Next, scrub the skin of six good-sized carrots. Don't peel the carrots because a lot of vitamins reside in their skin. Scrub the carrots with a vegetable brush or your hands to remove all the soil. Cut them into long strips and then cube them. Add them to the water.

- Remove the outer leaves of a small cabbage. Rinse its outer layer. Cut the cabbage head in half and then cut it into slices and then dice. Add a half or whole cabbage. You might want to add a sweet potato to thicken the broth. Scrub the sweet potato and then peel. Dice it into the pot. If you don't have a sweet potato, you can also use a bit of winter squash. Wash and peel the skin. Cut the squash into slices and then dice. Let these ingredients simmer for a while. Add several cups of cooked beans: I prefer pinto but white small beans are typically used. Add the variety you enjoy.
- In the meantime, rinse two to three bunches of collards. First trim off the stems. Submerge the collards in a big bowl of water. With running water, rinse every leaf on both sides. Trim the stems. Stack about three to four leaves. Roll up the stack tightly lengthwise. Use a paring knife to cut thin circles of collards. Place the ringlets in a bowl. Then cube the stems. Place these bits in the pot because they require a little more time to cook. Gently pour the collard ringlets into the stock pot and give a gentle stir. Let the soup simmer a bit longer.
- You can add a couple of tablespoons of Portuguese olive oil and salt to taste at the end. (It is not good to cook olive oil in high heat and for a long time because its beneficial qualities start to degrade. We usually bring the oil to the dinner table as a condiment. It can be added to the bowl.) Cover the pot and turn off the stove. The soup will finish cooking with the remaining heat.
- One option: *Chouriço* is an ingredient that you can add for flavor and additional protein. First, bring the *chouriço* to a boil. Drain out the water with fat residue. Add new water and bring it to a boil again. Drain that water and add new water and give it another boil. Pour out the water and place the whole sausage in the soup. When you are ready to serve the soup, cut the sausage into circles and place several circles on the top of each bowl.

- Another option: Add a tablespoonful of Portuguese fermented ground red pepper to the pot or a small dollop to each bowl of soup. This addition will give the soup spice, salt, and color.
- Yet, another option: Add torn stale bread to soup to thicken the broth.

Bom proveito! (Enjoy!) (The meaning of *proveito* is "a good benefit" and "make use of.")

References

Barad, K. (2007). *Meeting the universe halfway: Quantum physics and the entanglement of matter and meaning*. Duke University Press.

Davies, B. (2000). *A body of writing: 1990-1999*. AltaMira Press.

Deleuze, G., & Guattari, F. (1987). *A thousand plateaus: Capitalism and schizophrenia*. University of Minnesota Press.

Ellingson, L. L., & Sotirin, P. (2020). *Making data in qualitative research: Engagements, ethics, and entanglements*. Routledge.

Masny, D. (2013). Rhizoanalytic pathways in qualitative research. *Qualitative Inquiry, 19*(5), 339–348. https://doi.org/10.1177/1077800413479559.

Miller, J. P. (2014). *Teaching from the thinking heart: The practice of holistic education*. Information Age Publishing.

Pink, S. (2012). *Situating everyday life*. Sage Publications.

Richardson, L., & St. Pierre, E. A. (2005). Writing: A method of inquiry. In N. K. Denzin & Y. S. Lincoln (Eds.), *The Sage handbook of qualitative research* (3rd ed., pp. 959–978). Sage Publications.

Tillage, L. W. (1997). *Leon's story*. Farrar, Straus & Giroux.

CHAPTER 5

The Hawaiian Underground Imu: Possibilities Steaming Beneath the Surface of the Academy

KA ʻOHANA PERRY (KEKAILOA PERRY, KERI PERRY, AND MAKUALIʻI PERRY)

Introduction

Can cultural practices and the love of food support an emancipatory approach in academia while also rejecting the status quo? As academic folk who enjoy cooking and serving our family and friends good food, we embrace editors Brewer and Hayes's resolve to explore the academy "through the lens of food and the transferable lessons that can be gleaned from our grandmothers,' mothers,' fathers,' and our own kitchens" (Brewer & Hayes, 2024). The blending of our educational and cultural food practices challenges the academy's status quo approach. Establishing meaningful community spaces to engage cultural practices in academia raises the value of those academics who find themselves consistently occupying the "fugitive" spaces in the "undercommons of the university" (Harney & Moten, 2013, p. 28). To privilege the seemingly nonacademic cultural practice of preparing and sharing a meal and assert it must be integral to the life of academia is a transforming step we gladly take.

The irony that comes from the struggle of living a life partly in the academy and partly in the margins is intriguing for us who identify as minorities in both spaces. In the academy as members of the underrepresented minorities, we are unwelcomed, tolerated, or marketed as the institution's commitment to diversity. However, outside the academy, we thrive in our cultural spaces as we have cultivated a loving community consisting of family and friends that have respect for our sameness, as well as differences (Burgess, 2013). However, being educated in the academy, our degrees also make us a minority within a minority.

Our ʻohana (a family unit beyond the contrived Lilo and Stitch settler fantasy) entered higher education to fulfill the hopes and dreams of the previous generations. Our ʻohana also enjoys cooking, sharing, and eating good food. We each entered the academy knowing the degrees we earned empower the family and communities we represent. Collectively, our scholarly achievements counter the academy's negative tropes that maintain an "imperialist white supremacist capitalist [settler-occupier] patriarchy" (hooks, 2012, p. 4, brackets added). However, our scholarly achievements also empower the academy's neoliberal claim of ownership that celebrates Indigenous and marginalized academic accomplishments while doing nothing substantive to better the conditions of our communities (Franklin-Phipps & Stout-Sheridan, 2024; Pitawanakwat & Pedri-Spade, 2022).

The following Hawaiian Imu Methodology suggests the current U.S. higher education system be rejected for more generative and transforming possibilities (McGranahan, 2016; Simpson, 2017; Smith, 2002; Tuck & Yang, 2024). Our methodology encourages everyone to organize emancipatory outcomes that will delight our academic palates.

Traditional and Customary Food Practices

Na ke kanaka mahiʻai ka imu ō nui
(#2239)

E ʻai i kekahi, e kapi i kekahi
(#252)

The epigraphs are ʻōlelo noʻeau or Hawaiian proverbs relating to Hawaiian food practices (Pukuʻi, 1983). The first proverb references cooking in an imu, or underground oven, as knowledge that feeds the community through careful cultivation of ancestral memories (Puku'i, 1983). The second proverb tells us a healthy, balanced life requires tending to the needs of present and future generations (Puku'i, 1983). Hawaiian food ways can serve as a methodology for community-based academic sustainability in the academy.

The Hawaiian 'ohana is a multigenerational, multiethnic community conscientiously marshalling their food through the proper care and management of resources via traditional and customary practices (Handy & Puku'i, 1998). Although the social and economic conditions in Hawai'i have changed dramatically, making access to natural resources for traditional and customary food practices problematic, the resilience of the 'ohana provides wholesome responses to the demands of modern society (Delind, 2006; Parkins & Craig, 2009; Vivero-Pol, 2017).

Maintaining a healthy diet and lifestyle is complicated by the lack of access to traditional food sources or affordable foods (Sebai et al., 2024; von Seggern & von Poser, 2024) and healthy natural resources (Thattantavide & Kumar, 2024). For the native Hawaiian and Pacific Islander populations, community well-being and healthy food ways are tied directly to food sovereignty (Lukens, 2013). Food sovereignty is the community's ability to reclaim and maintain control over their own food ways and exercise greater self-determination in their communities (Lukens, 2013). Anthropologists von Seggem and von Poser (2024) explain "food ways" is an engagement with cultural food practices that reconnect and reinforce the social and cultural foundation of a people. This chapter accepts the authors' assertion where food production and sharing enforce stronger social connections, belonging, and sovereignty in the Hawaiian community and, by extension, all communities including those within the neoliberal, settler-occupier academy (von Seggem & von Poser, 2024). The academy is a neoliberal, settler-occupier institution that makes unsustainable demands upon faculty and student researchers in competition for economic and human resources (Brunette-Debassige, 2023; Davies et al., 2017; McLaren, 2010; A. Smith, 2009). In the present university system, Indigenous and marginalized academics find their value measured not by their skill and abilities but by how well they are able to parrot the status quo (Perry, 2023; A. Smith, 2009). We offer a Hawaiian Imu Methodology (Imu Methodology) to address the need for transforming academia through food ways to support cultural revitalization, self-determination, and justice approaches for Indigenous and marginalized academics (Huambachano, 2019).

The Hawaiian Underground Imu

The cooking technique guiding this chapter is the Hawaiian imu. The technology of the imu, or underground earthen oven (Handy, Handy, & Puku'i, 1995 Puku'i & Elbert, 1986), involves burning wood for fuel at an extreme temperature (300°F to 700°F) to heat porous basaltic stones that retain the heat for 8 to 20 hours (Handy, Handy, & Puku'i, 1991; Huebert et al., 2010). A steam-inducing medium of banana stumps and fresh ti-leaves are placed over the heated stones and wood coals. Food is added, covered with other fresh ti-leaves, woven mats, or soaked burlap, and topped with a heavy layer of dirt to seal in the steam and taste (Carson, 2002). The cooking process is like a smoke-flavored pressure cooker. The imu can feed a small family or an entire community.

Imu cooking requires community participation. The imu is a cooking medium used to prepare a variety of foods including proteins, vegetables, starches, or in terms of the Western palate, main dishes, side dishes, and even desserts. Overall, the imu cooking "system" is multigenerational and requires active participation from all family members regardless of age, gender, or race.

Food preparation is a community activity that includes gathering resources, setting the food in the imu, serving, and eating. For example, in June 2024 our 'ohana celebrated a grandchild's first birthday with 300 family and friends. To feed the 300 guests, pork cooked in the imu, poi, raw fish, crab, and various other dishes were prepared. Community participation is an integral part of the imu process. The imu is a focal point for community gathering, sharing of stories, and establishing new relationships. The imu process and food prep can last for several hours or several days depending on the size and occasion.

For this chapter, our ʻohana will focus on the preparation of a traditional meal using a variety of ingredients including taro leaves, animal protein, ti-leaves, and coconut milk. The quinssentential Hawaiian dish for imu cooking is called the laulau or lūʻau (Pukuʻi & Elbert, 1986). Its core ingredient, kalo leaves, or lau, are part of the Hawaiian staple plant kalo (Calocasia esculenta) (Whitney et al., 1939). Kalo is the genealogical elder sibling to humans according to the Kumulipo creation chant (Johnson, 1981). We recognize cooking with kalo reestablishes the reciprocal relationship between the elder (land, kalo plant) and younger siblings (people) whereby our care for the land will ensure future sustenance.

Laulau requires a large amount of lau. The lau are cleaned and then placed into bundles of six to eight pieces. Inside each bundle would be cuts of pork, beef, and fish carefully wrapped and tied with the outer ti-leaf, and placed in the imu for cooking. The cooking time in the imu is 6 to 12 hours, depending on the amount. When done, the bundles of steaming laulau are eaten in the entirety.

Our ʻohana are practitioners of imu cooking and food preparation spanning many generations. Each new ʻohana member (children, spouses, in-laws, and community acquaintances) is expected to learn the process and choose a functional role in the imu activity or food prep. The imu practice is a generative learning environment dependent on the community to ensure people are "well filled" with enough sustenance to care for their immediate and future needs. Thus the imu practice and accompanying cultural philosophy is a methodology for academics seeking ways to improve and build healthier possibilities in the academy. Our ʻohana calls this approach an "Imu Methdology."

A Hawaiian Imu Methodology and the Academic Underground

The Imu methodology asserts that all academics belong to and are influenced by the community. We are members of family units, civic groups, social societies, religious communities, or political parties, including the university system. As academics, we are a microcosm of the university ivory tower who educates or employs us. However, the academic community is limited and often neglects and undervalues the nonacademic community relative to research, teaching, or service. Thus the nonacademic community is relegated to being the subjects of research rather than vital research partners (Tuhiwai-Smith, 2021; Trask, 1999).

The Imu Methodology refuses the status quo approaches of the academy by posing new generative possibilities for research and learning. The essential elements of the Imu Methodology are (1) resource access and gathering, (2) community engagement/power sharing, (3) managing the heat of duty and responsibility, and (4) feeding the well-being of the whole. The hope is to provide greater possibilities to transforming academic relationships by centering life on communities in, around, and outside higher education.

Resource Access and Gathering

The imu practice requires several natural resources. First, land is needed to build the imu where an open fire can be ignited in a large subterranean cooking pit. Second, basaltic stones, firewood, and vegetation for food preparation are needed. These elements (land for the imu and cooking resources) reinforce the social and political conditions necessary to maintain imu cooking. Thus imu cooking is a food way that involves lessons in public policy, law, social engagement, and political activism.

For example, our ʻohana exercise traditional protocols in various locations to secure basaltic stones for imu cooking. The locations have since become gentrified with single family homes in the area exceeding $2 million. On one occasion police were called to investigate "strange Polynesian men stealing stones" from the stream bed. When police arrived, we were required to explain our practice and right to gather. The police were unaware our access rights were codified. Specifically, the Hawaiʻi State Constitution "reaffirms and shall protect all rights, customarily and traditionally exercised" by native Hawaiians (Forman & Serrano, 2012, p. 10; Forman & Serrano, 2015, pp. 786–798). Nevertheless, we were told to "hurry it up." We learned constitutional protections will not prevent ignorance fueled by power and privilege. Our example demonstrates the rules are subordinate to the economic and social constructs of the settler-occupier status quo (i.e., gentrification or university policies).

Similarly, Indigenous and marginalized academics find the policies in academia are restrictive and reinforce forms of cultural erasure (Brunette-Viczko, 2022; Kaomea, 2003; Martinez-Roldan & Quinones, 2016; Pitawanakwat & Pedri-Spade, 2022). While policies relating to research, teaching, and service appear benign, research shows these standards reinforce the neoliberal structures of domination and settler-occupier ideologies of difference (Davies et al., 2017; Lockford, 2017; Pedri-Spade & Pitawanakwat, 2022). Indigenous and marginalized scholars engage in community-focused research or cultural concepts often fall outside the academic research mainstream. Strategically, marginalized scholars will situate their work in familiar and acceptable mainstream concepts to matriculate in the academy, suppressing more salient research agendas or pigeon-holing their scholarship to narrow research tropes. However, diverging from mainstream academic approaches can also negatively affect employment, publications and teaching, or acceptance in the academic's discipline (Pedri-Spade, 2020; Pitawanakwat & Pedri-Spade, 2022).

Academics can create access and gathering approaches that identify spaces (land) to engage the community as valued members in higher education. The goal, however, is to claim the academy's spaces as rights to active learning that generates struggle and reconstitutes the power for all peoples in those community spaces. Therefore, an Imu Methodology in education offers the academic, the student researcher, and the community the right to access, gather, and/or share knowledge.

Community Engagement and Power Sharing

Imu cooking and food preparation are labor intensive because its intent is to feed families and the community. Hence, the imu requires ʻohana and community engagement and power sharing to ensure a successful imu (i.e., good food cooked well). Seasoned practitioners are essential members in the community. They guide and support the ʻohana in setting the firewood and stones, gathering resources for the imu cooking, and mentoring the inexperienced members to become valued resources for their ‘ohana and community. The process is generative, helping everyone become integral members of an extended ‘ohana.

In the preparation of food like laulau, the entire ‘ohana participates. Collectively the ‘ohana will gather to clean taro leaves, chop proteins, and bundle hundreds of laulau for cooking. The Hawaiian term often associated with this practice is “laulima,” which describes a process of cooperation. Like the creation of the imu, food preparation requires the full attention of all involved and is necessary to ensure food safety as well as good taste.

During the imu and food preparation processes, the community and ‘ohana participate in a vital cultural practice of social sharing and relationship development. Power is shared and learning is done collectively through a series of individual and group storytelling. Differences are learned and often debated. Overall the community is empowered and strengthened while engaged in the cooperative practice of laulima.

The academy seldom encourages a robust interdisciplinary relationship amongst departments and colleagues as required in imu cooking. Nonacademic communities are largely left out of the decision making, research, teaching, and service processes of academia. Often, student researchers and teachers find themselves in lonely spaces as a result of research foci that demand original ideas and often alienates others. The academics—especially those Indigenous and marginalized academics—are stronger and better prepared when engaged in or with ‘ohana and communities. However, the academy segregates itself from communities, making community engagement appear impossible, overwhelmingly difficult to maintain, or insignificant to its purpose. Understanding the intentional divisiveness between the academy and community is a fugitive insight for academics who yearn for greater shared power and community involvement. The academic has information challenging the existing structures with greater community participation in various elements of academic research, teaching, and service. Incorporating community participation and sharing intelligence—which may betray the privileged inner sanctum of the ivory tower—can greatly improve the conditions of the academy and promote a form of academic laulima.

The goal is to enfranchise the community by making them active members of the research, where teaching is reciprocal, multigenerational, and empowering.

Managing the Heat of Duty and Responsibility

The Hawaiian imu is hot. Standing in the pit or along its edges can easily cause second- and third-degree burns if one is not careful. However, an imu needs to generate a sustained heat of over 450°F for optimal steam cooking. The greater the heat, the better the cooking. To manage the heat, practitioners use plants like banana stumps and ti-leaves to prepare a cooking bed to keep the food from burning and create intense steam. Imu practitioners always get burned; it is part of the practice.The cooking process requires steam that causes meat to separate from the bone or vegetables to cook well enough to consume without chewing. Steaming is part of the Hawaiian imu cooking magic where elements of fire and water are carefully combined and pressurized for optimal flavorful results. Knowing how to manage the heat while carrying out duties and responsibilities is also part of the practice. While the process can be quite stressful, inexperienced practitioners need to learn the power of the imu fire and other dangers to avoid accidents and injury, or prevent food burning, as well as learn how to manage their duties and responsibilities collectively under intense pressure.

The key to managing the heat in the imu cooking process is knowing you are part of a larger ʻohana and community. Each person has a role to play intimately connected to the others. When there is need or uncertainty, one should humble themselves and reach back to ancestral knowledge and the community who are the keepers of ancestral knowledge. Where there is confidence, look to areas and people in the community who require help and lovingly support those needs. Frankly, what one person knows is just a part of the larger community relationship and knowledge bank. Individuals are made whole by the community. When the imu is completed, the community time continues. Stories and techniques are shared to build stronger foundations and expand the cooking practice to feed more people.

The academy is a pressure cooker process of a different kind. Community concerns are a lesser priority to individual research agendas and the funding processes (grants, publications, policy making) empower the neoliberal academy (Perry, 2023). Academics are taught to focus on areas of research, teaching, and service that benefit tenure, promotion, and academic notoriety. As a result, the communities outside the academy are seldom considered a valued part of the academic's professional trajectory. The Imu Methodology rejects the existing academic model of accomplishment because it limits the choices for healthy development and growth. The present academic process is an unsustainable model of scarcity and scorched earth where the cultural knowledge of Indigenous and marginalized communities is treated as an expendable resource extractible in the name of academic progress. Thomas argues that neoliberal institutions like the university extract knowledge from Indigenous and marginalized communities to the detriment of their health, culture, community cohesion, and self-determination. Even when the institutions are motivated by good intentions, "Very rarely does the knowledge shared by Indigenous people benefit them as much as it benefits the state" (Thomas, 2021, p. 2).

Transforming the structures of government, like the academy, will require a deconstruction of the institution's settler-occupier, neoliberal processes. Such an approach requires empowering the communities most affected and most able to start the transformation process (Muller, 2018). The Imu Methodology argues for an academic duty and responsibility greater than the limited confines of the present academic system. The heat required to cook up a healthier and more responsive academic life can be accomplished by burning the structures currently supporting settler-occupier and neoliberal logics of difference. Professors and researchers acting alone might spark a flame, but such a method is not sustainable and leads to burnout. The Imu Methodology calls for a community-focused approach inclusive of the ʻohana and larger community who are currently ignored or undervalued by the academy. The academic insiders (those who are tenured or in positions of relative power) can serve the role of seasoned practitioners in developing the Imu Methodology in academia.

Feeding the Well-being of the Whole

The final Imu Methodology element focuses on eating. After a long cooking time, the ʻohana and family carefully remove the dirt, burlap, and plant coverings exposing the cooked food. The food is brought to the serving table while the ʻohana cleans the imu by removing the charcoal and basaltic cooking stones and any other plant materials from the pit. The imu is then covered until the next gathering. The laulau is unwrapped and served with other dishes made in the imu or by ʻohana and community. In our ʻohana, we recognize the many hands who contributed to the gathering and preparation of food. We also ask everyone to offer words of love and thanks and then turn to our creator for guidance and blessings.

Next, we eat. The children and elderly are served first; then visitors, guests, and ʻohana; the hosts of the imu often eat last. Feasting time is a culmination of weeks of access and gathering, power sharing, and cooking in intense heat and pressure. The goal of feeding the ʻohana and community is accomplished in several ways. First, our bodies are nourished, providing sustenance for our continued well-being. Second, ʻohana and community are reunited to share stories and ideas and build relationships. In doing so, we affirm our commitment to each other and the broader cultural relationships, responsibilities, and duties that connect us. Third, we reestablish the practice of ʻohana and community openly and notoriously in a world that appears too eager to erase our worldviews and knowledge. In Hawaiʻi and other parts of the world, "Food practices are increasingly understood as cultural expressions of belonging" (von Seggem & von Poser, 2024, p. 2). Indeed, the process of learning to cook and eat imu food reinforces "taking care of the neighbours . . . and is also connected to transforming healthy people and communities that are more food-sovereign" (von Seggem & von Poser, 2024, p. 18).

The Imu Methodology aspires to refuse, reimagine, and create a culture of learning to empower the cultural knowledge and ideas generated by a cooperative relationship between the academic and the community within a marginalized society that does not appreciate, nor respect, culturally rich practices passed on for generations. Preparation requires a conscientized approach to the work spaces of the institution where knowledge can be shared openly and freely, and fed in emancipatory ways to nourish the whole community and not just the privileged few. The laulau is a dish best shared with ‘ohana and community because the ingredients are gathered from the land and the flavor is melded from the many hands that lovingly and carefully wrapped and cooked it. When the academic is able to share his/her food of knowledge it is due in large part to the collective engagement created and sustained in their community in the most positive way possible.

Planning the Next Meal

We conclude this chapter by referencing the ‘ōlelo no‘eau above, “e ‘ai i kekahi, e kapī i kekahi” (Puku‘i, 1983, p. 31). The proverb recognizes the need to cherish and protect the knowledge of our communities so it will be available to guide everyone moving forward. The Imu Methodology encourages academics to treat all of their knowledge respectfully and to honor the communities from whence that knowledge came. Therefore, we will prepare and eat some food now and ready the imu for the next time to sustain a healthy and beloved community (Burgess, 2013).

How might we know whether the Imu Methodology is working? By observing whether we are supporting or refusing the status quo. When some are well-fed while others are not, we know there is more work to do. Have we struggled enough to assert our rights and access to space, land, and ideas that promote our communities? Do we know where the resources are? Are we caring for those resources? Have we used our privilege as academics to build a shared governance and power relationship with each other and our communities? Is our fire hot enough to burn through the capitalist-driven, ego-laden trappings of academia so we can generate healthy options and meaningful approaches? Too little heat means minimal improvements and greater chances of being consumed by the settler-occupier ideologies of difference and domination. It means our generative ideas will not be fully cooked or ready to take on an empowered role in the academy and the academy will remain unchanged as a settler-occupier, neoliberal institution.

As educated Indigenous and marginalized academic authors and imu cooks/connoisseurs, we consider life in the academy's status quo unacceptable. Noted 19th century songwriter and poet Eleanor Pendergrast penned a protest song condemning the U.S.-led overthrow of the Hawaiian Kingdom and the Provisional Government it replaced. The song's name is "Kaulana Nā Pua" or "Ka Mele 'Ai Pohaku" (Nordyke & Noyes, 1993). The Provisional Government attempted to create a new status quo by demanding all government employees swear an oath of allegiance or be fired. Pendergrast wrote "Kaulana Nā Pua" in protest. Today, the song represents community resistance and refusal. A critical line of the song states, "ua lawa mākou i ka pōhaku a me ka 'ai kamaha'o o ka 'āina" (Basham, 2008, p. 163; Nordyke & Noyes, 1983, pp. 28–29). We understand the phrase to mean the people of Hawai'i would rather eat the stones and other resources of the land before accepting oppressive policies and ideologies of domination. The stones are the basaltic rocks that create the heat for our imu cooking and the implements for food preparation. The stones are a source of life and survival for our communities, therefore "eating the stones" can mean to eat from the imu and engage in the cultural practices that empower our communities. In the academy, Indigenous and marginalized academics can turn to their communities for sustenance and power and reject the academy's unhealthy, status quo approaches. Our communities are our stones—their knowledge and love represent the abundant resources that feed and sustain our world.

In the end, we need to ask: are academics and communities being fed by our Imu methodologies (our food ways) or by the status quo? The present system promotes predatory practices, scarcity, and starvation in an academic institution where resources reward the status quo while tolerating those willing to accept a subaltern life in the margins and undercommons. Such an approach is illogical and unsustainable. There is no denying the academy is an important part of our community but it is lacking. A healthy academic community must include everyone, not just some. The sooner academics and the institution learn this simple truth, the greater our chances of realizing a well-nourished university community.

Through a Hawaiian Imu Methodology, we believe it is possible for our food ways and love of culture to fuel a process that rejects the status quo and shifts us toward a more emancipatory framework in higher education. The process involves struggle, and chances are we will get burned from time to time, but the foods and knowledge we generate are quite delicious and well worth the effort.

References

Basham, L. (2008). Mele Lāhui: The importance of pono in Hawaiian poetry. *Te Kaharoa, 1*(1).

Brewer, T. J., & Hayes, C. (2024). Food stories: Navigating the academy with cultural lessons from the kitchen – Call for proposals. Retrieved from https://tjamesonbrewer.com/food-stories.

Brunette-Debassige, C. (2023). Indigenous refusals in educational leadership practices in Canadian universities. *AlterNative: An International Journal of Indigenous Peoples, 19*(2), 377–386.

Brunette-Debassige, C., & Viczko, M. (2022). Critical perspectives for educational leadership and policy in higher education. In *The Palgrave handbook on critical theories of education* (pp. 261–282). Cham: Springer International Publishing.

Burgess, P. (2013). Building the beloved community: A life practice. *Hūlili: Multidisciplinary Research on Hawaiian Well-Being, 9*, 11–34.

Carson, M.T. (2002). Tī ovens in polynesia: Ethnological and archaeological perspectives. *The Journal of the Polynesian Society, 111*(4), 339–370.

Davies, B., Somerville, M., & Claiborne, L. (2017). Feminist poststructuralisms and the neoliberal university. In *Qualitative inquiry in neoliberal times*, pp. 87–103. Routledge.

Delind, L.B. (2006). Of bodies, place, and culture: Re-situating local food. *Journal of Agriculture and Environmental Ethics, 19*, 121–146.

Forman, D. & Serrano, S. (2012). *Hoʻohana aku, a hoʻola aku: A legal primer for traditional and customary rights in Hawaii.* Ka Huli Ao Center for Excellence in Native Hawaiian Law.

Forman, D. M., & Serrano, S. K. (2015). Traditional and customary access and gathering rights. *Native Hawaiian Law: A Treatise*; Kamehameha Publishing: Honolulu, HI, USA, 779–854.

Franklin-Phipps, A., & Stout-Sheridan, R. (2024). Conditions of arrival: On refusing to be included. In *Working with Theories of Refusal and Decolonization in Higher Education* (pp. 15–27). Routledge.

Handy, E. S. C., & Pukuʻi, M. K. (1998). *The Polynesian family system in Kaʻū, Hawaiʻi.* Mutual Publishing.

Handy, E. S. C., Handy, E. G., & Puku'i, M. K. (1995). *Native planters in old Hawai'i: Their life, lore and environment*. Bishop Museum Press.

Harney, S. & Moten, F. (2013). *The undercommons: Fugitive planning & black study*. Minor Compositions.

hooks, B. (2012). *Writing beyond race*. In Writing beyond race (pp. 184–190). Routledge.

Huambachano, M. A. (2019). Indigenous food sovereignty. *New Zealand Journal of Ecology, 43*(3), 1–6.

Huebert, J. M., Allen, M. S., & Wallace, R. T. (2010). Polynesian earth ovens and their fuels: Wood carchoal remains from Anaho Valley, Nuku Hiva, Marquesas Islands. *The Journal of the Polynesian Society, 119*(1), 61–97.

Johnson, R. K. (1981). *Kumulipo, the Hawaiian hymn of creation* (Vol. 1). Topgallant Publishing Company.

Kaomea, J. (2003). Reading erasures and making the familiar strange: Defamiliarizing methods for research in formerly colonized and historically oppressed communities. *Educational researcher, 32*(2), 14–23.

Lockford, L. (2017). Welcome to the neoliberal university. *Cultural Studies↔Critical Methodologies, 17*(4), 361–363.

Lukens, A. B. (2013). "Theorizing food justice: Critical positionality and the political economy of community food systems." Thesis for the degree of Doctor of Philosophy (University of Hawai'i at Manoa). Political Science. University of Hawai'i at Manoa.

Martínez-Roldán, C. M., & Quiñones, S. (2016). Resisting erasure and developing networks of solidarity: Testimonios of two Puerto Rican scholars in the academy. *Journal of Language, Identity & Education, 15*(3), 151–164.

McGranahan, C. (2016). Theorizing refusal: An introduction. *Cultural Anthropology, 31*(3), 319–325.

McLaren, P. (2010). Revolutionary critical pedagogy. *InterActions: UCLA Journal of Education and Information Studies, 6*(2).

Muller, M. K. (2018). Promoting or protecting traditional knowledges? Tensions in the resurgence of Indigenous food practices on Vancouver Island. *The International Indigenous Policy Journal, 9*(4).

Nordyke, E. C., & Noyes, M. H. (1993). Kaulana Na Pua: A voice for sovereignty. *The Hawaiian Journal of History, 27*(1), 27–42.

Parkins, W., & Craig, G. (2009). Culture and the politics of alternative food networks. *Food, Culture & Society, 12*(1), 77–103.

Pedri-Spade, C. (2020). Centering the lived struggle of indigenous women in the academy: A performance autoethnography. *Decolonizing and indigenizing education in Canada*, 91–116.

Perry, K. (2023). The salient truthfulness of aloha 'āina theory and guerrilla praxis. In R. J. Tierney, F. Rizvi, & K. Erkican (Eds.), *International Encyclopedia of Education*, vol. 3. Elsevier. https://dx.doi.org/10.1016/B978-0-12-818630-5.06090-2.

Pitawanakwat, B. T., & Pedri-Spade, C. (2022). Indigenization in universities and its role in continuing settler-colonialism. *Janus Unbound: Journal of Critical Studies, 1*(2), 12–35.

Puku'i, M. K. (1983). *'Ōlelo No'eau: Hawaiian proverbs & poetical sayings.* Bishop Museum Press.

Puku'i, M. K., & Elbert, S. H. (1986). *Hawaiian dictionary: Hawaiian-English, English-Hawaiian*, Revised and Enlarged Edition. University of Hawai'i Press.

Sebai, I., Ing, A., Nardocci, M., Fediuk, K., Sadik, T., Chan, H. M., & Batal, M. (2024). Eating Traditional Foods Enhances Diet Quality Among First Nations in Canada: An Analysis Using the Healthy Eating Food Index-2019 (HEFI-2019) and the Canadian Healthy Eating Index 2007 (C-HEI 2007). *Applied Physiology, Nutrition, and Metabolism*, (ja).

Simpson, A. (2017). The ruse of consent and the anatomy of 'refusal': Cases from indigenous North America and Australia. *Postcolonial Studies, 20*(1), 18–33.

Smith, A. (2009). "Native studies and critical pedagogy: Beyond the academic-industrial complex." In J. Sudbury & M. Okazawa-Rey (Eds.), *Activist scholarship: Antiracism, feminism, and social change.* Paradigm Publishers.

Smith, G. H. (2002, April). Beyond Freire's political literacy: From conscientisation to transformative praxis. In *AERA Conference, New Orleans.*

Thattantavide, A., & Kumar, A. (2024). Local food systems as a resilient strategy to ensure sustainable food security in crisis: Lessons from COVID-19 pandemic and perspectives for the post-pandemic world. *CABI Reviews*, (2024).

Thomas, A. (2022). Indigenous knowledge is not an extractable resource. *Academia Letters, 2.* Article 3832. https://doi.org/10.20935/AL3832.

Trask, H.-K. (1999). *From a native daughter: Colonialism and sovereignty in Hawaii, revised edition.* University of Hawai'i Press.

Tuck, E. & Yang, K.W. (2024). Series Editor's Introduction. In P. Mikulan & M. Zembylas (Eds.), *Working with theories of refusal and decolonization in higher education.* Taylor & Francis Group.

Tuhiwai-Smith, L. (2021). *Decolonizing methodologies: Research and peoples, third edition.* Zed Books Limited.

Vivero-Pol, J. L. (2017). The idea of food as commons or commodity in academia. A systematic review of English scholarly texts. *Journal of Rural Studies, 53*, 182–201.

von Seggern, J., & von Poser, A. (2024). Re-engaging foodways: Life-courses of disconnection and reconnection with food, environment, and sociality in Hawai'i. In *Anthropological Forum* (pp. 1–23). Routledge.

Whitney, L. D., Bowers, F. A. I., & Takahashi, M. (1939). *Taro varieties in Hawaii.* Hawai'i Agricultural Experiment Station of the University of Hawai'i, Bulletin No. 84.

CHAPTER 6

Ditching the Pipeline and Living the Curriculum of Bread

LAURA JEWETT

I was just past the grind of the 11th-hour push for promotion to full. Contrary to Sparkes' (2021) description of "the deep affective somatic and spiritual crises that many academics are suffering from that threatens to overwhelm them" (p. 1027), full professorship found me feeling just a little flat. For years, I had been seeing to production—initiating research, presenting at conferences and attempting to publish as well as all the other tasks that keep the academic pipeline flowing. This pipeline metaphor modeled by my father, the professor, and pedagogically reinforced by graduate school mentors has scored me rank, material gain and other privileges. But at the same time, it seemed to be denuding my intellectual life. Similarly, McDaniel (2019) writes in *The Chronicle of Higher Education* that by the time she reached full professor her intellectual interests had "started to feel stale." This is where I turned to bread, or more specifically, sourdough. This chapter draws from a yearlong autoethnographic experiment in which I closely chronicled the process of cultivating a starter, baked lots of bread, and then applied these sourdough principles to the process of feeding, fermenting, stretching, folding, shaping, and leavening my intellectual life as a university professor. This chapter stretches and folds autoethnographic findings into narrative accounts of my yearlong process of tending my intellectual life based on the living curriculum of lactobacilli and the jointly embodied symbiosis of its fermentation as a way of cultivating more life-sustaining metaphors of intellectual life and scholarly productivity.

Metaphors play a powerful role in shaping our understanding and conceptualization of complex ideas. According to McGrew (2016), "metaphors are often helpful in conceptualizing and communicating complex social phenomena in a manner that is accessible (p. 354). In line with McGrew (2016), this chapter critiques what Kerr (2022) calls the "alluring discourse of the academic pipeline" as applied to notions of scholarly productivity. The pipeline metaphor is widely used to discuss the sequence or flow of academic productivity and has shaped institutional practices such as the development of research policies, granting procedures, funding priorities, and faculty evaluation. The pipeline metaphor conveys industrial values of efficiency, progress and linear progression codified as intellectual productivity. However, this metaphor is problematic on multiple levels. Husu (2001) argues that the pipeline metaphor fails to account for the dynamic and iterative nature of research, promotes standardization in ways that constrain diversity, and obscures nonlinear connections among scholarly processes. Further, Pérez (2022) and Stern, Vela, & Nakae (2023) argue that the pipeline metaphor is exploitative and its use offensive. Posthumanist critiques of extractivist logic from Bösel (2022), Davis (2019), and Palacios & Baldauf (2022) critically explore the extractivism at work in the pipeline discourse as "both an ideology and an economic system built on the understanding that the world, and all its beings, are inherently commodifiable, violently turned into 'things' operating as a standing reserve for the accumulation of profit and power" (Davis, 2019). Fairchild (2023) and Bauman (2020) critically explore "fossil fuel time of chronos" as a "uniform timeframe based upon efficient causality, parsimony," disconnected from the "complex thinking that a relational world of evolving, porous bodies require" (p. 97). Both authors critique the temporal logic at work in the pipeline metaphor and seek more expansive options of time. This chapter looks at the temporal and spatial assumptions of the pipeline metaphor and then attempts to counter them through alternative metaphors of academic growth from sourdough cultures. Towards these ends, I combine Aoki's (1993) notion of the lived curriculum with the living curriculum of sourdough and then ask what this might mean in terms of restructuring metaphors of the intellectual life and academic productivity or the curriculum vitae.

Method

This chapter explores data from a yearlong experimental inquiry in which I, along with a confederacy of microbes, cultivated a starter, baked lots of bread, and then applied these sourdough principles to the process of feeding, fermenting, stretching, folding, and shaping my intellectual life as a curriculum scholar. The methodological design shaping the experiment overlaps with those found in autoethnographic and autobiographical accounts of the academy such as Gill (2018), Moriarty (2019), and Sparkes (2021, 2007). In this vein, I constructed narrative accounts of my own experiences as a curriculum scholar in tandem with sourdough experiences and then conducted discourse analysis as described by Davies & Bansel (2010) in their exploration of the discursive practices through which "academic subjects are re-shaped and re-shape themselves, singly and collectively" (p. 5). Additionally, my methodological aims find inspiration from slow-food and other slow-living movements scored by notions of "deliberate, thoughtful, in-depth, and conscious" methodologies (Crabtree et al., 2020, p. 56). However, my inquiry also relies on surface reactions, accidental blooms, and the unconscious bubbling of becomings. Like Fairchild (2016), I see this methodological approach as one in which experimental inquiry "folds and unfolds to reveal becoming-researcher, becoming-methodology, becoming-data" (p. 21). And in this sense, the liveliness of these methodological interactions can be seen to spring back against "commodity-focused production-consumption systems" at work in the discursive and material practices associated with the academic pipeline through which intellectual resources are extracted and become commodified as productivity (Szanto, 2022, p. 189).

As St. Pierre, Jackson, & Mazzei (2016) describe, the process of this inquiry is also an experimental project that explores a "different plane of thought on which we can create new concepts that will help us live a different existence" (p. 100). In the case of this study, the aim is to experiment with alternative conceptions of intellectual productivity and concomitantly embody diverse ways to live curriculum and its inquiry. To conduct this experiment, I used my recent experience learning to bake sourdough bread to identify a constellation of fruitful material practices and then figuratively applied these to the discursive and material practices of my own curriculum scholarship via lived experience. This entailed altering my scholarly rhythm to mimic the sequenced activation, responsive care and feeding, and periods of dormancy sourdough requires. Toward these ends, I enacted a twice-daily series of intellectual "feedings" and "discardings" in which every 8 to 12 hours I would engage in reading or other intellectual, aesthetic, and creative acts aimed at activating my intellectual life and then "discard" via writing or other creative outputs for approximately a quarter of the time I spent feeding. For example, my autoethnographic journal reveals that on the first day of the experiment, my first feeding at 5:55 a.m. consisted of reading a chapter from Pallant's (2021) social history of bread for 25 minutes, and my discard consisted of 9 minutes spent crafting a bread haiku. Then at 4:00 p.m., I spent 2 hours reading from Serres' (2018) discussion of metaphysics and spent 30 minutes writing a response. This cycle was aimed at activating and maintaining my intellectual starter, in contrast to fueling a specific project of intellectual production. I continued this sequence of feeding, discarding, repurposing discard, fermenting, stretching, folding, resting, shaping, and yielding for a year.

I'm not a just-so baker or scholar. I often rely on substandard weights and measures. The results are, by and large, a bit rough and ready. So, at first glance sourdough method seemed at times overly scientific and too technical for my more intuitive oeuvre. Even a brief Google search into "sourdough for beginners" offers bushels of details designed to demystify the process of sourdough. As a preface to a discussion of findings from my year of living my academic life lactobacterially, I provide an overview of the general process I use to make a boule (round loaf) of sourdough bread, ideally without allowing the chemistry of sourdough to obscure its alchemy.

For over 5,000 years, sourdough breadmaking has started with a fermented mixture of flour, water, and naturally occurring wild yeast and bacteria (Corsetti, 2012). To activate, this starter—also called the mother—needs to be fed every 12 hours or so by removing some starter (discard) and stirring in fresh flour and water to the remaining starter. You can keep an active starter on the counter until you are ready to use it, or she can be left to nap in the fridge. I just rouse her with regular feedings 48 hours or so before I plan to bake. Sourdough bread needs an active, bubbly starter to ferment and rise. To make bread, I gently combine flour and water and let the mixture rest for an hour or sometimes several. This period of rest after gently mixing flour and water, but before adding salt and the starter or yeast, is called autolyze. The best bakes add the starter just before the apex of its rise, when it looks like a bubbling dome (Boddy, 2022). It took a while for me to get this timing down. Mother is not tethered to a timer. But generally, I feed her and then in the time it takes to answer morning emails, swim laps, and autolyze, she is ready. After autolyze, I add some starter to the dough and mix. I sprinkle salt across the top and pinch it in. The addition of starter to the dough initiates the stage known as bulk fermentation (Landis et al., 2021). With the exception of a series of slaps, stretches, folds, and rests at 30-minute intervals for the first 2 hours or until it looks right, the action of bulk fermentation appears subtle as the wild yeast and bacteria work to develop flavor and structure in the dough (Pallant, 2021). After bulk fermenting on the counter, I shape it into a ball by first turning it onto a scantily floured cutting board, lightly patting it into an oval, and folding it like an envelope. Next, I gather the envelope into a roundish shape and, cupping my hand around the dough ball, drag it in small, tense circles until it is very taut and round. Then I put the tight dough ball seam-side up in a spiraled cane banneton, swaddled in a damp tea towel, and leave it to sleep in the fridge overnight.

On baking day, I get up early, make coffee, and preheat a cast iron Dutch oven to 500 degrees for an hour or until it's screeching hot. In the minutes just before baking, I remove the fully proofed or fermented dough from the basket and put it on parchment. It has expanded and slackened overnight and demands quick attention between the fridge and the oven. Using a sharp blade called a lame, I usually try to make a single, confident slash in a semi-circle just left of center. Right before I put the scored boule—parchment and all—into the Dutch oven, I spritz it with water. Then I turn down the heat to 450, put the lid on, and bake for 30 minutes. Next, I remove the lid and bake uncovered until it looks done and sounds hollow when I knock on its undercrust. I like to let the crust almost burn, forming a deep burnished constellation of crackles. Then I let it cool on a rack and take lots of pictures. The entire process, from feeding the starter to pulling the finished loaf from the oven, takes me at least 24 hours.

Sourdough baking is emblematic of the slow-food movement, which seeks to contest "an industrial system that privileges efficiency and markets over holistic alternatives that encourage creativity and well-being" (Kauper & Jacobs, 2019, p. 339). According to Van der Sluis (2020), the notion of slow food offers "some tantalising arguments, providing a standpoint to critique contemporary Higher Education" (p. 1). Berg & Seeber (2016) draw from the slow-food movement in their critique of the neoliberal temporal sensibilities at work in the commodification of academic life and scholarly productivity. They draw from the slow food movement to critique pipeline time and argue for a new narrative in which time is seen "as a process of becoming . . . rather than thinking of time as an accumulation of lines on the CV" (Berg & Seeber, 2016, p. 59). In what follows, I draw parallels between the living curriculum of sourdough starter and the lived curriculum of my experimental inquiry and apply them to considering new narratives for feeding intellectual life and sustaining a more vital academic culture.

Of CVs and Wild Yeast

Starter is the foundation of sourdough bread. It's a living culture of wild yeast and lactic acid bacteria that ferments flour and water (Dees, 2020). This permeable microbial consortium is also called inoculant, *levain*, or *lievito naturale*. Some just call her mother. I started with two starters and named them after influential women in my life. The first I named Dean O'Toole in honor of a family friend and unofficial godmother who was the university dean of home economics when I was growing up. She was a powerful academic and a sophisticated world traveler. I still wear the string of carnelian beads she brought me from Egypt 40 years ago. The second I named Sussy after my mother's hippie business partner. I credit her with fostering many of my crunchier proclivities. I don't remember Sussy making sourdough bread, though I do remember a mason jar of starter sitting on her kitchen counter. There is a long tradition of naming starters after loved ones. Naming my starters in this way allowed them to serve as animated, matrilineal metaphors for the emotional connections among women and the satisfaction that accompanies nurturing a living culture through consistent care and feeding: Take care of her. Feed her. Let her rest.

I killed them both. They died separately in the same manner. Coaxing activity out of a sleepy starter takes patience, attention, and warmth. In the beginning, I used to rush my mothers too much. I would warm their ceramic crocks or keep them in a cold oven (with the oven light on) in hopes of accelerating their activity. I forgot about Dean O'Toole and accidentally baked her while preheating the oven for leftovers. Six weeks later, Sussy died the same way. I started over. Two years later she doesn't have a name, though she represents a distinct and ever-changing and interdependent colony of relations with an evolving personality and mercurial behavior. She contains multitudes. Describing this phenomenon, Fournier (2020) asserts "The fermenting body takes in bacteria and yeast from its environment and integrates it into its constitution, becoming something different than it was before" (p. 91). But as research has illustrated, it is not only the microbial bodies of the mother that are changed through their fermentation. Lidz (2020) describes a comprehensive study in which researchers found that "the microbes on the hands of the bakers mirrored the microbes within their starters" (p. 5). Ultimately inseparable from their mothers, "bakers had, in some sense, become their bread and vice-versa" (Lidz, 2020, p. 5). As Fournier (2020) reminds, "the creation of a good sourdough is a symbiosis between baker and microbes" (p. 176).

My idea for this experimental inquiry, like my sourdough journey, started with the care and feeding of my metaphoric mother and my blooming consciousness of myself as a co-evolutionary being imbricated in what Trigg (2023) and other scholars describes as, cultures representing interconnected strains of bacterial life and human lifeways (Arantes, 2020; Crane, 2021; Trigg, 2022, Woo, 2022). According to Katz (2011), "The Ferment itself, and our ability to produce it, is as much a product of co-evolution as the person, plant, yeast, or bacteria. Thus, co-evolution encompasses even culture" (p. 167). I began to see myself as a co-creator of a culture based on a central mode of production that connected me to histories of women's work as brewers, bakers, scholars, and other conjurers, and which defied easy dichotomies like wild versus domesticated. After all, from the microbes' point of view, I too was becoming domesticated by wild yeast, and wild yeast was becoming me (Fournier, 2020). I contrast this mode of production with the unidirectional pipeline metaphor and its concomitant metaphor of a "line of scholarship." The latter sees scholarship as a commodity to be extracted and refined in standardized ways to ensure a product that meets the external standards of research. For the next year, I sought to reconceptualize my scholarship as inspired by my relationship with sourdough starter and our mode of coproduction that embodies "both preservation and transformation" (Fournier, 2020, p. 106). This meant paying attention to the processes of activating, feeding, and fermenting my scholarship in ways that meant caring for the scholarship was nearly inseparable from caring for the scholar.

Fundamental to my study was the twice-daily tending to the vitality of my scholarly life/culture beyond the annual production schedule represented in time by academic year and in text by materials for annual review. For the year of this study, I worked to ferment my scholarship with twice-daily feedings. These constituted textual inputs. For this study, I deliberately engaged with texts with the aim of activating and sustaining, as opposed to extracting ideas from literature exclusively for their use in service of a research line reliant on lock-step alignment of inputs and outputs. To activate and sustain, I also attended a diverse variety of 40-plus scholarly workshops, conferences, and talks in which I was not presenting, and which might only be peripherally related to my research line. The aim was to activate, not disseminate. This aim resists the logic of the pipeline as codified through discursive practices of the CV in which the vitality of a scholarly course of life is reduced to a tightly aligned set of activities and deliverables, in which everything up the line must be in direct service of the final product (Forsberg, 2016; Smyth, 2017).

In her research on the literacy of sourdough, McConnell (2021) quotes food activist Michael Pollan's (2013) assertion that "to ferment your own food is to lodge a small but eloquent protest—on behalf of the senses and the microbes—against . . . homogenization" and a "declaration of independence from an economy that would much prefer we remain passive consumers of its standardized commodities" (Pollan, 2013, p. 414–415 in McConnell, 2021, p. 3). Likewise, approaching my scholarship as ferment—the rapidly co-evolving yet slow-moving, not fully domesticated, life-preserving interrelation among the mother acting jointly with diverse living histories and cultures of co-producers, seen and unseen—can be viewed as a cozy rebellion against a scholarly life clocked and measured against the extractive labor required necessary for the overproduction of harshly refined forms of scholarly productivity reified as research lines.

The Paradoxical Productivity of Discard

The process of discarding is as central to the preservation and the transformation of sourdough cultures as feeding is. Removing and feeding at regular intervals helps sustain a consistent level of fermentation and microbial activity (Arantes, 2020). Removing a portion of starter helps maintain a balanced ratio of flour, water, and microorganisms. This balance is crucial for the vitality of the culture (Landis et al., 2021). McConnell (2021) describes this process as a cycle:

> The starter is a ghost of itself every time. The yeasts and bacteria in the starter are old and new each time I feed it. It's a lesson in the cyclical nature of life and death. Something is born and grows and then dies when I discard it, but in the portion of starter I've saved, the ghosts of the previous starters remain, giving it life. (p. 67)

I too enact this cycle. I discard three-quarters of the starter and feed the remaining one-quarter twice a day. Sometimes I throw the discard out as McConnell describes above, but often I use this prolific byproduct to add tang to pancakes or pizza dough. It makes the most pillow-y naan. Keep in mind that this process of discarding is also central to maintaining the active starter, which I then apply to flour and water and salt to make bread. While sourdough loaves, boules, and bâtards depend on an active, bubbly mother for their doubling and rising and holy crumb, the productivity of discard is not diminished by its dormancy.

This messy ritual of removal punctuates my days, and sticky starter speckles the surfaces of my life. Discard winds up in my hair, on my cats, and between the spaces of my keyboard. It is a living thing that resists being contained. I also give discard away. Thus it becomes the mother of another. According to Van Oyen (2021), "a starter 'born' in one kitchen can make its way through many others by way of being shared; within it are 'borne' the traces of other bodies it has lived alongside" (p. 16). In this way, the mother is both preserved and transformed as she is distributed across relational and spatial networks of embodied knowledge. She gets around. In her discarding she loses parts of herself, she changes, and is remade. For the year of my experimental inquiry, I expanded this concept beyond the reach of individual manuscripts and instead applied it as an embodied process of cultivating intellectual life from discarded ferments of my work's more central strain. This meant putting the discard from the twice-daily creative feedings to pragmatic use while maintaining the capacity of the mother culture to give rise to and sustain longer-term intellectual projects. My creative discard found new life in conversations with colleagues and students, journal entries, haikus, social-media posts, essays, and theorizings, while its fertile flecks often wound up in my teaching. Without even a line on my CV, do these out-of-line intellectual activities aimed at sustaining the mother even count as work? Maxwell (2020) sees such work "as a vital and revolutionary act" that "lays in a quiet site" of discard (p. 9). So do I. The labor of discard can be seen as a paradoxically subtractive process, through which the materialities of sourdough cultures, their decompositions, and the joint embodied knowledges among them divide, multiply, redistribute, and reconstitute. Alluding to sourdough and its discard, Maxwell (2020) suggests that "perhaps through such subversive, household practices, we can craft the power to decompose our institutions and cultural narratives" (p. 17).

Living the Curriculum of Bread

According to Szanto (2023):

> Even as such cultures are consumed by a production process, they are renewed by it: a piece of lively starter is taken away for a batch of, say, sourdough bread and is then replaced by new food (flour), itself a product of a previous death (wheat harvest). To remain alive, a culture must be used, cared for, performed with, annihilated, reborn, and reset. (p. 40)

It is not hard to draw parallels between Szanto's (2023) discussion of the productive capacity of sourdough starter and modes of scholarly production. In my yearlong experiment, I pushed these parallels by actually trying to mirror the cultures of sourdough production and apply them to my scholarly life. I gleaned many things from my autoethnographic experiment trying to connect the symbiotic material practices embodied jointly by me and a confederacy of microbes at work in the domestic sphere of my kitchen to my own material and discursive configurations of my intellectual life as a curriculum theorist, both inside and outside the fossil-fueled temporal assumptions and extractive logic of scholarly productivity represented by the academic pipeline metaphor. First, I learned to feed the mother. An active starter is essential to a well-risen loaf and, at least in my experiment, a more fully leavened intellectual life. Proper feeding at the right time, over time, is key to promoting activity. Bauman (2020), borrowing from Haraway (2016), pleads that "we must find ways to carve spaces outside of the fossil-fueled time of chrono. We must not rush away" (p. 94). My findings provide an opportunity for scholars to acknowledge if and to what degree notions of the pipeline commodify time, promote an academic "hurry culture" and constrain the timelines of their research as well as those of their own scholarly becoming (Berg & Seeber, 2016; Gil, 2018; Vostal, 2015). Findings also carve out space for thinking through alternative ways that time spent feeding our intellectual life and theorizing outside the pipeline might be punctuated.

In a separate but related finding, activating the starter is a slow process that entails a multiple-embodied sequence of reserving and discarding parts of the mother (or starter) herself and then feeding the reserve in response to the mother's own daily activities of bubbling, rising, and falling. Practices of discarding are imbricated in the process of feeding the starter, which is in turn stretched and folded into the main object of production, which for me is almost always a round loaf called a boule. But discard also serves as a material resource in alternative modes of production peripheral to the central aim of production, but which yield more varied and diverse products. As applied to my academic production, this meant spending my intellectual chi on feeding and maintaining and ultimately re-activating my theoretical energy, not as an inert resource to be extracted and exploited through an academic pipeline of production, but sustained as a renewable, living set of embodied interactions or "cultures" contingent, in part, on the paradoxical productivity of discard.

Szanto (2022) sums up this cycle here: "To remain alive, a culture must be used, cared for, performed with, annihilated, reborn, and reset" (p. 189). Findings from my study remind that conditions must be right in order for cultures of intellectual as well as academic life to ferment, activate, reproduce, and yield. I want to suggest that, in contrast to the constellation of life-sustaining metaphors my time with sourdough cultures gave rise to, the pipeline metaphor works to obscure the conditions through which the extractive logic of academic production, the labor of sustaining it, and the laboring subjectivities which constitute its cultures are reproduced. Likewise, Gill (2018) writes that "the conditions in which research is produced, our experiences as 'knowledge workers,' and our labouring subjectivities—these seemed among the biggest and most systematic silences about research" (p. 1). While a wide body of educational scholarship focuses on the laboring subjectivities of teachers, such inquiry less often focuses on the laboring subjectivities of educational scholars and the conditions through which research products are produced. Heeding Haraway (1988), educational research "must not rush away." Such efforts might help us ditch the resource-stripping, extractivist pipeline metaphor in favor of discursive embodiments of a more fully leavened intellectual life in tandem with more vibrant academic culture perpetually in bloom.

References

Aoki, T. T. (1993). Legitimating lived curriculum: Towards a curricular landscape of multiplicity. *Journal of Curriculum & Supervision, 8*(3).

Arantes, L. M. (2020). Learning to dwell with micro-organisms: corporeality, relationality, temporality. *Anthropology in Action, 27*(2), 40–44.

Bauman, W. (2020). Sourdough time and the time of protest: Reflections on the pace of planetary becoming. *Minding Nature, 13*(3), 94–99.

Berg, M., & Seeber, B. K. (2016). *The slow professor: Challenging the culture of speed in the academy*. University of Toronto Press.

Boddy, E. (2022). *The sourdough whisperer: The secrets to no fail baking with epic results*. Page Street Publishing.

Bösel, B. (2022). Affective extractivism: The dispositional challenge to feel differently. In S. Herbrechter, I. Callus, M. Rossini, M. Grech, M. de Bruin-Molé, & C. J. Müller (Eds.), *Palgrave handbook of critical posthumanism* (pp. 1–20). Springer International Publishing.

Calvert, M. D., Madden, A. A., Nichols, L. M., Haddad, N. M., Lahne, J., Dunn, R. R., & McKenney, E. A. (2021). A review of sourdough starters: Ecology, practices, and sensory quality with applications for baking and recommendations for future research. *Peer J, 9*, Article e11389. https://doi.org/10.7717/peerj.11389.

Cappelle, S., Guylaine, L., Gänzle, M., & Gobbetti, M. (2023). History and social aspects of sourdough. In *Handbook on sourdough biotechnology* (pp. 1–13). Springer International Publishing.

Corsetti, A. (2012). Technology of sourdough fermentation and sourdough applications. In *Handbook on sourdough biotechnology* (pp. 85–103). Springer US.

Crabtree, S. A., Hemingway, A., Sudbury, S., Quinney, A., Hutchings, M., Esteves, L., & Norton, L. (2020). Donning the "Slow Professor." *The Radical Teacher*, (116), 55–65.

Crane, K. (2021). Thinking fungi, or random considerations. *Comparative Critical Studies, 18*(2–3), 239–258.

Davies, B., & Bansel, P. (2010). Governmentality and academic work: Shaping the hearts and minds of academic workers. *Journal of Curriculum Theorizing, 26*(3), 5–20.

Davis, H. (2019). Blue, bling: On extractivism. *Afterall: A Journal of Art, Context and Enquiry, 48*(1), 12–19.

Dees, J. (2020). The sourdough microbiome. American Society for Microbiology. https://asm.org/Articles/2020/June/The-Sourdough-Microbiome.

Fairchild, N. (2023). Multiverse, feminist materialist relational time, and multiple future(s): (Re)configuring possibilities for qualitative inquiry. *Qualitative Inquiry, 30*(6). https://doi.org/10.1177/10778004231176753.

Fairchild, N. (2016). Plugging into the umbra: Creative experimentation (in)(on) the boundaries of knowledge production in ECEC research. *Reconceptualizing Educational Research Methodology, 7*(1), 16–30.

Forsberg, E. (2016). Curriculum vitae – The course of life. *Nordic Journal of Studies in Educational Policy, 2016*(2–3). https://doi.org/10.3402/nstep.v2.33742.

Fournier, L. (2020). Fermenting feminism as methodology and metaphor: Approaching transnational feminist practices through microbial transformation. *Environmental Humanities, 12*(1), 88–112.

Gill, R. (2018). Beyond individualism: The psychosocial life of the neoliberal university. In M. Spooner & J. McNinch (Eds.), *Dissident knowledge in higher education* (pp. 194–216). University of Regina Press.

Haraway, D. J. (2016). Staying with the trouble: Making kin in the Chthulucene. In *Staying with the Trouble*. Duke University Press.

Haraway, D. J. (1988). Situated knowledges: The science question in feminism and the privilege of partial perspective. *Feminist Studies, 14*(3), 575–599. https://doi.org/10.2307/3178066.

Husu, L. (2001). On metaphors on the position of women in academia and science. *NORA: Nordic Journal of Women's Studies, 9*(3), 172–181.

Katz, S. E. (2011). Fermentation as a co-evolutionary force. In *Cured, smoked, and fermented: Proceedings of the Oxford Symposium on Food and Cookery* (pp. 165–174). Oxford Symposium.

Kauper, K., & Jacobs, M. M. (2019). The case for slow curriculum: Creative subversion and the curriculum mind. In C. A. Mullen (Ed.), *Creativity Under Duress in Education?* (pp. 339–360). Springer, Cham. https://doi.org/10.1007/978-3-319-90272-2_18.

Kerr, P. (2022). Academic pipeline or academic treadmill? Postdoctoral fellowships and the circular logic of "development." *South African Journal of Higher Education, 36*(3), 72–90. https://journals.co.za/doi/full/10.20853/36-3-5080.

Landis, E. A., Oliverio, A. M., McKenney, E. A., Nichols, L. M., Kfoury, N., Biango-Daniels, M., Shell, L. K., Madden, A. A., Shapiro, L., Sakunala, S., Drake, K., Robbat, A., Booker, M., Dunn, R. R., Fierer, N., & Wolfe, B. E. (2021). The diversity and function of sourdough starter microbiomes. *eLife, 10*, e61644. https://doi.org/10.7554/eLife.61644

Lidz, F. (2020, April 11). At the sourdough library, with some very old mothers. *The New York Times*. https://www.nytimes.com/2020/04/11/science/sourdough-bread-starter-library.html.

Maxwell, A. (2020). On witches, shrooms, and sourdough: A critical reimagining of the white settler relationship to land. *Journal of International Women's Studies, 21*(7), 8–22.

McConnell, M. (2021). *From Starter to Finish: Learning the Literacy of Sourdough* (Doctoral dissertation). Department of English: Dissertations, Theses, and Student Research | English, Department of | University of Nebraska - Lincoln (unl.edu).

McDaniel, K. N. (2019). You're a full professor. Now what? *The Chronicle of Higher Education, 65*(21).

McGrew, K. (2016). The dangers of pipeline thinking: How the school-to-prison pipeline metaphor squeezes out complexity. *Educational Theory, 66*(3), 341–367.

Moriarty, J. (2019). *Autoethnographies from the neoliberal academy: Rewilding, writing and resistance in higher education.* Routledge .

Palacios, M., & Baldauf, A. (2022). From extractivism to adjacency: A research manifesto. *Emancipations: A Journal of Critical Social Analysis, 2*(1), 9.

Pallant, E. (2021). *Sourdough culture: A history of breadmaking from ancient to modern bakers.* Agate.

Pollan, M. (2013). Air: The education of an amateur baker; Earth: Fermentation's cold fire. In *Cooked: A natural history of transformation* (pp. 291–416). The Penguin Press. https://archive.org/details/cookednaturalhis00mich/page/290/mode/1up

Pérez, M. P. (2022). Can academia be decolonized beyond the metaphor? *Journal for Critical Education Policy Studies, 20*(3), 21–40.

Serres, M. (2018). *The incandescent.* Bloomsbury.

Smyth, J. (2017). *The toxic university.* Palgrave Macmillan.

Sparkes, A. C. (2021). Making a spectacle of oneself in the academy using the H-Index: From becoming an artificial person to laughing at absurdities. *Qualitative Inquiry, 27*(8–9), 1027–1039.

Sparkes, A. (2007). Embodiment, academics, and the audit culture: A story seeking consideration. *Qualitative Research, 7*(4), 519–548.

Stern, N., Vela, M., & Nakae, S. (2023). Eliminating the pipeline metaphor in framing workforce equity for American Indian and Alaska Native communities. *JAMA Network Open, 6*(7), Article e2321926. https://doi.org/10.1001/jamanetwork open.2023.21926.

St. Pierre, E. A., Jackson, A. Y., & Mazzei, L. A. (2016). New empiricisms and new materialisms: Conditions for new inquiry. *Cultural Studies↔Critical Methodologies, 16*(2), 99–110.

Szanto, D. (2022). Staff of life: Preserving yeast, memory, and humanity. *Canadian Theatre Review, 189*, 40–44.

Trigg, M. (2023). Kneading bodies. In H. Sauzet & S. Ziegler (Eds.), *Posthumanism in practice* (p. 95). Routledge.

Trigg, M. (2022). *From dough to wheat: A posthuman performance practice with companion species* [Doctoral dissertation, Massey University]. Massey Research Online. https://mro.massey.ac.nz/handle/10179/17777.

Van der Sluis, H. (2020). Slow higher education. *New Vistas, 6*(1), 4–9.

Van Oyen, J. (2021). *Nested bodies: Fermentation as embodied praxis.* (Master's Thesis, Emily Carr University). doi:10.35010/ecuad:17028.

Vostal, F. (2015). Academic life in the fast lane: The experience of time and speed in British academia. *Time & Society, 24*(1), 71–95.

Woo, E. (2022). *Breaking bread: Building community and resiliency through sourdough bread* [Doctoral dissertation]. ProQuest Dissertations and Theses Global.

CHAPTER 7

Louisiana Lagniappe

ANISSA GUERIN, KALA BURRELL-CRAFT,
JOVAN T. THOMAS, AND KRISTIN ROBAIR

Growing up in Louisiana, our upbringing was deeply intertwined with the rich tapestry of Cajun and Creole cuisine. From learning to craft the perfect roux alongside our elders to reveling in the communal joy of crawfish boils with loved ones, food wasn't just nourishment; it was a vibrant expression of culture and connection. It served as our universal language, transcending differences and grounding us in our shared heritage. As Louisiana natives who have pursued doctoral studies in our beloved region, we've witnessed firsthand how academic rigor intertwines with our rich cultural tapestry. Academia, much like our diverse cuisine, thrives on the fusion of ideas, perspectives, and disciplines, enriching the intellectual landscape with every interaction. Our deep immersion in Louisiana cooking informs our scholarly approach, emphasizing interdisciplinary collaboration, community engagement, and the preservation of cultural traditions. In this chapter, we draw parallels between some of our favorite Louisiana foods and the solidarity cultivated in our academic pursuits. We illuminate the challenges and triumphs of our academic and personal journeys, revealing profound lessons that resonate within our cultural heritage and scholarly pursuits. By dissecting the ingredients and techniques that define our cuisine's complexity, we uncover insights into the importance of diversity, collaboration, and inclusion in academic endeavors. Just as each dish tells a story, our academic journey reflects our dedication to preserving traditions, nurturing community, and pursuing knowledge with unwavering passion and purpose.

Keeping the "Holy Trinity" of Work–Life Balance

In Louisiana, the holy trinity, or "chopped onions, peppers, and celery" is considered to be the "heart" of the ingredients in all Creole and Cajun dishes. It's such a staple of the culture and cuisine that many successful global businesses have created Creole seasonings from the baseline of the "Holy Trinity" such as Tony Chachere's, Zatarain's, Slap Ya Mama, etc. If the dishes don't have the right mixture of seasonings, it can have an adverse effect and possibly ruin the dish to where the chef would have to start from scratch. The holy trinity is sauteed in butter (with or without garlic) to begin the infusion in other ingredients to make a flavorful dish. Similar to cooking, in the academic field, work–life balance is essential to ensuring that one has well-balanced obligations in life. Thus, work–life balance is the prerequisite for a successful matriculation in any doctoral program, or academia career field.

During the journey of being doctoral students, we experienced many obstacles as it related to work–life balance while juggling the multiple roles of doctoral students, parent or surrogate, and full-time jobs. During this time, it is important to know that there is no perfect way of finding a balance except making sure that the skills of time management and goal setting while having a healthy well-being support system is implemented. This is essential to the success of scholarly advancement and making it to the finish line of graduation. Prior research shows that retention rates in doctoral education are far from optimal; depending on the discipline, 30% to 70% of doctoral students never [make it] to complete their PhD degree (Gardner & Gopaul, 2012; Ivankova & Stick, 2007). Those who do complete their degree show consistent determination through persistence in their studies by facing and overcoming long line of challenges that may without sufficient support turn into stressors (Barry et al., 2018; Cotterall, 2013).

Just as you sauté the "holy trinity" to prepare the base of the dish, students find themselves in a period of growing and developing in their field. Time management is necessary for work–life balance as it can provide the experience of navigating the spaces of collaboration and research while making sure to achieve the milestones that it takes to graduate. However, throughout this journey, students can often get imposter syndrome based on the responsibilities that one decides to take on despite being a full-time or part-time student. The Council of Graduate Schools (2005) comments on this expectation saying that full-time study "allows students to concentrate exclusively on course work or research; to acquire the habits, attitudes, skills, and insights necessary for attaining the Ph.D.; and to find opportunities to work closely with the professors and other students" (p. 21). However, opportunities may vary depending on extra responsibility such as full-time employment and parental or family responsibilities while being a part-time or full-time student. As a full-time student, I often struggled with managing tasks as many of those opportunities such as conferences, teaching, or research were offered during a time when I was unable to participate due to my full-time job and parental responsibility. Additionally, I also grappled with finding the time to participate in consistent journal articles and other scholarly writing opportunities due to those same focus commitments. Throughout the halls, there were many conversations about "being a good graduate student," one must conduct research, produce journal articles, and conduct oneself as a future academia mentee learning how to navigate the faculty world. Even though it's possible, as a woman preparing for future academia, there is always the constant thought as to "How to make the most of your time at work and with family?" "How do I protect my time as a grad student?" "Will the lack of experience in publishing affect my career development after graduation?" According to Munn (2013), promoting work–life balance requires an employee to understand the provision of their work scope and responsibilities and how it could bring meaning to them and others. This means for academics to acquire work–life balance, there is a need for them to feel empowered by their profession and to fully understand its significance (Badri, 2024).

As I constantly compared my journey to those that were full-time students with graduate assistantships, this led me to a place where I believe that I would not be as successful as my other cohort members. Moreover, it provided me with a sense of stressors that allowed me to believe in the imposter syndrome that most graduate students get. If we are to be perceived as good graduate students, we must then go to the conferences we are told to, attend the lectures, speaker series, or colloquium suggested by our advisors despite the, often, incompatibility with our own schedules of family, childcare, or limited finances (Cope-Watson & Betts, 2010).

Despite these unspoken rules, the pathway that is forged is not limited due to these factors. Goal setting is just as important as making sure that the time management of balancing multiple projects is handled. To make sure there is a track for success, it would be more advantageous for students to create a timeline/checklist of tasks, or goals that they want to accomplish as they matriculate through the program. Support groups are beneficial to the work–life balance challenge that many graduate students and faculty members have. Devenish et al. (2009) stated that collaborative peer support has been one of the most valuable enablers to our progress. Collaborative support has encouraged and supported a mutual interest in extending our areas of learning, knowledge, and participation in the academic world (p. 61). To maintain a healthy well-being, graduate students and faculty can offer the opportunity to collaborate and support one another by listening, giving feedback, offering suggestions, and building a mentor/mentee relationship. As students begin to transition from student to the academia field, one needs to make sure that the skills of time management, goal setting, and having a peer support group is essential to the success of progressing through your program, or even through the collaboration of academic pursuits. Graduate students who proactively imagine multiple possible futures, define the story they want to tell about the transferability of skills they have already mastered, and create opportunities to gain additional skills become especially attractive and competitive candidates for the positions they pursue (Smith, 2016). Just as someone begins to purchase the ingredients to prepare for a good meal of red beans, gumbo, or even crawfish étouffeé, the holy trinity is needed to ensure that the ingredients for the meal will be flavorful and well balanced.

Traditions, Communal Bonds, and Red Beans and Rice

Red beans and rice, a staple in Creole cuisine, has long been a symbol of comfort and community. Originating from Louisiana, this dish is traditionally served on Mondays, utilizing leftovers from Sunday's dinner, typically including salt meat, ham hocks, pig tails, and/or sausage. The simplicity of its ingredients belies the complexity of its flavors, which develop over hours of slow cooking. Similarly, the journey through a doctoral program is an intricate blend of personal and shared experiences, culminating in a deeply rewarding academic and personal achievement.

The process of making red beans and rice starts with selecting ingredients. Each choice reflects personal preferences and available resources, analogous to a doctoral student selecting a research topic or methodology. Just as the beans must be sorted, rinsed, and soaked, doctoral candidates must prepare through coursework and literature review, laying a solid foundation for their research. Scholars note the parallel between ingredient preparation and initial academic preparations as foundational to both culinary and academic success (Smith, 2020). In the kitchen, the choice of ingredients often depends on the cook's personal tastes, the availability of resources, and the intended outcome of the meal. Similarly, a doctoral student selects a research topic based on personal interests, academic background, and the availability of resources such as data, funding, and faculty expertise. Just as some ingredients can be hard to find, requiring adjustments or substitutions, so too can certain research topics be constrained by the availability of resources or ethical considerations.

After sorting and rinsing, the beans are typically soaked, sometimes overnight, which softens them and reduces cooking time. This soaking process symbolizes the training and coursework that doctoral students undergo before they fully engage with their research. Just as soaking enhances the beans' readiness for cooking, coursework, and comprehensive exams prepare students by deepening their knowledge base and honing their analytical skills, priming them for the rigorous demands of dissertation work.

The selection of spices and the type of meat (ham hocks, salt meat, pig tails, or sausage) in red beans and rice can vary widely, influenced by regional tastes and cultural backgrounds. This diversity mirrors how doctoral research is shaped by the cultural and societal context in which a student operates. Researchers bring their own cultural identities and personal experiences to their work, influencing their perspective and approach. This aspect of research highlights the importance of diversity in academia, as different backgrounds lead to a richer variety of research topics and methodologies. As with any dish, seasoning is critical. The cook must adjust spices to achieve the desired flavor profile, similar to how doctoral students must continuously refine their hypotheses and arguments in response to feedback and new insights. This individual seasoning process highlights the customization of the doctoral experience, where each journey is unique and tailored to personal academic goals and aspirations (Lee, 2021).

In many cultures, cooking is a communal activity, and red beans and rice is often cooked in large pots to feed a community. Similarly, doctoral programs are not solitary endeavors; they are communal, with peers, mentors, and academic advisors playing crucial roles. Finding one's tribe within the academic community provides support and enriches the doctoral experience, promoting both personal and professional growth. The significance of building a strong network of peers, mentors, and advisors in a doctoral program cannot be overstated. This network acts as a scaffold that supports students through the challenges of rigorous academic work. As Martinez (2018, p. 12) notes, "the academic journey is both a personal challenge and a community achievement, where the collective input and mutual support play crucial roles in individual success." This network is not just about academic support but also emotional and motivational support, mirroring the way a meal like red beans and rice provides not just sustenance but also comfort.

Just as sharing a meal of red beans and rice can reinforce social bonds, collaborative projects, and shared academic challenges can strengthen ties between doctoral students. These relationships are pivotal, providing emotional support and fostering an environment of mutual aid and inspiration. Martinez (2018) emphasizes the importance of academic networks as a source of both support and necessary challenge, akin to the shared meals that strengthen communal ties. The sharing of meals in many cultures is an act of unity and community building. In the context of a doctoral program, this analogy extends to the collaborative research projects, study groups, and peer-review sessions that form the core of academic life. These collaborative efforts are not merely academic exercises; they represent the coming together of diverse minds to challenge, refine, and support one another's work. Research by Thompson (2022, p. 13) underscores this, noting that "collaboration in academic settings enhances learning outcomes, as students leverage diverse skill sets and perspectives to tackle complex problems." This process is akin to how different ingredients in a dish like red beans and rice complement each other, each adding depth and flavor to create a balanced and satisfying meal.

Soul Food and Fellowship

Food and fellowship are truly good for our souls. A few of the authors of this chapter grew up in rural areas where Walmart remains the staple, the Sonic drive through is the hangout spot, local shops and grocery stores still survive, and Friday nights are all about football. Needless to say, a lot of things centered around food because in rural areas you have to create your own entertainment. Many memories growing up revolved around catfish Fridays, seafood, casseroles, Kool-Aid, and sweet tea. We grew up eating fried catfish (or white perch, or buffalo) at least once a week. Growing up there were not a lot of baked or grilled fish options, everything was fried. Fried fish alone represented fellowship whether you were eating catfish in the school cafeteria amongst friends, gathering at the local fish house, or eating it at home (or someone else's); fish was always there (both bone in and filet). Bonding over getting choked off fish bones is a whole different story. Families and friends fished together at local lakes, bayous, or rivers. Fishing was an activity that brought everyone together and allowed them to share stories, dreams, and other family and local gossip. Fishing was about sharing. Not only did everyone share information and stories while fishing, but they also shared their catch of the day with the community. Fishing was an activity that demonstrated love and respect for oneself and others just like the food and fellowship of our African traditions. Fish is mainly considered a finger food that you eat with your hands. One of the only times you use a fork is to pull the meat from the bones when eating whole fish. Fish remains a staple in our community in Louisiana regardless of geographical location across the state, and an old wise tale you often hear when referencing fish is "it's good for your brain." Don't know if there is any truth in that or not, but a large majority of the doctors and professional people we know all love fish.

Seafood and seafood boils also represented togetherness, but also patience. Seafood is prepared in a variety of delicious ways like in creoles, etouffees, meat pies, gumbos, chargrilled oysters, boudin, salmon croquettes, jambalaya, and boils just to name a few. The patience it takes to harvest the seafood is just as time consuming as it is to fish. The dishes we prepare are thoughtful, intentional, and almost always inclusive of the holy trinity (onions, celery, green peppers). The blending of seasonings and the careful attention and focus it takes not to burn your roux is an art. Our seafood staples are shrimp, crabs, crawfish, and oysters. Yes, we do have access to other seafood, but our dishes usually center around one or more of these options. For a seafood boil, you can have absolutely everything in there. The blending of the seafood and fixings into a flavorful, spicy boil is nothing short of amazing and is hard to perfect for a non-native Louisianan. The seasoning combination must be perfect to achieve the right amount of flavor and heat. Then the seafood and trimmings must follow in a methodical way and can include everything that was mentioned above to include sausage, potatoes, corn, and turkey necks. A boil itself is one dish that is prepared usually outside surrounded by family, friends, and the community. Why waste a good boil for just yourself? No, everyone brings stuff to throw into the pot. Afterall, what is better than food and fellowship?

Louisiana is considered the cultural mixing pot because it is unique to Native American, Creole, and Acadian cultures (Explore Louisiana, n.d.). It is from the blending of these cultures that our culinary styles and foods represent and overlap. Each group of people brought their own flavors and ingredients to Louisiana. Today, we can see their influence through our foods. For example: Native Americans lived off the land and waters. Because of this, seafood, wild game, and rice (grains in general) are central to our diet. The Creoles historically had money to spend on food and trade and were able to take advantage of adding additional spices and sometimes meat/seafood to their dishes because of their access. The Acadians used a lot of one-pot dishes (hence that's probably where casseroles evolved) to feed the family and the community. They were a poorer group of people and used whatever was readily available and what they had learned from the Native Americans; however, they incorporated more pork which is why sausage (traditionally a cheaper pork option) became a staple in many dishes like seafood boils, red beans and rice, and boudin. We Louisianans use everything, and we know how to come together to celebrate life. We literally have a festival to celebrate everything that makes our culture unique and flavorful. From rice, to strawberries, to sugar, and soul food everything is appreciated and recognized (a trait akin to our Native American culture).

Gumbo Wisdom: Navigating the Academic Kitchen With Quality Mentors

Gumbo, a staple of Louisiana Creole cuisine, symbolizes the blending of diverse traditions, reflecting the multicultural essence of its origins. In Louisiana, gumbo is more than just a dish; it's a cultural symbol that requires quality ingredients and careful preparation. This mirrors the academic journey, where patience, resilience, and diverse perspectives are key. Just as gumbo's complexity comes from its ingredients and technique, academia thrives on the fusion of ideas and collaboration. Assistant professors, like novice chefs, depend on mentors for guidance and support, learning to navigate and contribute to the academic field. This mentorship is crucial for both personal growth and the continuity of scholarship, ensuring that knowledge is passed on and enriched for future generations. By embracing the tradition of giving back through mentorship and service, assistant professors contribute to the continuity and vitality of academic scholarship, ensuring that the flavors of knowledge are continually refined and shared for generations to come.

In the rich tapestry of academic life, much like the meticulous crafting of a flavorful gumbo, the presence of quality ingredients is paramount. Just as fresh seafood, spices, and roux are essential to the gumbo's depth and richness, assistant professors rely on seasoned mentors to navigate the complexities of academia. Much like the careful selection of ingredients shapes the taste of a gumbo, the guidance and support of mentors play a crucial role in an assistant professor's career. Assistant professors face a myriad of challenges as they navigate the complexities of research, teaching, and professional development (Larson et al., 2019). Amidst these challenges, the presence of quality mentors emerges as not just beneficial, but crucial to their success and growth within the academic landscape. Mentorship serves as a guiding beacon in the often-turbulent waters of academia, providing assistant professors with invaluable support, wisdom, and perspective. At its core, mentorship is more than just passing knowledge; it is about fostering relationships built on trust and mutual respect, where experienced faculty members invest in the personal and professional development of their mentees.

One of the primary roles of a mentor is to impart insider knowledge and share institutional wisdom. Senior faculty members who have traversed the academic hierarchy possess a wealth of experience, lessons learned from both successes and setbacks, insights into navigating departmental politics, and understanding the unspoken norms and expectations within their field (Lunsford et al., 2018). This insider knowledge can significantly shorten the learning curve for assistant professors, allowing them to make informed decisions and avoid common pitfalls that might otherwise impede their progress. Furthermore, mentors play a pivotal role in helping assistant professors develop their scholarly identity and establish a clear research agenda. They offer critical feedback on research proposals, grant applications, and manuscripts, guiding their mentees toward producing high-quality scholarly work (Lunsford et al., 2018). This guidance is particularly crucial during the early stages of an academic career when building a robust publication record and securing external funding is paramount. Beyond research and publications, mentors also support assistant professors in honing their teaching skills and navigating the challenges of academic pedagogy. Effective teaching requires more than subject matter expertise; it necessitates the ability to engage students, adapt teaching methods to diverse learning styles, and assess learning outcomes effectively (Moschis, 2024). Mentorship provides a platform for discussing innovative teaching strategies, classroom management techniques, and ways to integrate cutting-edge research into curriculum development (Templeton et al., 2021). Mentors can also serve as advocates for their mentees within the academic community. They can open doors to professional networks, introduce them to key stakeholders in their field, and nominate them for prestigious awards and leadership opportunities. This advocacy not only enhances the visibility and reputation of assistant professors but also positions them for advancement within their institutions and broader academic circles. Moreover, their emotional and psychological support is paramount to those who may face isolation, imposter syndrome, or burnout amidst the pressures of tenure-track positions (Duke et al., 2013). Mentors provide a safe space for candid discussions about career aspirations, work–life balance, and personal challenges, offering empathy and encouragement based on their own experiences navigating similar hurdles.

In conclusion, the importance of quality mentors for assistant professors cannot be overstated. As Black academics navigating this journey, our mentors have profoundly shaped our paths. Their guidance, support, and advocacy have been instrumental in helping us navigate the complexities of academia and embrace our identities and voices as scholars. Much like the intricate process of cooking gumbo, which reflects a blend of diverse ingredients, academia requires a careful balance of ingredients, knowledge, resilience, and cultural awareness. Our mentors have provided invaluable insights into navigating institutional challenges, developing a robust research agenda rooted in my cultural experiences, and refining my teaching methods to engage and empower students. Importantly, their mentorship has inspired a dedication to paying it forward. As we grow in our respective roles, we are committed to supporting and mentoring other assistant professors and graduate students, particularly those from underrepresented backgrounds. Mentorship goes beyond transmitting knowledge; it is about nurturing a sense of community and solidarity within academia, where diverse perspectives are valued and celebrated. Through active engagement in mentorship, we can collectively work towards creating a more inclusive and equitable academic environment where all scholars can thrive and contribute their unique flavors to the academic gumbo.

Conclusion

The journey through a doctoral program, much like the cooking of our Louisiana cuisine, is a deeply personal experience that thrives within a communal context. Both processes are characterized by individual choices, slow development, and the seasoning of personal growth. By embracing the unique journey of each doctoral student within the supportive framework of their academic community, the path to academic success becomes a fulfilling process of personal and collective achievement. Sharing meals, in both literal and metaphorical senses, is integral to building and sustaining communities. In doctoral programs, where the academic and personal challenges are significant, these shared experiences are crucial. They foster an environment of collaboration and support, which not only enhances the educational experience but also prepares students for future professional endeavors. Food and fellowship are so intertwined together in Louisiana that we cannot experience anything outside of it. It is what we grew up doing, and it is the essence of what got us successfully through our various undergraduate programs and our Ph.D. program together as a Krewe at Louisiana State University. Food and fellowship were even a written and unwritten tradition in our syllabi and classes. That is how deep this love for food and fellowship nurtures our soul and deserves space to be highlighted and celebrated.

References

Badri, S. K. Z. (2024). Evaluating higher education (HE) work design to sustain academics' work-life balance. *Journal of Applied Research in Higher Education, 16*(1), 134–149. https://doi.org/10.1108/JARHE-04-2022-0116.

Barry, K. M., Woods, M., Warnecke, E., Stirling, C., & Martin, A. (2018). Psychological health of doctoral candidates, study related challenges and perceived performance. *Higher Education Research & Development, 37*(3), 468–483.

Cope-Watson, G., & Betts, A. S. (2010). Confronting otherness: An e-conversation between doctoral students living with the Imposter Syndrome. *Canadian Journal for New Scholars in Education/Revue canadienne des jeunes chercheures et chercheurs en éducation, 3*(1).

Council of Graduate Schools. (2005). *The doctor of philosophy degree: A policy statement.* Author.

Cotterall, S. (2013). More than just a brain: Emotions and the doctoral experience. *Higher Education Research & Development, 32*(2), 174–187.

Devenish, R., Dyer, S., Jefferson, T., Lord, L., van Leeuwen, S., & Fakerley, V. (2009). Peer to peer support: The disappearing work in the doctoral student experience. *Higher Education Research and Development, 28*(1), 59–70.

Duke, N. N., Gross, A., Moran, A., Hodsdon, J., Demirel, N., Osterholm, E., Sunni, M., & Pitt, M. B. (2019). Institutional factors associated with burnout among assistant professors. *Teaching and Learning in Medicine, 32*(1), 61–70. https://doi.org/10.1080/10401334.2019.1638263.

Explore Louisiana. (n.d.). *Welcome to explore Louisiana.* Retrieved from https://www.explorelouisiana.com/.

Gardner, S. K. & Gopaul, B. (2012). "The Part-time Doctoral Student Experience." *International Journal of Doctoral Studies 7*: 63–78.

Ivankova, N. V. & Stick, S. L. (2007). Students' Persistence in a Distributed Doctoral Program in Educational Leadership in Higher Education: A Mixed Methods Study. *Research in Higher Education 48* (1): 93–135.

Larson, L. R., Duffy, L. N., Fernandez, M., Sturts, J., Gray, J., & Powell, G. M. (2019). Getting started on the tenure track: Challenges and strategies for success. *SCHOLE: A Journal of Leisure Studies and Recreation Education, 34*(1), 36–51. https://doi.org/10.1080/1937156X.2019.1589804.

Lee, C. (2021). Personalizing the academic journey in doctoral education. *Educational Horizons.*

Lunsford, L., Baker, V., & Pifer, M. (2018). Faculty mentoring faculty: Career stages, relationship quality, and job satisfaction. *International Journal of Mentoring and Coaching in Education, 7*(2), 139–154. https://doi.org/10.1108/IJMCE-08-2017-0055.

Martinez, D. (2018). *Community and collaboration in doctoral programs: The support network.* Academic Studies Press.

Moschis, G. P. (2024). Preparing for academic career. In *Academic research in business and the social sciences.* Springer. https://doi.org/10.1007/978-3-031-56548-9_2.

Munn, S. L. (2013), "Unveiling the work-life system: the influence of work-life balance on meaningful work", *Advances in Developing Human Resources, 15*(4), 401–417.

Smith, S. (2016). A 21st-Century Doctoral Education. In Manifesto for the Humanities: *Transforming Doctoral Education in Good Enough Times* (pp. 155–164). University of Michigan Press. https://doi.org/10.2307/j.ctv65sw68.18.

Smith, J. (2020). Foundational techniques in cooking and academia. *Journal of Culinary Education.*

Templeton, N. R., Jeong, S., & Pugliese, E. (2021). Mentoring for continuous improvement in teaching and learning. *Mentoring & Tutoring: Partnership in Learning, 29*(1), 1–5. https://doi.org/10.1080/13611267.2021.1902709.

Thompson, L. (2022). Interdisciplinary approaches in graduate education. *Educational Research Journal.*

CHAPTER 8

Sihk jó faahn meih a?: Collectivist Healing Wisdom Lineages Embedded in Asian Foods

GRACE POON GHAFFARI

Introduction

In Asian culture, food is constructed as more than just a biological necessity. Rather, food is an embodied form of collective support and relational healing wisdom that can nourish the social, emotional, and spiritual needs of one's body. This chapter will illuminate the ways Asian cultural foods, and the collectivist ethos that is tethered to such foods, are forms of cultural wealth (Yosso, 2005) for navigating higher education. Yosso (2005) describes community cultural wealth as the "accumulated assets and resources in the histories and lives of Communities of Color" (p. 77). Before presenting the collectivist healing wisdom and cultural wealth embedded in Asian food culture, I will situate my positionality as a Chinese American woman, who is in, but not of, the academy (Moten & Harney, 2004; Patel, 2021). Next, I will open in ritual to honor the lineage of ancestors, elders, and community who have brought me, and who I bring with me (T. Jones Jolivet, personal communication, February 5, 2024). Rooted in my lived experiences and those of my dissertation research collaborators, I will outline three areas of collectivist healing wisdom embedded in Asian foods: rest, resistance, and care. This chapter will end with imaginative possibilities gleaned from Asian cultural food wisdom that can nourish and sustain educators, students, and others in and beyond the academy.

Positionality

I am a Chinese American woman, daughter of immigrants, and mother to a daughter. Growing up, Asian cultural knowledge systems were embodied and interwoven into how I interacted with others in community and across generations. Rooted in intergenerational and ancestral wisdom, Mama and Baba communicated their love through embodied cultural practices of handmaking wontons; slicing fruit; and wok-tossing garlic, ginger, red wine vinegar, black sesame oil, and soy sauce. Food in my community often acted as spiritual portals, such as lighting joss sticks and placing fruit at the alters of ancestors, and ceremonial blessings, including Chinese tea ceremonies and eating 餃子 (dumplings) for good fortune on Lunar New Year. I come from a lineage of healing, survival, and resistance that situated food as synonymous with care, medicine, empowerment, ancestral and intergenerational connections, and belonging.

I am also a scholar-practitioner who has worked for over a decade in student affairs and currently serves as an assistant professor of counselor education. In higher education, I have spent the majority of my time supporting survivors of sexual and relationship violence and educating and researching sexual and societal trauma and healing, with a particular centering of Women of Color. Navigating educational environments has illuminated how Eurocentric colonial positivist frameworks pervade educational systems (Bhattacharya, 2019; Chávez et al., 2012) and position the individual mind as separate and above my ancestral, intergenerational, and collective ways of knowing. The combination of my personal and professional experiences has illuminated the carcerality and coloniality that operates throughout the machinery of higher education (Patel, 2021). By situating myself as a scholar-practitioner, I assert that I am not separate but rather part of the collective struggle in and beyond academia to reclaim our humanity, embodied knowledge, and lineage of healing wisdom.

Opening Tea Ritual

Because Western-centric colonial agendas in education often appropriate knowledge from the margins (Smith, 2013), it is vital to open in ritual to honor the sacredness of Asian food-related wisdom. Honoring the sanctity of our food-related wisdom also resists racial capitalism (Robinson, 2020) and settler colonial violence, genocide, and the abuse of enslaved Africans and Indigenous communities, which have long been perpetuated by and within the academy (Smith, 2013; Wilder, 2013). In this spirit, I invite readers to not extract and repackage the following wisdom into a checklist of tasks or quick programs that are devoid of the ancestral, collective, and intergenerational roots that circulate throughout Asian food wisdom.

With this in mind, I take a deep breath in and out and begin this opening tea ritual. In Chinese culture, we always pour tea for elders before we pour tea for ourselves and others as a practice of collective care and intergenerational respect. I will similarly pour tea for my Maa Maa, Po Po, Gong Gong, Je Je, Mama, Ba Ba, and other blood and spirit elders and ancestors, who are the roots and rivers that formed my inherited connections to food as an embodied pathway for healing. I pour tea for my collective Asian diasporic community of scholars, activists, and healers who have helped me to reclaim the ancestral lineages embedded in Asian epistemology. I also pour tea for the similarities and differences in language, culture, histories, and racialization within the pan-ethnic Asian/Asian American community. I pour tea to myself to honor the ways I am a part of this pan-ethnic community and yet do not represent all Asian/Asian American individuals and communities. As such, I resist dominant narratives of homogeneity that are often perpetuated against the Asian diaspora. As I take a soothing sip of tea, I close my eyes and slightly bow my head in deep gratitude for the wisdom I inherited that was not of my own individual making (T. Jones Jolivet, personal communication, June 14, 2024).

Asian Cultural Foods as Collectivist Healing Wisdom

Collectivist wisdom exists and permeates throughout Asian food traditions. Collectivist values emphasize interconnectedness and interpersonal harmony and frame well-being and healing as inseparable from one's environment (Yeh et al., 2006). As a result, collectivist approaches consider one's relational and reciprocal connection to others and one's mind-body-spirit connections as both interrelated and central to responding to distress and cultivating wholeness (Yeh et al., 2006). When applied to healing, Asian food itself and the culture that surrounds Asian food is both a way to heal and a way to glean healing wisdom from peers, elders, ancestors, and community. This section explores three ways that collectivist healing wisdom is situated through food: rest, resistance, and care.

Collective Rest

Growing up, I regularly engaged in collective rest through rituals like yum cha, where fried rice, dumplings, ginger, tofu, sesame oil, sweet bread, and soy sauce intermingled with stories in Cantonese English around a circular table. In ancient China, yum cha began as a way for Chinese people to rest and converse in traditional tea houses, especially during long and arduous journeys. More than simply meals to nourish the physical body, yum cha was and is a reprieve from the daily machinery of capitalism and an invitation to slow down and heal through relational, communal, and intergenerational connections. Gathering with blood and chosen kin to yum cha and share stories taught me the centrality of radical rest (Hersey, 2022) as a method of resistance against academic capitalism and the necessity of collective community.

The following is a composite narrative that illustrates this idea of collective rest through the experiences of multiple Asian American women survivors. I met Tracy, a multiracial Chinese Vietnamese woman who experienced sexual violence, through my dissertation study. Tracy described how she grew up in a multigenerational household where her grandmother often prepared delicious meals using ingredients from their family garden. Tracy's grandmother did not have a formal education and spent most of her younger years growing fruits and vegetables in the same fields that her parents, siblings, and ancestors labored from early in the morning to late in the evening. After a full day of labor, Tracy's grandmother always gathered each evening with family and friends to eat, rest, and share stories. Rooted in her grandmother's legacy, Tracy described how her grandmother similarly taught her the importance of resting with food and family after a long day of labor or moments of distress. Tracy explained that whenever she was distressed, her grandmother, sensing her emotional state, would often offer to make dumplings to rest and ground collectively. Searching the photos on her phone, Tracy found a photo that showcased rows and rows of dumplings that she and her grandmother made for a recent family gathering. Her eyes lit up as she continued to share how food was a form of self-care and how her grandmother taught her that dumpling making can help release tension, self-regulate, and rest in community. Tracy illuminates how Asian cultural food practices that are passed through ancestral and intergenerational lineages are forms of healing wisdom that prioritize rest and rejuvenation. Because Asian cultural foods are often prepared and shared collectively, traditional practices of preparing food with others can also be both physically and relationally grounding.

Collective rest practices and ideologies embedded in Asian cultural foods can serve to resist the grind culture that exists in academia. In *Rest Is Resistance: A Manifesto*, Hersey (2022) argues that "academia is the headquarters for grind culture . . . Our everyday behaviors and false beliefs about productivity drive us into behaving in a robotic, machine-like way." (p. 25). As an apparatus of grind culture, academia functions to machinify scholars and anyone who resides in the institutional machinery (la paperson, 2017). Treating our bodies as human machines, toxic academic systems normalize productivity, exhaustion, and busyness and force our bodies to the edges of collapse and decimation. However, Asian cultural knowledge systems illustrate that taking refuge in collective rest can actively resist systems of disconnection that reduce our bodies, especially the bodies of Communities of Color, into vehicles of labor and profit. As Tracey illuminated above, preparing, sharing, and eating culturally relevant foods can also be used as contemplative and embodied practices for grounding in response to distress and trauma among Communities of Color in higher education.

Collective Resistance

In Asian cultures, food is situated as a communal, reciprocal, and relational experience (Mayuzumi, 2006). Positioning meals as a relational concept invites and facilitates opportunities to not only share food but also ancestral, intergenerational, and collective wisdom to resist coloniality and White dominance. Around the dinner table, holding our bowls of rice, I often saw how Baba transported us to his childhood memories of eating rice with his family while living in British colonial Hong Kong. Looking at his bowl of rice, Baba reflected on feeling abundant as a child even during times of scarcity where they only had a small bowl of rice to eat. As immigrants, my Baba and Mama navigated xenophobic and White dominant environments, where they often experienced anti-Asian racism while supporting my siblings and me with limited resources. Recalling his felt sense of abundance, Baba illustrated to my siblings and I how to experience joy amidst institutional challenges and uncertainty.

Collective resistance is necessary to subvert the dominant narratives in higher education that frame students, staff, and faculty, especially Communities of Color, as deficient and inferior. Moreover, as a colonial White dominant enterprise, educational systems are riddled with deficit-oriented ideologies that blame individuals for their own struggle (García & Guerra, 2004). Deficit-oriented views mask structural inequities as individual challenges rooted in meritocracy, anti-Blackness, and White dominance (Poon et al., 2016). Such ideologies are rooted in systems of domination that especially silence, manipulate, disembody, and erase epistemologies of Communities of Color (Poon Ghaffari, 2024). Therefore, deficit ideologies are a prevalent manifestation of racism and racialized violence in schooling systems that continue to construct Communities of Color as weak, inferior, and deprived (Yosso, 2005). However, reconnecting to collective resistant wisdom can challenge racism in the academy and resist dominant discourses of deficiency. Resistant capital is an expression of cultural wealth that Communities of Color possess and is often passed from one generation to the next (Yosso, 2005). As illustrated in Baba's bowls of rice, culturally relevant foods often reveal counterstories of self-worth and lessons of survival.

Because educational systems erase and invalidate the resistant technologies that Communities of Color possess, the act of reclaiming wisdom that has been forgotten or never known can be an essential act of subversion and homecoming (Bhattacharya, 2023; Bryant, 2022). Tasting and sharing cultural foods with others can often conjure up ancestral and intergenerational ways of knowing that hold collective resistant stories and strategies. Eating rice every night with my Baba called forth a lineage of dreaming beyond present circumstances and struggles. Embedded in our food stories were strategies that ancestors and elders used to traverse hostile terrains and xenophobic landscapes.

Collective Care

Asian cultural wisdom situates food as part of a legacy of collectivist care and connection practiced within Asian communities (Mayuzumi, 2006). In particular, this connective approach to food is highlighted in the ways Asian/Asian American communities commonly greet one another with, "Have you eaten yet?" This phrase transcends questioning what someone had for their last meal and is instead a caring expression of "I love you" (Matsuoka, 2022). Expressions of "Sihk jó faahn meih a?" or "Have you eaten (rice) yet?" were frequently heard among my family, friends, and elders as a way of expressing care for my psychological well-being as connected to my physical body. This relational inquiry often reminded me of the ways my personal well-being was also interconnected with our collective well-being—if I eat, then you must eat too. "Have you eaten yet?" also revealed how collective care didn't need to overly rely on verbal or explicit forms of communication. Instead, care could be a *felt* sense in my body that enveloped me in the sights, flavors, smells, and presence of mutuality.

Collective care was also highlighted by several collaborators in my dissertation study. Fern, a queer Filipina woman survivor of sexual violence, was one collaborator who particularly described how food was both a vehicle for relational care and a form of healing. Fern grew up in Central Jersey in a close-knit Filipino immigrant community that would often gather for celebrations and holidays, many of whom she called her aunts, uncles, and cousins that expanded beyond blood-kin. Referencing these gatherings, she described how she "grew up always surrounded by the food and people and singing and dancing." Fern further explained the ethos that undergirded these community gatherings:

> Community and togetherness and collectivism are really important in Filipino culture. There is so much emphasis placed on hospitality and hosting and being welcoming and always offering food, sending people home with Tupperware, having Tupperware set aside that is specifically for guests.

In this quote, Fern highlights the centrality of collective care through the regular accessibility of Tupperware to ensure that everyone is always fed now and in the future. Later in our conversation, Fern highlighted how the collective care embedded in her Filipino food culture drove her to connect with others to heal after experiencing sexual violence. Fern's ability to receive collective care through food was not predicated on external agencies, government entities, and organizations. Considering the barriers that marginalized communities often experience when navigating campus and community resources, Fern highlights how food as collective care can be a tool for healing that is by and for minoritized communities. Because care is tethered to food, Fern also shared how she had regularly volunteered for a food pantry while living in New York City, which aimed to bring together culturally diverse communities through food. Collective care as synonymous with feeding others was also echoed by other collaborators in my dissertation research, who shared stories of providing and sharing food with others as a pathway for healing.

In higher education, there can be several barriers to receiving care from others in and beyond the academy. For faculty who are navigating trauma and distress, it can often be difficult to disclose to others due to norms of academic professionalism that prevent faculty from bringing their full selves to teaching and research (Marine et al., 2021). Faculty, especially pre-tenured faculty with marginalized identities, often face pressures to maintain a specific image and are often concerned with how they are perceived by their academic peers (Martinez & Welton, 2017). Discussing sensitive topics and asking others for help may also be culturally incongruent, which is often the case for communities across the Asian diaspora (Kim &

Ward, 2007; Okazaki, 2002). Help-seeking often necessitates one to acknowledge that they need help and that they are worthy of receiving help from others. Unfortunately, trauma can often prevent individuals from acknowledging traumatic experiences and can affect their sense of self-worth (Bryant, 2022). However, food can be a vehicle for collective care that is not predicated on vulnerable disclosures and culturally incongruent forms of help-seeking.

Collective wisdom lineages in Asian food culture highlight how food can be an embodied way to receive collective care and support for those navigating challenging circumstances. Such relational ways of being that situate the needs of our *whole* bodies, as interconnected to the needs of others, can help those navigating the academy to be accountable to one another. In doing so, we can collectively resist the individualistic, competitive, and mind-supremacist (Wagner & Shahjahan, 2015) culture that permeates in and beyond the academy. As a basic human necessity, food can also be a vehicle to rehumanize those who the academy often attempts to dehumanize, including Communities of Color, trans and queer communities, and people with disabilities. By inquiring whether someone has eaten, we express care for their real human needs. When receiving food from others, we can also experience the *felt* sense of care and love that often transcends words.

Collectivist Imaginings for Higher Education

> *After a long day, I hold a warm cha siu bao in my hand and look toward my daughter, taking in the sweet and savory fragrance of Chinese barbeque sauce and soft milk bread. As we take our first bites together, she whispers, "I love you, mommy. I love bao." I whisper back, "I love you too sweetheart. Did you know that our ancestors also ate these same baos that we are eating today?"*

As illustrated in the above vignette with my daughter, collectivist rest, resistance, and care are interwoven within Asian food culture and part of diverse wisdom lineages across the broader Asian diaspora. Such ways of being have fueled and continue to feed our social, emotional, and spiritual needs throughout the generations. However, our needs and ways of being are often erased and invalidated within higher education spaces that are seeped with White supremacy culture, which prioritizes machine-like productivity and runs on racial capitalism (Okun, 1999). Moreover, colonial, imperial, and White-dominant logics in the academy have attempted and continue to attempt to erase, co-opt, and extract the embodied wisdom of Communities of Color (Kim, 2020; Patel, 2015; Smith, 2013).

To resist the colonial and capitalistic machine of higher education (la paperson, 2017), Communities of Color who are in, but not of, the institution must remember and reclaim the ancestral, collective, and intergenerational wisdom that we possess. Hence, this chapter is an illustration and a political praxis of re/embodying the lineage of collectivist healing wisdom embedded in Asian cultural food systems. In particular, I, in collaboration with my ancestors, elders, and community, highlight the wisdom of collectivist rest, resistance, and care that has been passed through generations of struggle and healing. Such wisdom is part of the interconnected constellations of culturally situated and transformative healing wisdom that Communities of Color practice and embody on a daily basis. As an educator, I apply this lineage of wisdom to imagine and co-create collectivist healing spaces for and with myself, my students, and my colleagues. Therefore, I present the following collectivist imagining that is rooted in Asian cultural food wisdom for our collective liberation and healing in and well beyond the academy. When we engage in the praxis of imagination, we can collectively transform higher education into sites of healing and freedom.

Imagining Higher Education as a Site of Collectivist Rest, Resistance, and Care

I close my eyes, take a sip of my jasmine tea, and imagine a higher education that is no longer a harmful and violent enterprise that erases and minimizes ways of knowing and being that are practiced across the Asian diaspora and other Communities of Color. Instead, I imagine higher education as a site of collectivist rest, resistance, and care that honors the healing wisdom embodied in the lineage of Asian food culture. Rooted and connected to my wisdom lineages, I wake up each morning feeling nourished, well rested, and deeply connected to others. I regularly rest and eat with my colleagues and students, sharing stories of wisdom from our community and ancestors. We openly and willingly exchange ideas, questions, and curiosities because each of us is rooted in mutuality and reciprocity. Regardless of educational background, age, and other identities and experiences, we know that each person has something that can be offered and learned from. We work not out of individualistic competition nor to demonstrate our value through productivity, but we work so that we can tend to ourselves and one another through our gifts and medicines. Although oppressive forces are no longer trying to break us, we remain vigilant and alert because we have heard the stories of resistance and survival from our ancestors. We teach, write, mentor, research, ideate, and lead in and through education because we wish to express care and love for those who wish to learn with us.

Invitations and Reflections

I invite fellow academic comrades to rest, resist, and care for one another as we navigate the colonial machinery that permeates in and beyond the academy. This chapter illustrates the collectivist healing wisdom that is at the center of Asian foods. Collective rest invites us to slow down and prioritize resting together, instead of abiding by the rules of academic grind culture. Collective resistance invites us to tune into the stories of survival, abundance, hope, and strength that are embedded in food, especially culturally relevant foods. Collective care invites us to care for the needs of our *whole* bodies—physical, spiritual, emotional, and relational—as interrelated to the needs of others and to engage with food as a relational way of being. To cultivate these invitations to collectively rest, resist, and care for one another, I invite readers to reflect on the following questions:

- How might I integrate collective rest to resist academic grind culture and ground in community during moments of distress?
- What stories of collective resistance are tethered to the foods that I have eaten with others in community?

- What might change if I truly cared for the basic needs (like food) for myself and others?

Special acknowledgement to Dr. Tabatha Jones Jolivet, my dissertation chair and spirit mama. Thank you for watering the seeds of this work within my soul and for helping me tune into my embodied wisdom.

References

Bhattacharya, K. (2019). Theorizing from the streets: De/colonizing, contemplative, and creative approaches and consideration of quality in arts-based qualitative research. In N. K. Denzin & M. D. Giardina (Eds.), *Qualitative inquiry at a crossroads: Political, performative, and methodological reflections* (pp. 109–125). Routledge. https://doi.org/10.4324/9780429056796-9.

Bhattacharya, K. (2023). Homecoming with culturally situated philosophies of being in qualitative inquiry. *Qualitative Inquiry, 29*(1), 117–125. https://doi.org/10.1177/10778004221111378.

Bryant, T. (2022). *Homecoming: Overcome fear and trauma to reclaim your whole, authentic self.* TarcherPerigee.

Chávez, A. F., Ke, F., & Herrera, F. A. (2012). Clan, sage, and sky: Indigenous, Hispano, and Mestizo narratives of learning in New Mexico context. *American Educational Research Journal, 49*(4), 775–806. https://doi.org/10.3102/0002831212441498.

García, S. B., & Guerra, P. L. (2004). Deconstructing deficit thinking: Working with educators to create more equitable learning environments. *Education and Urban Society, 36*(2), 150–168. https://doi.org/10.1177/0013124503261322.

Hersey, T. (2022). *Rest is resistance: A manifesto*. Little, Brown.

Kim, H. J. (2020). "Where are you from? Your English is so good": A Korean female scholar's autoethnography of academic imperialism in U.S. higher education. *International Journal of Qualitative Studies in Education, 33*(5), 491–507. https://doi.org/10.1080/09518398.2019.1681551.

Kim, J. L., & Ward, L. M. (2007). Silence speaks volumes: Parental sexual communication among Asian American emerging adults. *Journal of Adolescent Research, 22*(1), 3–31. https://doi.org/10.1177/0743558406294916.

Marine, S. B., Hurtado, S., & McCoy-Simmons, C. (2021). Survivor-faculty and the lived experience of disclosure. *Journal of Women and Gender in Higher Education, 14*(3), 245–264. https://doi.org/10.1080/26379112.2021.1990777.

Martinez, M. A., & Welton, A. D. (2017). Straddling cultures, identities, and inconsistencies: Voices of pre-tenure faculty of color in educational leadership. *Journal of Research on Leadership Education, 12*(2), 122–142. https://doi.org/10.1177/1942775115606177.

Matsuoka, S. (2022, May 11). *"Have you eaten yet?" Is the Asian "I love you."* Verywell Mind. https://www.verywellmind.com/have-you-eaten-yet-food-is-the-ultimate-asian-love-language-5270875.

Mayuzumi, K. (2006). The tea ceremony as a decolonizing epistemology: Healing and Japanese women. *Journal of Transformative Education, 4*(1), 8–26. https://doi.org/10.1177/1541344605282856.

Moten, F., & Harney, S. (2004). The university and the undercommons: Seven theses. *Social Text, 22*(2), 101–115.

Okazaki, S. (2002). Influences of culture on Asian Americans' sexuality. *The Journal of Sex Research, 39*(1), 34–41. https://doi.org/10.1080/00224490209552117.

Okun, T. (1999). *White supremacy culture.* dRworks. https://www.whitesupremacyculture.info/uploads/4/3/5/7/43579015/okun_-_white_sup_culture.pdf.

la paperson. (2017). *A third university is possible.* University of Minnesota Press. https://manifold.umn.edu/projects/a-third-university-is-possible.

Patel, L. (2015). *Decolonizing educational research: From ownership to answerability*. Routledge.

Patel, L. (2021). *No study without struggle: Confronting settler colonialism in higher education.* Beacon Press.

Poon, O., Squire, D., Kodama, C., Byrd, A., Chan, J., Manzano, L., Furr, S., & Bishundat, D. (2016). A critical review of the model minority myth in selected literature on Asian Americans and Pacific Islanders in higher education. *Review of Educational Research, 86*(2), 469–502. https://doi.org/10.3102/0034654315612205.

Poon Ghaffari, G. (2024). Theories in the flesh: The embodied lives of Asian/American women survivors of sexual and relationship violence [Ph.D./HE, Azusa Pacific University]. In *ProQuest Dissertations and Theses* (2916247794). ProQuest Dissertations & Theses Global. https://www.proquest.com/dissertations-theses/theories-flesh-embodied-lives-asian-american/docview/2916247794/se-2?accountid=14026.

Robinson, C. J. (2020). *Black marxism: The making of the Black radical tradition* (3rd ed.). UNC Press Books.

Smith, L. T. (2013). *Decolonizing methodologies: Research and Indigenous peoples* (2nd ed.). Zed Books.

Wagner, A. E., & Shahjahan, R. A. (2015). Centering embodied learning in anti-oppressive pedagogy. *Teaching in Higher Education,* 20(3), 244–254. https://doi.org/10.1080/13562517.2014.993963.

Wilder, C. S. (2013). *Ebony and ivy: Race, slavery, and the troubled history of America's universities.* Bloomsbury Press.

Yeh, C. J., Arora, A. K., & Wu, K. A. (2006). A new theoretical model of collectivistic coping. In P. T. P. Wong & L. C. J. Wong (Eds.), *Handbook of Multicultural Perspectives on Stress and Coping* (pp. 55–72). Springer US. https://doi.org/10.1007/0-387-26238-5_3.

Yosso, T. J. (2005). Whose culture has capital? A critical race theory discussion of community cultural wealth. *Race Ethnicity and Education, 8*(1), 69–91. https://doi.org/10.1080/1361332052000341006.

CHAPTER 9

The Southern Kitchen: Resistance Epistemologies Cultivated Through "Soul Food"

BRANDON BECK

Durocher and Knezevic (2023) assert that

> Food culture as part of a broader socio-cultural context informs which types of knowledge and practices (such as food production and harvesting, circulation, preparation, control, and consumption) are rendered possible, and what issues are created, debated, or made invisible. (p. 849)

As a third-year African American male Ph.D. student, I have had my share of challenges trying to teach and conduct research at a large predominately white institution (PWI) research institution in the American South. Whether those challenges stem from systemic oppression, racial bias, or a lack of navigational capital, I have dealt with many of the same issues that other Black scholars have had to deal with. As a new scholar and young adult, I struggled to gain a footing in this social institution that was historically created to exclude people like me. To succeed, I recalled much of the wisdom my mother shared with me about how to navigate systems of oppression as well as the guidance I received from a prominent female Black mentor and scholar in the academy. As a single Black woman, my mother faced interlocking systems of multiple oppressions rooted in racism and sexism as she navigated differing societal institutions (Collins, 2009; Collins et al., 2021). My mother served as one of the only Black municipal court judges in a small city in the South; she often experienced dehumanizing and racist experiences due to her gender, class, and race. Conversely, my mentor has faced similar systems of oppression as she continues to combat Whiteness, anti-Blackness, and racial discrimination that exist in the academy.

After spending long, exhausting days my mother was often eager to escape the White-dominated space of her job and replace that environment with the Black-dominated cultural space of her kitchen. Historically, Black men and women have found the kitchen, BBQ pits, or places of food preparation as dynamic places where the goal is not merely to survive, fit in, or to cope but rather to feel ownership and accountability (Collins, 2009; Miller, 2021; Wilkinson, 2024). Conversely, from the Antebellum period to the present the Southern kitchen has been a place of comfort for Black individuals but also a place of resistance to systemic oppression in the face of racism. The southern kitchen of American slavery often served as a symbolic struggle of power and oppression due to it being "a confining place which signified the relational conflicts between White and Black women and their negotiation of space within the plantation household" (Davis, 1999, p. 367).

The 18th century Southern plantation system was structured to separate the kitchen from the rest of the larger planation (Halloran, 2012). White plantation mistresses often showcased their place in the power structure due to their increased supervision and domination of enslaved Black women within the Southern kitchen (Durocher & Knezevic, 2023; Leveen, 2001). Enslaved women used the Southern kitchen as place to sustain and provide sustenance for the entire human family including the white and Black family, while also cultivating a safe place for Black women and subtly redefining their newly transformed space into a place of resistance (Durocher & Knezevic, 2023). Historians argue that although this separation was mainly due to the heat, noise, and orders often associated with cooking and the kitchen, the spatial separation away from the main house physically separated kitchen slaves from members of the plantation family (Leveen, 2001; Ryan, 1999; Vlach, 1995). Coupled with the plantation mistress's role as overseer of tasks and chores associated around the planation home, the role of cook was one of inferiority and subservience (Egerton & Egerton, 1993). Within this place of banishment, Black women resisted hatred and oppression and transformed the kitchen into a site of ethical care and serenity (McCutcheon, 2015). Thus the kitchen became a cultural significance in the African American community due to its ability to provide a space for Black women to pass down survival skills to their daughters and later sons on navigating systems of oppression (Garth & Reese, 2020).

The historic relationship between the kitchen and the Academy informs the experiences of the Black community as they have struggled to navigate institutions of White dominance. Similar to the Southern plantation kitchen, White faculty often hold the power and control for entry, success, and promotion in the academy (Schuster & Finkelstein, 2006). Entry into the academic institutions has often been withheld from Black academics. Their experience is often similar to the experiences of the enslaved women in plantation kitchens, in that like the cooking skills of the enslaved Black women, the Black academic's knowledge and scholarship are often valued but they are often distanced from the values of the institution (Hendrix, 2021; Thomas, 2020).

These values are held in juxtaposition with the experiences my mother often shared with me in her safe place of the kitchen. Throughout the years, my role changed from observer to sous-chef, but the stories and life lessons told during our time in the kitchen influenced how I navigated systems of oppressions. Like the foremothers in plantation kitchen in the Antebellum South, my mother and other Black scholars gave me the social, linguistic, and navigational capital to carve out my own place in the academy (Clayton et al., 2023; Martinez et al., 2017). Although the work of Black scholars is often regulated to the "kitchen space," through my mother's wisdom and the wisdom of other Black scholars, I have been given the tools needed to create a space outside the mainstream departments and the intellectual dinner table of the Big House or the "academy" (Durocher & Knezevic, 2023; Martinez et al., 2017).

My experience within the walls of the ivory tower echo many of the experiences Black academics face daily. I would soon go on to realize that while penetrating the walls of the ivory tower and gaining employment are difficult, the most difficult part of my journey lies in negotiating staff and student perceptions which often reside against a backdrop of normative Whiteness and dominant Eurocentric curricula (Arday & Mirza, 2018). My journey into the field of academia began during the Fall of 2021, as I was accepted into and started my doctoral program focusing on teaching and learning at one of the larger research universities in the southeast. Initially, due to my experience and success in the classroom as a middle school social studies teacher, I had been persuaded to enter the educational leadership program to expedite my career into K-12 administration. Like many that are new to the field of education, I was unaware of the experiences that I would face in this new institution. While I was not naive to the idea that I would be facing some sort of inequity due to the prevailing attempts to center Whiteness within institutions of education and systems of power, I was unaware of how deeply rooted anti-Blackness was within these predominantly White institutions (PWIs) (Pérez Huber & Solorzano, 2015).

Seeds of Resistance

Growing up as the son of single Black female in the American South brought its own set of unique challenges. My mother was the first in our family to graduate from college in 1989. She would go on to be one of the first Black women to hold the title of municipal court judge in a small conservative town in the South. Her appointment to this position brought constant microaggressions and blatant displays of racism from her superiors, peers, and subordinates. As my mother came home from work, she would express her profound frustrations at the systemic racism she faced. As she would tell me about her day, she would also begin her debrief while she was in the kitchen preparing our dinner. While she was often the main cook in our home kitchen, my role was to sous chef and help her prepare the meal. Many of the conversations we would have within the kitchen would often center on the barriers to success she faced as a Black person but also the barriers she faced as a female. While at the time I was not aware of the term intersectionality, I was aware of the duality in which the forms of hatred seem to come for my mother.

I do believe that it is important that I acknowledge that as a Black male I will never fully be able to understand the plight of Black females, but I do recognize their unique struggle and look to speak to the experiences faced by mother. Davis (1999) states that "that the kitchen provided a space in which Black women passed on survival skills down to their daughters and helped them develop ways to confront oppressive conditions" (p. 369). During our therapeutic cooking sessions, my mother often planted seeds of resistance within me. Our conversations often consisted of roleplaying scenarios that she would often use to facilitate discussions that look to show me how to navigate institutions of oppression. She would often situate these roleplaying scenarios within her daily experiences. These scenarios ranged from us discussing how she handled the misogynistic co-workers, or how she handled the racist verbal assaults from her superiors. She also used these times to discuss how the issues she faced might translate to me in my future profession. Essentially, she transformed the kitchen space as a place absent of outsiders and central for "ritual nurturance and African American identity" (Davis, 1999, p. 370).

Her stories embodied the resistance practices of enslaved Africans during the transatlantic slave trade. Our kitchen conversations consistently allowed me to realize the importance of embracing my race and culture in the face of adversity. They also allowed me to recognize Anti-Blackness, while critiquing White power and privilege. As a Black historian, I later realized the connection between my mother's active resistance and the resistance of the enslaved Black woman. Like most things in White-dominated spaces, the narrative surrounding slavery situates enslaved Africans as being barbaric and having access to little or no culture upon their removal from the continent of Africa (Nunn & Wantchekon, 2011; Richardson, 2009).

As enslaved Black families were taken from their homelands during the days of the transatlantic slave trade, they left so much of their shared culture in their West African villages. As an act of resistance to save aspects of their community and culture, Black enslaved women braided the seeds of crops like sugarcane, West African yams, collard greens, and rice into their hair. Consequently, these seeds were the foundation for anti-White resistance as they were eventually planted, nurtured on the lands of the enslavers. Concurrently, these seeds of resistance made their way to plantation kitchens as enslaved Black women used their knowledge and expertise of these foods to craft cultural dishes that were unique to the Black experience.

These historic experiences balanced with the experiences of my mother's experiences helped me navigate my experiences trying to navigate the ivory tower of academia. Like many Black Americans, I entered this often-unforgiven space armed with the ancestral seeds of resistance from my enslaved ancestors. I was aware that I would be surrounded with scholars that did not look like me, did not understand my culture or lived experiences, or teach epistemologies that were rooted in diversity.

Audre Lorde asserts that the master's tools will never dismantle the master's house (Lorde & Lorde, 2018). Lorde's words have been used to explain the concept that while the master (White leaders) will look to embody Black people with tools they could use in order to perform the task they needed to be successful, they would never use those tools to exceed their place within the social hierarchy (Jackson, 2022; Jannesari, 2023). Through my kitchen conversations with my mother, I walked into the academy armed with this knowledge. I was also keenly aware that while I had to learn how to operate within the structure of the White academy, I could use the tools that had been given to me to craft my own space. This can best be seen through the work of critical scholars as they used their entry into the academia to create their own unique spaces for research centering the diverse experiences of those that do not hold power.

A metaphorical example of Black resistance within the construct of the academy lies in the description of soul food. To do a complete analysis of the term soul food we would need to include contributions from African, American, and European influences in the production, collection, preparation, and consumption of foods (Whit, 1999). Scholarship and access into the academy has always been rooted in Whiteness (Matias et al., 2019; Pérez Huber & Solorzano, 2015). Thus, when Black academics and other academics of color gain access into the ivory tower, they are met with notions of assimilating their scholarship to fit the model of the White academic (Moore et al., 2018). In turn, this tactic is reminiscent of the nutrition offered to many enslaved Africans. Slaveowners notably gave the scraps or unwanted selections of food to their enslaved Africans. These "scraps" were deemed unfit for human consumption but were deemed as acceptable for the enslaved (Witt, 2004). In the eyes of the enslaved these scraps would produce food that would later embody Black resistance, as often disregarded food like the greens from the tops of beets were eaten, as were dandelions (Kittler and Sucher, 1989). The enslaved also proved resourceful in appropriating vegetable sustenance with chard, collard greens, kale, mustard greens, marsh marigold leaves, milkweed, pokeweed, and purslane (Kittler and Sucher, 1989). Pigs provided most of the meat for the diet of the enslaved as edible or desirable parts were often claimed by the slave owners and the inedible parts were often given to the slaves. These scraps consisted of the pigs' stomach, ears, feet, other intestines, head cheese (brains), ribs, fat back, and hocks (Whit, 1999). All these meats influenced what came to be called soul food and are currently considered delicacies in many cultures outside of the Black community (Williams-Forson & Sharpless, 2015).

We see the similarity within the academy as Black scholars have looked to take the White-dominated teachings of these predominantly PWIs and create theories that give importance to the Black experiences. Scholars like Derek Bell, Gloria Ladson Billings, Cedrick Robinson, and Patricia Hill Collins have created research that looks to center the Black experience within White-dominated spaces. Yet we continue to see Black academics take the scraps (White-dominated literature and academic practices) and transform them into epistemological and ontological masterpieces that look to separate and celebrate the Black experiences. In my own journey within the ivory tower, I was introduced to theoretical and conceptual ideas rooted in Whiteness. As a novice scholar I was unaware of the amount of Black literature that was available to me; I was primarily taught how to conduct, analyze, and synthesize research through a White-Eurocentric lens. It was not until the second year within my doctoral program that I was able to take a course from a Black female scholar who specialized in critical theory. She allowed me to see beyond the scraps I was given and allowed me the opportunity to craft a space within the academy using my own unique talents backed with research from my community and culture. Whit (1999) asserts that "most important to the nature of Soul Food is the tradition of spicing by which bland food is made interesting" (p. 38). This professor taught me to see the true nature of my work; in essence she allowed me to spice up the naturally bland work that I had been taught in the academy.

Soul Food, the Academy, and Black Identity

The definition of term soul food has several different meanings. The complexity of the definition of the term metaphorically expounds the struggle for direct ownership of the word. Fredrick Douglass Opie (2010) asserts that while soul food is unique to the African American experience, it has been influenced by other cultures. However, it is the intellectual invention and property of African Americans due to its connection to the Black struggle and its expression of resilience in the face of adversity and oppression. Despite the obvious historical and cultural connections and contributions of Black people to this style of cooking, soul food has often been solely defined as "Good, Ole-Fashioned, Southern Cooking" (Graves, 2015; Whit, 1999).

Historically, there has been little mention of the basic division between the food often fed to enslaved Blacks and the food usually prepared for the White master's family. The White family would often eat the finest cuts and produce with dishes often resembling something like "fired chicken, fired pies, potato salad, hot biscuits and yeast rolls" (Ferguson, 1989, p. xxvi). Enslaved Blacks would often be forced to be creative and invent new dishes with the food that they were given. In turn, many of the White enslavers became envious of the resiliency of their enslaved Blacks, as they often demanded that this "slave food" be served at the kitchen table in the big house (Whit, 1999). These enslaved Black individuals were also forced to teach their White owners the various methods and ways of food production as well as write "cookbooks" with many of the enslaved never receiving credit (Whit, 1999). Emancipation brought an end to chattel slavery, and as White slave owners began to experience life without the enslaved, the mistresses began to utilize many of the food preparation and cooking techniques taught to them by their slaves (Williams-Forson & Sharpless, 2015). Consequently, we see these techniques and recipes became tremendously valued and co-opted. Ergo, the former White enslavers took "ownership" of this style of cooking (Davis, 1999; Egerton & Egerton, 1993). The idea of Southern food and modern soul food took shape, as the contributions of the Black Americans were diminished and discredited (Miller, 2021; Richardson, 2009).

Within the academy we see similar issues arise as the institution of the academy, and many of the actors within that space, continue to operate to preserve the unrepentant Whiteness of the academy. The Whiteness I speak to is not solely represented by the disparity in racial demographics at college or universities often describes as PWIs. The Whiteness I speak to focuses on the way White ignorance is a normal part of academic life. The creation and inclusion of DEI statements, land grant acknowledgements, and committees structured to promote the recruitment of Black faculty and staff are mere illusions of progress (Lewis et al., 2023). They center the idea that while there is an outward focus diversity within the ivory tower, this White space will always be patrolled for dark intruders, whose very presence is a smear on the civilized Whiteness that encompasses the White academy (Mills, 2011).

This concept of White ignorance differentiates from the general definition of ignorance in that it is strategic, structural, and in the service of sustaining White power and privilege (Lewis et al., 2023). Similar to the co-option of soul food as part of the White southern identity, there is often little to no recognition given to the accomplishments and work done by Black scholars within the academy. While there have been acknowledgements of the scholarship of Du Bois, Ladson Billings, Woodson, Mills, and Bell within the academy, we continue to see their work co-opted to fit a never-ending White narrative (Nishi, 2022).

As I entered the field of academia, there was much discussion from those within my institution about the need for addition of core curriculum and courses rooted in diversity. Hearing this I was excited to hear that Black scholarship would be a fixture in my doctoral coursework. What I came to experience during my coursework was vastly different than the narrative I was sold on. Many of the courses I was given centered the theories and concepts of great White thinkers in the field of education. I often would hear of the works of Vygotsky, Bruner, and the like as we discussed educational philosophy. When scholars of color were mentioned, it was often surface level, and they would choose to include the simplistic aspects of culturally responsive or sustaining pedagogies. Many of the scholars who taught these courses were nurtured in their academic career by Black scholars. They had been introduced to exceptional Black research and theory but choose to perpetuate the theories and ideologies of other White scholars as they taught graduate level course. Many adopted anti-racist, culturally responsive, or critical approaches to their academic persona. I often would find tremendous disparity in the work they published versus how they taught their classes. Thus, we see the connection between the co-option of soul food as southern food and the co-option of diverse and critical scholarship as White owned.

In conclusion, as I navigated the predominantly White space of the academy, I leaned on the teachings of both my mother and my mentor within the academy. Both were Black women who faced interconnecting forms of oppression, flourished within predominantly White spaces, and looked to spread their knowledge about how to succeed within these spaces within their community through, and with, the lessons learned in the kitchen and around food. The African proverb, "She who learns must teach," echoes the importance that Black women in positions of power have had on my life but also the importance they continue to have within White spaces.

References

Arday, J., & Mirza, H. S. (2018). *Dismantling race in higher education: Racism, Whiteness and decolonising the academy*. Palgrave Macmillan.

Clayton, A. B., Breeden, R. L., & Davis, T. J. (2023). "My entire support system for graduate school": Black students' experiences in a McNair Scholars Program. *Journal of College Student Retention: Research, Theory & Practice*, 15210251231182683.

Collins, P. H. (2009). *Black feminist thought: Knowledge, consciousness, and the politics of empowerment* (2nd ed.). Routledge.

Collins, P. H., Da Silva, E. C. G., Ergun, E., Furseth, I., Bond, K. D., & Martínez-Palacios, J. (2021). Intersectionality as critical social theory: Intersectionality as critical social theory, Patricia Hill Collins, Duke University Press, 2019. *Contemporary Political Theory, 20*(3), 690–725. https://doi.org/10.1057/s41296-021-00490-0.

Davis, O. I. (1999). In the kitchen: Transforming the academy through safe spaces of resistance. *Western Journal of Communication, 63*(3), 364–381. https://doi.org/10.1080/10570319909374647.

Durocher, M., & Knezevic, I. (2023). Food matters and materialities: Critical understandings of food cultures. *Food, Culture & Society, 26*(4), 844–855.

Egerton, J., & Egerton, A. B. (1993). *Southern food: At home, on the road, in history*. University of North Carolina Press.

Ferguson, S. (1989). *Soul food: Classic cuisine from the deep South* (1st ed). Weidenfeld & Nicolson.

Garth, H., & Reese, A. M. (2020). *Black food matters: Racial justice in the wake of food justice*. University of Minnesota Press.

Graves, B. (2015). You are what you beat: Food metaphors and Southern Black identity in twentieth-century African American literature and Goodie Mob's "soul food." *Studies in Popular Culture, 38*(1), 123–137. JSTOR.

Halloran, V. N. (2012). Recipes as memory work: Slave food. *Culture, Theory and Critique, 53*(2), 147–161. https://doi.org/10.1080/14735784.2012.682791.

Hendrix, K. G. (2021). There are no awards for surviving racism, sexism, and ageism in the academy: Contemplations of a senior faculty member. *Communication and Critical/Cultural Studies, 18*(3), 246–262. https://doi.org/10.1080/14791420.2020.1865551.

Jackson, T. M. (2022). Dismantling the master's house with the master's tools. In E. Pérez, T. E. Brown, & W. Irwin (Eds.), *Black Panther and philosophy: What can Wakanda offer the world?* (pp. 211–220). Wiley-Blackwell.

Jannesari, S. (2023). Dismantling the master's house: An introduction to our first issue. *Stolen Tools, 1*(1), 1–3.

Kittler, P. G., & Sucher, K. (1989). *Food and culture in America: A nutrition handbook*. Van Nostrand Reinhold.

Leveen, L. (2001). Dwelling in the house of oppression: The spatial, racial, and textual dynamics of Harriet Wilson's our nig. *African American Review, 35*(4), 561–580.

Lewis, A. E., Forman, T. A., & Hagerman, M. A. (2023). Charles Mills ain't dead! Keeping the spirit of Mills' work alive by understanding and challenging the unrepentant Whiteness of the academy. *Race Ethnicity and Education, 26*(4), 553–564. https://doi.org/10.1080/13613324.2023.2207986.

Lorde, A., & Lorde, A. (2018). *The master's tools will never dismantle the master's house*. Penguin Books.

Martinez, M. A., Chang, A., & Welton, A. D. (2017). Assistant professors of color confront the inequitable terrain of academia: A community cultural wealth perspective. *Race Ethnicity and Education, 20*(5), 696–710.

Matias, C., Walker, D., & del Hierro, M. (2019). Tales from the ivory tower: Women of color's resistance to Whiteness in academia. *Taboo: The Journal of Culture and Education*, 18(1), 4.

McCutcheon, P. (2015). Food, faith, and the everyday struggle for Black urban community. *Social & Cultural Geography, 16*(4), 385–406. https://doi.org/10.1080/14649365.2014.991749.

Miller, A. (2021). *Black smoke: African Americans and the United States of barbecue.* The University of North Carolina Press.

Mills, C. W. (2011). *The racial contract* (Nachdr.). Cornell University Press.

Moore, K. K., Cid-Martinez, I., Toney, J., Smith, J. A., Kalb, A. C., Shin, J. H., & Spalter-Roth, R. M. (2018). Who climbs the academic ladder? Race and gender stratification in a world of Whiteness. *The Review of Black Political Economy, 45*(3), 216–244.

Nishi, N. W. (2022). Imperialistic reclamation of higher education diversity initiatives through semantic co-option and concession. *Race Ethnicity and Education, 25*(2), 249–267.

Nunn, N., & Wantchekon, L. (2011). The slave trade and the origins of mistrust in Africa. *American Economic Review, 101*(7), 3221–3252.

Opie, F. D. (2010). *Hog and hominy: Soul food from Africa to America.* Columbia University Press.

Pérez Huber, L., & Solorzano, D. G. (2015). Racial microaggressions as a tool for critical race research. *Race Ethnicity and Education, 18*(3), 297–320. https://doi.org/10.1080/13613324.2014.994173.

Richardson, D. (2009). Cultures of exchange: Atlantic Africa in the era of the slave trade. *Transactions of the Royal Historical Society, 19*, 151–179.

Ryan, B. (1999). Kitchen testimony: Ex-slaves' narratives in new company. *Callaloo, 22*(1), 141–156.

Schuster, J., & Finkelstein, M. J. (2006). *The American faculty.* Johns Hopkins University Press. https://doi.org/10.1353/book.3484.

Thomas, V. (2020). "How dare you!" African American faculty and the power struggle with White students. *Journal of Cases in Educational Leadership, 23*(4), 115–126. https://doi.org/10.1177/1555458920945762.

Vlach, J. M. (1995). "Snug li'l house with flue and oven": Nineteenth-century reforms in plantation slave housing. *Perspectives in Vernacular Architecture, 5*, 118–129.

Whit, W. C. (1999). Soul food as cultural creation. *Journal for the Study of Food and Society, 3*(1), 37–47. https://doi.org/10.2752/152897999786690717.

Wilkinson, C. (2024). *Praisesong for the kitchen ghosts: Stories and recipes from five generations of Black country cooks* (First edition). Clarkson Potter.

Williams-Forson, P., & Sharpless, R. (2015). *Dethroning the deceitful pork chop: Rethinking African American foodways from slavery to Obama.* University of Arkansas Press.

Witt, D. (2004). *Black hunger: Soul food and America* (1st University of Minnesota Press ed). University of Minnesota Press.

CHAPTER 10

Feeling and Feeding the Immigrant Void in Academia

MADINA DJURAEVA, LAURA WALLS,
FERIAL PEARSON, AND
SANDRA RODRÍGUEZ-ARROYO

This chapter tells the food stories of four women in academia: Madina—an Uzbek, Ferial—a Kenyan Muhindi, Laura—a Chicana, and Sandra—a Boricua/Puerto Rican. We come together in Midwestern America from seemingly disparate places through *testimonios* (Delgado Bernal, Burciaga, & Flores Carmona, 2012). In these narratives, we find that being far from home has created a void and a feeling of longing—*añoranza*—within ourselves.

Even after years of living in the United States, we feed this *añoranza* with food and conversation about food; it is a connection to our families, lives, cultures, and homes that we are compelled to bring to this land that feels foreign at times. Food is spatial, temporal, and ubiquitous, integral to our dispositions as educators, writers, friends, and members of our personal and academic communities. As we engage in dialogues through this chapter, we ask ourselves how we navigate academia and beyond with authenticity, transnational perspectives, care, and cooking.

Many fields link food to the body through the concept of embodiment. In language studies, embodiment manifests through body management and other physical attributes to perform group membership (Bucholtz & Hall, 2016; Eckert, 1989). In food studies, narratives embody cultural identity (Abarca & Colby, 2016). In examining narratives of food (Holtzman, 2006) and language (Mendoza-Denton,

2014), scholars showed how embodied discursive practices of migration transcend identity beyond cultural practices into a lived, gendered, and moral experience that is intertwined with geographies of space and memories of place. In addition to embodiment, nostalgia is another concept central to our food *testimonios*. Holtzman (2006) defines nostalgia as a memory of embodied events that people recall and undertake to communicate in the present, showing how food and memory confluence is based on past generosity and dispositions embodied in memories around particular foods. Other have shown how food keeps nostalgia on an alien soil for diasporic immigrants (Sakkthi & Aruna, 2021) and how "in telling what 'We eat,' we are showing who we are" (Abarca & Colby, 2016, p. 7). We draw from these articulations of embodiment and nostalgia to analyze the language and discourse in our food *testimonios*.

A genre accepted for "methodology, pedagogy, research, and reflection within a social justice education framework" (Delgado Bernal, Burciaga, & Flores Carmona, 2012, p. 363), *testimonio* pushes against dominant discourses and allows racialized communities to critically reflect on their practices (Mizell & Flores Carmona, 2023). As we engage in *testimonio*, we share our oral, written, and digital narratives to engage in critical reflection within socio-political contextual realities. In analyzing these reflections, we borrow from affect theory (Fielding, 2022) to examine the impact that history and heritage can have on our thinking at the crossroads of food and academia. We also attend to the affective discourse (Arnold, 2011) to explore the pride, ownership, belonging, and resistance constructed through our *testimonios* (Djuraeva, Nguyen, & Castro, 2022). We invite you to join us in our exploration of the relationship between food and navigating the academy and feed our *añoranza* as scholars and educators far from home.

Our Testimonios

Madina: The Most Expensive Gasoline That Ensures I Do Not Break Down

As a busy single mother and tenure-track professor who loves her career and adores her daughter, I must manage demanding roles without a village to support me. Food is the most expensive gasoline that fuels my body, soul, and brain so I do not break down. Living in the United States for over a decade, I am still not used to drinking iced water or eating sandwiches for every meal. I need the hybrid cuisine of Central Asia—*borsch, sho'rbo, osh, manti, kefir*, green and black tea with a touch of fresh mint and lemon to help me keep up with my scholarship and be the mother my daughter deserves. As a scholar who studies multilingualism, I am no stranger to diverse cuisines, some of which are my cooking staples—*kimchi, sauerkraut, naan*, and *tostones*. My body is healthy, my soul joyous, and my mind at peace when I cook these foods and bring them to work.

While Uzbek cuisine is rich in spices and flavors, it is well cooked and thoroughly prepared so that every ingredient tastes like the best version of itself; the lamb tastes like the best lamb, and the potato tastes like the best potato. Nothing is a mystery, and everything is designed to improve the experience. The resemblance of my cuisine to my academic persona is uncanny: straightforward, honest, nourishing, and transparent. My colleagues and students appreciate my honesty and transparency. My community partners, including refugees in high school, value the care, time, and food I put into our service-learning sessions. Recently, a preservice teacher said she found me rude; I wonder if this is because I am not a fan of sandwiches and iced water.

I embody my cuisine across different domains of my life. I choose my research collaborators carefully—based on their ability to reciprocate, follow through, and relate. At home, my cooking can be an attempt to recreate childhood memories of eating with my mother, now with my daughter, and at the university; it is the locus of connection. Uzbek hospitality is famous, and I try to showcase it to my colleagues by bringing my food to work, inviting them to my home, and never going empty handed to my colleagues' homes.

Ferial: Karibuni

Our elders always fed visitors, even if they were enemies or if it was the last of our favorite dishes. We cooked more than necessary in case someone came by and sent food home with them. In Kenya, visitors verbally knock shouting, "*Hodi*!" in Swahili. We yell back,

"*Karibu*!" and they join us for chai, a snack, or a meal. We always prepare for guests so shopping lists include snacks, tea, milk, and sugar. If someone new came we would ask about their favorite foods and any religious or medical food restrictions so they would not only be able to eat but would also enjoy the food. This inclusion and hospitality extended beyond home. We took food to gatherings, helped hosts with preparations, fed those who could not afford it or were sick, and never returned dishware empty. However, if we went elsewhere and did not trust the cook, we would not even taste it as it might make us sick or sad.

Like Kenyan culture and indigenous ways, religion also influenced our food practices. Muslims share food with family, friends, neighbors, and those in need. It is said that followers of the Prophet Muhammad (peace be upon him) would gift him with food, which he would distribute to people experiencing poverty. So, on Fridays, we, as *Ismail'i* Muslims, make a plate for our *Nāndi* ceremony, auctioned off at *Jamatkhana* after prayers, and proceeds go to people in need.

Today, I do not cook for someone I love if I have hate, anger, or sadness in my heart; it affects the taste of the food and the mood of the person consuming it. I cook more than necessary in case someone drops by. I send food to friends, family, students, even strangers. Slaughtering a lamb and roasting it in my front yard would be frowned upon here, so I make loads of mutton biriyani to share during Eid. I consider food restrictions and remember people's favorites when cooking, constantly learning about different foods and cultures from students and new friends.

These traditions have taught me to care about, feed, and welcome the most vulnerable in my home and classroom with cultural humility, service, inclusivity, and justice. My traditions connect me to my values and lessons passed down by my ancestors, religion, and culture, even while I learn new shortcuts and different preparations. Food is culture, superstition, religion, tradition, emotion, and magic—the essence of me as a person, mother, community member, teacher, and scholar.

Laura: Quintessentially Necessary for Home

Throughout my life, my experiences with food have made me feel loved, disdained, excluded, and included. In academia, it proved a sense of inclusion. As a graduate student, I was invited to the homes of my professors, where they cooked elaborate meals for us. One professor, knowing my taste for more uncommon foods, shared meals of *chapulines*, black pudding, and sweetbreads with me. However, not all professors enjoyed cooking, so my dissertation advisor and I often ate out. Through her, I discovered my love of various cuisines.

Food also played a key role in my relationships with fellow graduate students. Weekly outings for shawarma with my closest friends gave me a sense of belonging during my solitary dissertation work. These Monday dinners, where we laughed and caught up on gossip and goings on, were my only social connection. I may not have survived my program without it. Leaving Los Angeles for Omaha, I missed these gatherings but eventually found a new group of friends at the University of Nebraska at Omaha (UNO), where I continue the tradition of sharing meals.

Food was equally important in my family life. My Mexican-born mother cooked Mexican food daily, while my American father prepared southern-style American cuisine on holidays. He introduced her to traditional Thanksgiving meals, which always included cornbread stuffing. This dish has become a staple at Thanksgiving dinners I spend with my UNO family, and they too include what is quintessentially necessary for them to feel at home at these dinners. This helps to reproduce the emotional and social support I need to continue in a place where my birth family is so far away.

As a graduate student and now as a faculty member at UNO, I have realized the significant role food plays in fostering a sense of community and belonging. It is this feeling that kept me sane and keeps me sane. I strive to create a similar experience for my students, so I share food with them as well. I bring Mexican hot chocolate and *pan de muerto* for *El Día de los Muertos* and dishes from my childhood like *albóndigas, empanadas*. I hope to create a community for my students, so they too can feel like they belong.

Sandra: Reaffirming My Puerto Rican Identity Through Food

When I moved to the "mainland" to work on my master's, I discovered *potlucks*. There were potlucks for everything, including classes and social gatherings. However, I was culturally shocked and felt insulted whenever leftovers from my dishes were returned to me instead of shared with others. Potlucks have continued after graduate school, but something has become clear: people should learn the difference between Mexican and Puerto Rican food as they always ask about the ingredients.

I have made it my mission to share Puerto Rican food with my students. I could not share food during the pandemic, but I still told students that Puerto Rican food had spices but was not spicy and that sofrito made everything taste better. I explained that sofrito, a combination of onions, peppers, *ajies*, garlic, and *recao*, is the base of Puerto Rican food. Two sofrito ingredients are unfamiliar, *ajies* and *recao*, but they make all the difference in the flavor. I have been asked why I cook for my classes, and the answer is that it is my way of combating stereotypes in our Latinx community. We are a diverse community, but we are many times lumped together as one; we become Mexican or Hispanic, and I do not want my students to continue this stereotype that leads to microaggressions. As a former professor told us, "It is HIS panic, not MY panic."

I also acknowledge my privilege as a Puerto Rican and recognize I am in a unique position where I have learned the majority culture as a U.S. citizen. Still, at the same time, I did not grow up on the mainland. I am in this in-between, hybrid space where I am part of two worlds, and as Puerto Rican food, I combine familiar ingredients with unique ones from the island. This hybrid space guides me to advise, mentor, and support Black, Indigenous, and People of Color (BIPOC) students and faculty who often feel like outsiders as they navigate the majority-dominant culture of academia. As my food, I will tell them the truth, but with mild sauces to introduce gently and diplomatically the challenges they might face. I also encourage BIPOC students and faculty to never leave behind their unique identities. Like the sofrito in my food, an unusual and delicious combination of familiar ingredients, I want them to maintain their spirit and sparkle.

You Are What You Eat: Navigating Academia Through Food

In examining our *testimonios*, three themes were prevalent: (1) food and health, (2) food and personal qualities, and (3) relationship building in academia. Below we showcase our analysis and findings vis-a-vis navigating academia through food.

Food and Health

Madina and Laura discussed the theme of food and health and, especially, the role of food in their well-being and academic survival. In Madina's narrative, food is a direct cause of her physical well-being, whereas in Laura's, it is a tool through which she maintains her mental health.

Madina uses fuel as a metaphor for food: "So I do not break down," describing it as expensive but necessary to perform the dispositions of an academic and mother. In doing so, she uses evaluative language as "the most expensive gasoline," "health," "joy," and peace" to emphasize the central role of food in her body. At the same time, Madina indexes her *añoranza* for her cultural identity by discussing balancing her various identities as a scholar, single mother, Central Asian immigrant, tenure-track assistant professor, and cosmopolitan woman. Madina recognizes that to perform these distinct but intersecting group memberships, she needs a healthy body and a joyous soul. Food does that for her.

Laura describes her weekly gatherings with friends while performing the dispositions of a graduate student, such as writing her dissertation, as an opportunity to laugh and catch up "on gossip and goings on." These meetings helped her survive by contributing to her mental well-being. She uses language like "laughing," "love," "catching up," and "hope" to reconstruct her experiences during challenging periods. Laura feeds this *añoranza* for the good old days by reconstructing these positive moments with her students.

Food and Personal Qualities

While we all connected food to our personal qualities, the distinction between positive and negative personal qualities constructed through food stood out in our analysis.

For Ferial, her personality embodies the traditions associated with cooking in her culture, for example, "taught me to care about, feed, and welcome the most vulnerable into my home and classroom." Here, Ferial constructs an affective discourse of pride through the act of feeding and performing the moral act of a symbolic mother of those in need. That Ferial employs the concepts of cultural humility, inclusivity, and justice in her work, as inspired by her roots, further demonstrates her pride in belonging to her community "there" and in enacting the associated values in her community "here."

For Sandra, her Puerto Ricanness is central to her identity, which she mentions several times in her narrative. As a transnational scholar, Latina, and migrant acculturating and integrating into the United States, food is critical to informing who she is and where she stands as an academic. For Sandra, sofrito is at the heart of Puerto Rican cooking and symbolizes not losing her connection to her embodied self. She tries to impart this knowledge to her students and junior faculty mentees: "[l]ike the sofrito in my food . . . I do not want them to lose their spirit and sparkle."

Sandra's and Ferial's positive discourses contrast with Madina's encounter with a preservice teacher. In retelling the event, Madina distances herself from the unfamiliar "iced water" and "sandwiches," using this analogy to demonstrate how her resistance to these American foods is symbolic of her being positioned as "other" and thus perceived negatively by the preservice teacher. She hints that this may have resulted from a lack of congruency between cultures and their understanding of politeness.

Relationship Building in Academia

As BIPOC women, we found that our ethnic backgrounds and cultural foods shape how we understand relationship building. For this reason, nostalgia and our embodied memories of food inform how we engage and build our current relationships at home, work, and in the community. We showcase examples from all four narratives to highlight the centrality of this theme in all our *testimonios*.

Just like the Uzbek cuisine that is well cooked and thoroughly prepared, Madina translates these qualities to highlight the dispositions she values in her research partners "based on their ability to reciprocate, follow through, and relate." These qualities lie at the heart of Uzbek hospitality. Madina applies these qualities to her relationships with her colleagues by "inviting them to my home, and never going empty-handed to my colleagues' homes." Ferial's father, religion, and community in Kenya taught her to use food as the primary pathway to connection and relationship building with others. These past experiences still hold true for her work and life balance in the United States. She sends "food to friends, family, students, even strangers when there is a need." In describing how she celebrates Eid, an important Muslim holiday in the United States, she becomes nostalgic for the sacrificing and sharing of a lamb with the broader community. This embodied memory of food inspires her to "instead make loads of mutton biriyani."

Food is central to belonging and inclusion in Laura's academic life. Laura embodies this inclusion and belonging by preparing specific Thanksgiving meals she learned from her father and sharing them with her found Omaha family, who also bring their Thanksgiving dishes to the celebratory meal. Following her professors' footsteps, she reenacts the disposition of inclusion with her current students "so that they too can feel like they belong." Laura brings food dear to her heart, such as Mexican hot chocolate, *pan de muerto*, *albóndigas*, and *empanadas*. Like Laura, Sandra remembers the potlucks she was included in as a student and professor; however, what stood out for Sandra was that many people in those potlucks "should learn the difference between Mexican and Puerto Rican food." Her resistance to stereotypes is exemplified by educating people around her, especially her pre- and in-service teachers, about what Puerto Rican food tastes like. We found a resemblance in our experiences and understanding of how we ought to build relationships in academia. Consequently, we wonder if this is because we are all women of color living in a new and unfamiliar place or because we all come from nondominant collective cultures. Perhaps it is the constellation of many more factors that create such resemblance.

Filling the Añoranza Through Embodies Food Practices

In this chapter, four BIPOC women in academia have come together to discuss the significance of food and its impact on our lives in a predominantly white Midwestern state. Through sharing our stories, we employ *testimonio* to resist dominant cultures and narratives, enabling us to engage in critical reflection. Using food as a lens allowed us to explore how we embody our experiences of and through food and how this embodiment manifests in our personal and academic lives, evoking nostalgia in our daily food-related actions. Our stories highlight a sense of void/*añoranza* within us, which we attempt to fill through food—a foundational link to our roots.

Our first finding showed the close connection between food and our bodies. We discussed how our comfort foods serve as a vehicle for physical and mental health, to manage Madina's demanding roles as a mother and academic, and Laura's sanity throughout her doctoral program. Therefore, our primary recommendation applies to our colleagues, particularly those beginning their careers. Because of the limited tenure-track positions, we do not always choose where we work, landing in estranged places without our villages to support us. Hence, we need to keep our roots thriving by feeding our void. A few ways we have found are to have a few healthy staples like *kimchi* and *kefir*, engage in meal preparations for the rest of the week, or create large food batches, freezing them for later. It is essential to learn your surroundings in a new place and develop a food map of your city, highlighting the grocery stores, eateries, etc., that may carry familiar ingredients to your cuisine. Assign time for meals and friends just like we do for meetings and consult with established colleagues regarding the local availability of familiar ingredients.

Our most significant finding highlighted that despite cultural differences, food is intertwined with how we build and foster relationships in academia and beyond. In our *testimonios*, food symbolizes generosity, care, giving back, including and helping others, the moral dispositions that we learned in childhood and continue to embody as critical scholars of color by "going beyond what is traditionally considered the limits of our field, by following the lead of marginalized voices" (Catedral & Djuraeva, 2022, p. 18). As we have found ways to engage in critical pedagogy (e.g., learning people's food preferences, using food to include and educate students), we advocate for using your traditions and familiar practices in performing criticality because our bodies know those ingrained dispositions best. Consequently, we recommend reflecting critically on standard food practices in academia, such as potlucks and boxed lunches that are often used to feed and include and that make sandwiches and returning empty dishes universal practices. Instead, we suggest learning about nondominant food practices and the language of hospitality in other cultures, for example, offering a hot beverage.

Learning via *testimonio* about the deep connection between food and our personal qualities was one of our most interesting findings. Through the affective discourses of pride, ownership, camaraderie, and resistance, we constructed our academic identities in relationship to our food and food practices. Our culinary choices and rituals embody our moral dispositions, linking the qualities we assign to our food and food practices with the ethos of transparent and welcoming teaching, reliable and responsive research, and inclusive and caring service. In exploring the connections highlighted by *testimonios* that prioritize oral, communal, and moral storytelling, we advocate for methodologies grounded in Indigenous ways of knowing as essential tools for research. Embracing diverse ways of knowing validates and honors the richness of academia, moving beyond traditional paradigms. In spaces not inherently designed for us or our cultures, it becomes imperative to carve out authentic practices. Just as we counsel preservice teachers to honor their individuality, we propose that our colleagues, particularly those navigating foreign territories that are gradually becoming home, do the same. Reflecting on our food practices is a powerful reminder of our roots and routes, aiding in the navigation of nostalgia and *añoranza*, both felt and nourished, as we forge our spaces and identities.

In this chapter, we explore our testimonies as BIPOC women scholars navigating the complexities of academia within a commuter/urban campus in the heart of a midsize Midwestern city whose food culture often feels foreign to us. We aim to scrutinize food's role in shaping our academic journeys. Through reflections on teas, soups, spices, and tortillas, we uncover the profound nostalgic significance of our food practices, which intertwine with our health, personalities, and social connections. These culinary rituals serve as homage to our ancestors, infuse our lives with excitement, and bridge the gap left by the immigrant experience. They are sources of healing, reminders of our origins, and tools for resistance against assimilation while embracing acculturation. This fusion of academic and personal realms sustains us and educates others about our identities, ensuring we do not forsake our cultural heritage. Moreover, it fills the void of separation from our loved ones. Crafting this chapter has proven to be a deeply fulfilling endeavor, akin to discovering a place where we can nourish our souls; as Madina aptly puts it, "We seek places where we fuel ourselves." Indeed, this chapter stands as one such sanctuary.

References

Abarca, M. E., & Colby, J. R. (2016). Food memories seasoning the narratives of our lives. *Food and Foodways, 24*(1–2), 1–8. https://doi.org/10.1080/07409710.2016.1150101.

Arnold, J. (2011). Attention to affect in language learning. *Anglistik: International Journal of English Studies, 22*(1), 11–22.

Bucholtz, M., & Hall, K. (2016). Embodied sociolinguistics. *Sociolinguistics: theoretical debates, 1*(1), 173–200.

Catedral, L., & Djuraeva, M. (2022). Whose voice matters? Chronotopic position(ing)s and the dialogic inclusion of marginalized stakeholders in critical applied linguistics. *Applied Linguistics, 44* (3), 420–441. https://doi.org/10.1093/applin/amac052.

Delgado Bernal, D., Burciaga, R., & Flores Carmona, J. (2012). Chicana/Latina testimonios: Mapping the methodological, pedagogical, and political. *Equity & Excellence in Education, 45*(3), 363–372. https://doi.org/10.1080/10665684.2012.698149.

Djuraeva, M., Nguyen, D., & Castro, M. (2022). Bilingual investments of dual-language immersion program alumni. *International Journal of Bilingual Education and Bilingualism, 25*(9), 3214–3227. https://doi.org/10.1080/13670050.2022.2039095.

Eckert, P. (1989). *Jocks and burnouts: Social categories and identity in the high school.* Teachers College Press.

Fielding, A. (2022). Going deeper than 'emotional impact:' Heritage, academic collaboration and affective engagements. *History, 107*(375), 408–435. https://doi.org/10.1111/1468-229X.13271.

Holtzman, J. D. (2006). Food and memory. *Annual Review of Anthropology, 35*, 361–378.

Mendoza-Denton, N. (2014). *Homegirls: Language and cultural practice among Latina youth gangs*. John Wiley & Sons.

Mizell, J. D., & Flores Carmona, J. (2023). Testimonios as a methodological third space: Disrupting epistemological racism in applied linguistics. *Journal of Latinos and Education, 23*(2), 829–842. https://doi.org/10.1080/15348431.2023.2187619.

Sakkthi, M. S., and Aruna, M. J. (2021). Food as a catalyst: Binding culture, nostalgia and identity in Sandeepa Mukherjee Datta's Those Delicious Letters. *Teresian Journal of English Studies, 13*(1), 50–55.

CHAPTER 11

Inclusion Is Not a Microwavable Meal: Cooking Up Critical Embrace in Academic Communities

DENNIS L. RUDNICK

This chapter aims to provide a comprehensive exploration of the theme "inclusion is not a microwaveable meal" by delving into the complexities, challenges, and rewards of fostering genuine inclusion in higher education communities. Too often, academic life is rife with perfunctory, quick-fix efforts at inclusion; institutional mission statements, frameworks, and policies, even with determined leadership and the noblest of intentions, often fall privy to larger, status quo ideologies, norms, cultures, policies, practices, and sociopolitical contexts (Barkley et al., 2017; Linder & Cooper, 2016). Such efforts may demand immediate results or focus on optics rather than investing in the deep, substantive work needed to foster authentic inclusion in what, how, and why we research, teach, and serve. Through a combination of theoretical insights and practical strategies, this chapter offers the concept of *critical embrace* to empower academics to foster, cultivate, and "cook up" more inclusive educational environments.

Inclusion is Not a Microwavable Meal

In higher education, there is a growing expectation for instant results and quick fixes across various domains. This "microwavable meal" culture, characterized by the desire for immediate gratification, is pervasive in academic spaces such as committee work and classroom interactions. Meaningfully, this culture manifests within the desire for immediate results from diversity and inclusion initiatives. For instance, committees tasked with promoting inclusion may be pressured to produce tangible outcomes quickly, often at the expense of thorough, thoughtful, and sustainable strategies. Similarly, classroom interactions may reflect a superficial approach to inclusion, where token gestures are mistaken for meaningful engagement with diverse perspectives.

The expectation for instant results in inclusion efforts is deeply tied to larger societal ideologies of neoliberalism and White supremacy. For example, Taylorism, or scientific management, emphasizes efficiency and productivity, often at the expense of humanistic values. In the context of inclusion, this ideology can manifest as a focus on measurable outcomes, such as demographic statistics, rather than the qualitative experiences of marginalized individuals (Fasenfest, 2021). This pursuit of efficiency often undermines the relational and experiential aspects of inclusion, which require time, reflection, and ongoing dialogue. As a byproduct, it often obviates qualitative research and researchers. Drawing on a bastardization of food, McDonaldization, or the principles of the fast-food industry being applied to various sectors of society, including education (Ritzer, 2021), emphasizes standardization, predictability, and control, which collectively can stifle the creativity and flexibility needed for genuine inclusion. When inclusion efforts are reduced to a checklist of best practices, they risk becoming performative rather than transformative. Consider how diversity, equity, and inclusion mission statements or student and faculty demographic data are often presented as menu items for the consumer, proof of already accomplished results rather than sobering and aspirational objectives. Race evasiveness involves the avoidance of direct engagement with issues of race and racism, often leading to surface-level solutions that do not address underlying systemic inequalities (Bonilla-Silva, 2022; Chang-Bacon, 2022; Rudnick, 2019). Collectively, these ideologies manifest via a "microwavable meal" culture, prioritizing quick, perfunctory fixes in the interests of avoiding, evading, and resisting reckoning with and investing in sustained intrapersonal, interpersonal, and systemic change.

Inclusive education is inherently complex and cannot be simplified or hurried. It involves addressing deep-seated biases, power dynamics, and structural inequalities that have developed over centuries. This process requires ongoing critical reflection, willingness to engage in uncomfortable conversations, and a commitment to continuous learning and unlearning. In higher education classrooms, fostering an inclusive environment goes beyond incorporating diverse materials or celebrating cultural holidays. It involves creating a space where all students feel valued, heard, and respected. This requires faculty and staff to be attuned to the diverse needs and experiences of their students and to adapt their teaching practices accordingly. It also necessitates a willingness to confront and address instances of exclusion or discrimination when they arise.

Achieving genuine inclusion in higher education requires patience, dedication, and a long-term commitment. Like many recipes handed down through the generations or high-end cuisine, meaningful inclusion is not a goal that can be achieved overnight or through isolated initiatives. Rather, it is an ongoing process that demands sustained effort and attention. Institutions must be willing to invest time and resources into developing and implementing comprehensive inclusion strategies. This includes providing professional development opportunities for faculty and staff, creating support systems for marginalized students, and continuously assessing and improving policies and practices. Moreover, individuals within the academic community must be willing to engage in the difficult and often uncomfortable work of self-reflection and personal growth. This involves recognizing and challenging one's own biases, listening to and learning from the experiences of others, and being open to change.

Salt, Fat, Acid, Heat: Understanding the Ingredients of Inclusion

Inclusion in academic communities is a multifaceted and dynamic process, akin to the culinary principles outlined in Samin Nosrat's

"Salt, Fat, Acid, Heat" (as cited in Khorana, 2024). We may define and operationalize what constitutes the core ingredients of inclusion as *deliberation, reflection, humility*, and *authenticity* (Bauer, 2017; Butler, 2018; Hardt, 2009). These ingredients are crucial to "cooking" up iterative structures and cultures of *diversity, equity, accessibility*, and *belonging*.

Inclusion goes beyond surface-level diversity initiatives to create an environment where all members feel valued, respected, and empowered. It involves a commitment to understanding and addressing the unique needs and experiences of individuals from diverse backgrounds. According to Bauer (2017), inclusion requires deliberate and sustained efforts to dismantle systemic barriers and create equitable opportunities for all. Butler (2018) emphasizes the importance of reflection and humility in this process, urging academic communities to continually reassess their practices and policies. Hardt (2009) highlights the need for authenticity, advocating for genuine engagement with inclusion rather than performative actions.

Similarly, the pursuit of authentic inclusion in higher education involves a careful balance of various elements. *Deliberation* requires intentionality and thoughtfulness. Deliberation involves considering the diverse perspectives, power dynamics, and lived experiences of all community members in decision-making processes. This attribute ensures that inclusion efforts are not tokenistic but are deeply embedded in the institution's values and practices. *Reflection* requires ongoing critical self- and systemic-assessment as crucial for fostering an inclusive environment. Academic communities must regularly evaluate their policies, practices, and interactions to identify areas for improvement. Reflection enables institutions to learn from past mistakes and adapt their strategies to better serve their diverse populations.

Humility requires recognizing the limitations of one's knowledge and being open to learning from others is essential for authentic inclusion. Humility fosters a culture of continuous improvement and encourages individuals to seek out diverse perspectives. This attribute helps to create a respectful and empathetic environment where all voices are heard and valued. *Authenticity* requires a genuine commitment to inclusion, more than just checking off boxes on a diversity checklist. Authenticity involves deeply engaging with the principles of equity and justice and striving to create meaningful and lasting change. Authentic inclusion is not about appearances but about creating a truly equitable and supportive environment for all. A key consideration is that minoritized community members, having to constantly navigate systems and practices of perfunctory inclusion efforts, are far more likely to ascertain authenticity and inauthenticity as they arise.

Diversity is the presence of individuals from a wide range of backgrounds, including different races, ethnicities, genders, sexual orientations, abilities, and socioeconomic statuses. While diversity is a critical component of inclusion, it alone is not sufficient. True inclusion requires actively valuing and leveraging this diversity to enrich the academic community. *Equity* involves ensuring that all individuals have access to the same opportunities and resources. This requires recognizing and addressing the systemic barriers that may prevent certain groups from fully participating in the academic community. Equity is about leveling the playing field and providing targeted support to those who need it. Equity often finds itself at odds with neoliberal, white-supremacy notions of decontextualized fairness and merit discourse (e.g., hire the best person for the job) (Bonilla-Silva, 2022).

Accessibility means removing physical, technological, and attitudinal barriers that may hinder participation. Accessibility ensures that all individuals, regardless of their abilities, can fully engage in academic activities. This includes providing accommodations, designing inclusive curricula, and fostering an inclusive campus culture. *Belonging* is the sense of being accepted, valued, and included within the academic community. It involves creating a supportive and inclusive culture where individuals feel a sense of connection and ownership. Belonging is fostered through inclusive policies, supportive relationships, and a substantive commitment to diversity *and* social justice.

The Interconnectedness of Inclusion Ingredients

Deliberation, reflection, humility, and authenticity are deeply interconnected with and essential to diversity, equity, accessibility, and belonging efforts. They collectively form the foundation of inclusive cultures and structures. Diversity without equity can lead to tokenism, where diverse individuals are present but not fully supported. Equity without accessibility can result in barriers that prevent individuals from fully participating. Accessibility without belonging can create an environment where individuals feel isolated despite being able to engage. Belonging without diversity can lead to a homogenous environment where different perspectives are not represented.

Achieving cultures and structures of inclusion requires careful planning, collaboration, and ongoing evaluation. Institutions must develop comprehensive inclusion strategies that address the unique needs of their communities. Collaboration among faculty, staff, students, and administrators is essential for creating a cohesive and supportive environment. Ongoing evaluation ensures that inclusion efforts are effective and responsive to changing needs.

Nourishing an Inclusive Environment: Cooking Up Critical Embrace

Faculty have a pivotal role and responsibility in creating inclusive spaces, with colleagues, with students, and with community (Laird, 2014). Faculty interactions with colleagues, students, and the wider community shape the culture and climate of the institution, including the seriousness to which inclusion efforts are considered and implemented. This section explores strategies for fostering cultures of dignity, respect, and understanding, mitigating against status quo, surface-level, often unidirectional and self-serving efforts (Fradella, 2018). In doing so, it introduces the concept of *critical embrace* as a means to engage about and across identity, difference, and power, and strategies to apply the principles of deliberation, reflection, humility, and authenticity in the pursuit of inclusion.

Faculty members are uniquely positioned to influence the inclusivity of their academic institutions. Our role extends beyond delivering curriculum to modeling inclusive behavior, facilitating open dialogue, and challenging the status quo. According to Laird (2018), faculty have a responsibility to actively engage in creating environments where all individuals feel valued and respected. This responsibility encompasses interactions with colleagues, students, and the broader community, each of which requires specific strategies and commitments.

The concept of *critical embrace* offers a framework that meaningfully interconnects the above ingredients of deliberation, reflection, humility, and authenticity towards aims of diversity, equity, accessibility, and belonging. Specifically, critical embrace mitigates against surface-level and superficial approaches and meaningfully navigates systems and cultures with attention to identity, difference, and power (Kirk & Okazawa-Rey, 2018). Critical embrace involves actively seeking to understand and appreciate the diverse experiences and perspectives of others and moves beyond surface-level, often unidirectional, and self-serving efforts. Fradella (2018) criticizes such superficial approaches, arguing that they fail to address the root causes of exclusion and inequity. Instead, faculty should strive to implement strategies that are thoughtful, deliberate, and rooted in a deep understanding of diversity and inclusion. It requires a willingness to engage in difficult conversations, challenge one's own biases, and work towards systemic change. One might consider the need for a healthier dose of *seasoning*; do with that allegory what you will.

Regarding deliberation, faculty should approach inclusion with intentionality and purpose—not unlike a chef at a Michelin star restaurant. This involves setting clear goals, developing comprehensive strategies, and regularly assessing progress. Deliberation ensures that inclusion efforts are thoughtful and well planned rather than reactive or performative. Regarding reflection, continuous self-assessment and critical reflection are essential for personal and institutional growth. Faculty should regularly evaluate their own practices and seek feedback from colleagues and students. Reflection helps identify areas for improvement and fosters a culture of ongoing learning and development.

Regarding humility, recognizing the limitations of one's knowledge and being open to learning from others is crucial for fostering an inclusive environment. Humility allows faculty to approach diversity and inclusion with a genuine willingness to grow and change.

Admittedly, humility is a grand challenge in higher education, perhaps even more so with faculty, who may feel the constant pressures of expertise and perfectionism (see almost any academic conference or faculty meeting). Regarding authenticity, genuine commitment to inclusion requires more than just following best practices or meeting institutional mandates. Authenticity involves deeply engaging with the principles of equity and justice and striving to create meaningful and lasting change. Faculty should be honest about their own biases and work towards building an inclusive environment that truly reflects their values.

In my home, we have all become better cooks in the kitchen by listening to and respecting one another; these principles hold true in higher education, too. Building an inclusive environment among faculty requires a commitment to collaboration and mutual respect. Faculty should engage in regular discussions with colleagues about diversity and inclusion, share best practices, and support one another in their efforts to create inclusive classrooms and departments. Professional development opportunities focused on equity and inclusion can provide valuable insights and tools for faculty to implement in their daily interactions.

Faculty–student interactions are central to the student experience. Creating an inclusive classroom involves recognizing and valuing the diverse backgrounds and perspectives that students bring. This can be achieved through inclusive teaching practices, such as incorporating diverse materials into the curriculum, using inclusive language, and creating opportunities for all students to participate in discussions. Additionally, faculty should be approachable and open to feedback, demonstrating a genuine interest in the success and well-being of all students.

Faculty can extend their influence beyond the campus by engaging with the broader community. This includes building partnerships with local organizations, participating in community events, and advocating for social justice initiatives. By connecting academic work with community needs, faculty can promote inclusivity and social responsibility.

What's Really Cooking? Overcoming Challenges to Building Inclusive Academic Communities

Building inclusive academic communities is essential for fostering supportive and equitable environments. However, this task is fraught with challenges rooted in societal attitudes, systemic inequities, and lack of resources (NERCHE, n.d.; Wall & Obear, 2008; Witham et al., 2015; Yosso et al., 2009). Prevailing societal attitudes can hinder efforts to create inclusive academic spaces. Prejudices and stereotypes about race, gender, sexuality, and ability often permeate educational settings, influencing the behavior and expectations of both students and educators. These attitudes can lead to exclusionary practices and create a hostile environment for marginalized students. Educational systems are often structured in ways that perpetuate inequities. Historical and ongoing discrimination has resulted in disparities in access to quality education, resources, and opportunities. Systemic barriers such as standardized testing, biased curricula, and unequal funding contribute to the marginalization of certain groups of students. Limited resources can impede efforts to build inclusive classroom communities. Campuses with smaller endowments and/or research funds, less prestige and/or desirable living communities, often lack the financial, human, and material resources necessary to meaningfully address and redress larger social ills. While the goal of creating inclusive educational environments is vital, sustaining these efforts requires resilience, the ability to overcome setbacks, and strategies to avoid burnout. How might we recognize and respond to context and power dynamics as sites of possibility, rather than sites of avoidance? Addressing these challenges requires a shift in perspective. Instead of viewing context and power dynamics as obstacles, educators and institutions should see them as sites of possibility. By critically engaging with these dynamics, we can identify opportunities for transformation and empowerment.

At the individual level, faculty play a crucial role in fostering inclusive classroom communities. Faculty can implement various strategies within our spheres of influence to overcome challenges related to societal attitudes and biases. Faculty can adopt culturally relevant, responsive, sustaining, and revitalizing teaching practices that recognize and value the diverse backgrounds of their students. This approach involves incorporating diverse perspectives into the curriculum, using inclusive language, and creating a classroom environment where all students feel seen and heard. Ongoing professional development focused on diversity, equity, and inclusion can help faculty develop the knowledge and skills needed to create inclusive classrooms. Training on topics such as implicit bias, anti-racism, and culturally relevant pedagogy can enhance their ability to support diverse students.

While faculty have an essential role and responsibility towards inclusion, the weight should not rest solely on our shoulders, either. Institutions must commit to systemic changes that address inequities and support inclusive practices. Departments, schools, colleges, and universities should develop and implement policies that promote equity and inclusion. This includes revising admissions criteria, diversifying faculty and staff, and providing resources for marginalized students. Institutions can also establish support systems such as mentoring programs, affinity groups, and counseling services to help students navigate challenges and succeed academically. Crucially, this all includes equitable resource allocation. Allocating resources equitably is essential for supporting inclusive classroom communities. This involves ensuring necessary funding, materials, and practices; campus leadership must be active in this procurement process. If not, the most thoughtfully crafted commitment to inclusion or faculty job description are rendered meaningless.

Addressing the broader societal context is crucial for critical embrace. Faculty, staff, and especially leadership should advocate for policy changes at the local, state, and national levels to address systemic inequities in education. This includes pushing for equitable funding, challenging discriminatory practices, and supporting legislation that promotes diversity and inclusion. Building partnerships with community organizations, businesses, and other stakeholders can further enhance efforts to create inclusive campus communities. These partnerships can provide additional resources, support services, and opportunities for students. Engaging with the community also helps to create a broader culture of inclusion and support.

Several additional factors must be considered. Sustained efforts to promote inclusion can lead to burnout, especially when faced with persistent resistance, limited resources, or slow progress. Educators and administrators often experience fatigue from the emotional and physical demands of this work. Keeping the momentum going for inclusion initiatives can be difficult, particularly when initial enthusiasm wanes or when faced with institutional inertia. Ongoing commitment and energy are required to keep efforts alive and impactful. Setbacks, such as policy changes, budget cuts, or backlash from stakeholders, can derail inclusion efforts. These challenges require adaptability and perseverance to navigate effectively. Performative allyship and climate surveys that diagnose but don't attempt to redress larger inequities exhaust and dishearten minoritized community members and foster a culture of apathy and survival.

Prioritizing self-care is essential for preventing burnout. Educators and administrators should establish boundaries, take breaks, and engage in activities that promote their physical and mental health. Mindfulness practices, exercise, and hobbies can help maintain balance and reduce stress. Continuous learning is crucial for staying informed and motivated. Professional development opportunities focused on diversity, equity, and inclusion (DEI) can provide new insights, skills, and inspiration. Workshops, conferences, and online courses can help educators stay engaged and committed to their inclusion goals. Building and maintaining support networks is vital for sustaining long-term inclusion efforts. Peer support groups, mentorship relationships, and professional communities can offer encouragement, advice, and shared resources. These networks provide a sense of solidarity and help individuals navigate challenges together.

Faculty should establish clear, achievable goals to maintain focus and momentum. Short-term objectives can provide immediate wins, while long-term goals ensure sustained progress. Regularly reviewing and adjusting these goals keeps the efforts relevant and manageable. Faculty recognizing and celebrating achievements, no matter how small, can boost morale and motivation. Highlighting success stories and milestones helps maintain a positive outlook and demonstrates the impact of inclusion efforts. Faculty should consider being adaptable and open to change as crucial for overcoming setbacks. When faced with obstacles, it's important to reassess strategies, seek alternative solutions, and remain resilient. Flexibility allows for creative problem-solving and ensures that efforts can continue despite challenges. Again, this work is ongoing; anyone expecting quick fixes or their durability ought to re-read this chapter in its entirety.

Collaboration among faculty, staff, students, and community members is essential for creating inclusive environments. Engaging a diverse range of stakeholders ensures that multiple perspectives are considered and that efforts are more comprehensive and effective. Establishing partnerships with external organizations, businesses, and community groups can provide additional resources and support for inclusion initiatives. These collaborations can enhance the reach and impact of efforts and create a broader culture of inclusion. Promoting a sense of shared responsibility for inclusion fosters a collective commitment. When all members of the academic community understand their role in creating an inclusive environment, the burden does not fall on a few individuals, and efforts are more sustainable.

Akin to meal prep, faculty should create a personal action plan outlining their specific goals, strategies, and timelines for promoting inclusion. This plan should include self-care practices, professional development activities, and steps for engaging with support networks. Faculty should identify and utilize available resources. Numerous resources are available to support inclusion efforts. These include toolkits, guides, and online platforms dedicated to DEI practices. Leveraging these resources can provide valuable insights and practical tools for implementation. Finally, faculty should commit to lifelong learning and doing. Lifelong learning is essential for staying current with best practices and emerging trends in inclusion. Lifelong doing recognizes that exclusionary realities exist and persist, and we should not, cannot, engage with inclusion only when it is palatable or convenient. Instead, we must critically embrace our will and skill to keep on cooking.

Conclusion: Beyond the Microwave

The "microwavable meal" culture, with its emphasis on instant results and quick fixes, is ill-suited to the complexities and nuances of inclusion efforts in higher education. Achieving genuine inclusion requires a departure from this mindset and a commitment to patience, dedication, and long-term effort. By recognizing the deeper societal ideologies that shape our expectations and embracing the complexities of inclusive education, we can work towards creating academic communities that are truly inclusive, equitable, and just.

Inclusion in academic communities is a complex and dynamic process that requires a deliberate and sustained commitment. By understanding and balancing the ingredients of diversity, equity, accessibility, and belonging, institutions can create a truly inclusive environment. Attributes such as deliberation, reflection, humility, and authenticity are essential for fostering meaningful and lasting change. Through careful planning, collaboration, and ongoing evaluation, academic communities can work towards achieving authentic inclusion and creating a supportive and equitable environment for all.

Creating inclusive spaces within academic communities is a complex and ongoing process that requires the active involvement and commitment of faculty. By critically embracing the ingredients of deliberation, reflection, humility, and authenticity, faculty can play a crucial role in promoting genuine inclusion. The concept of critical embrace offers a powerful framework for engaging with identity, difference, and power, and for building a more inclusive and equitable academic environment. Through thoughtful planning, collaboration, and ongoing evaluation, faculty can work towards creating academic communities that are truly inclusive, supportive, and just.

Building inclusive classroom communities requires addressing challenges related to societal attitudes, systemic inequities, and lack of resources. By recognizing and responding to context and power dynamics as sites of possibility, educators and institutions can implement strategies to overcome these barriers. Through culturally responsive teaching, equitable policies and practices, resource allocation, advocacy, and community engagement, it is possible to create supportive and equitable learning environments that benefit all students.

Implementing inclusive practices over the long term is a challenging but rewarding endeavor. By building resilience, avoiding burnout, maintaining momentum, and overcoming setbacks, educators and administrators can sustain their efforts to create inclusive educational environments. Ongoing professional development, support networks, and collaboration among stakeholders are crucial for achieving these goals. By following practical tips and utilizing available resources, academics can continue their journey towards fostering a more inclusive educational landscape. Let's get cooking.

References

Barkley, M., Burciaga, A., Couch, M., Desmond, C., Huddleston, S., Kinsinger, J., Labadie, T., Nwosu, I., & Williams, K. (2017). Inclusive excellence: Moving beyond diversity. *At Issue, 7*(1), 1–12.

Bauer, K. (2017). To be or not to be authentic. In defence of authenticity as an ethical ideal. *Ethical Theory and Moral Practice, 20*(30), 567–580.

Bonilla-Silva, E. (2022). *Racism without racists: Color-blind racism and the persistence of racial inequality in America* (6th ed.). Rowman & Littlefield.

Butler, S. L. (2018). The authenticity movement: Lies we tell ourselves and other truths that matter. https://www.higheredjobs.com/Articles/articleDisplay.cfm?ID=1709&utm_source=09_19_2018&utm_medium=email&utm_campaign=InsiderUpdate

Chang-Bacon, C. K. (2022). "We sort of dance around the race thing": Race-evasiveness in teacher education. *Journal of Teacher Education, 73*(1), 8–22.

Fasenfest, D. (2021). Reflections on the decline of academia: Large problems and small minds. *Critical Sociology, 47*(7–8), 1057–1063.

Fradella, H. F. (2018). Supporting strategies for equity, diversity, and inclusion in higher education faculty hiring. *Diversity and inclusion in higher education and societal contexts: International and interdisciplinary approaches* (p. 119–151). Springer International Publishing. https://doi.org/10.1007/978-3-319-70175-2_7

Hardt, H. (2009). Authenticity, communication, and critical theory. *Critical Studies in Mass Communication, 10*(1), 49–69.

Kirk, G., & Okazawa-Rey, M. (2018). Identities and social locations: Who am I? Who are my people? In M. Adams, W. J. Blumenfeld, C. Castaneda, H. W. Hackman, M. L. Peters, & X. Zuniga (Eds.), *Readings for diversity and social justice* (4th ed., pp. 10–15). Routledge.

Khorana, S. (2024). Samin Nosrat's *Salt, Fat, Acid, Heat*: Cooking on TV gets a decolonial makeover. *Food, Culture & Society, 27*(2), 326–341.

Laird, T. F. N. (2014). Reconsidering the inclusion of diversity in the curriculum. *Diversity & Democracy, 17*(4).

Linder, C., & Cooper, D. L. (2016). From cultural competence to critical consciousness: Creating inclusive campus environments. In M. J. Cuyjet, C. Linder, M. F. Howard-Hamilton, & D. L. Cooper (Eds.), *Multiculturalism on campus: Theory, models, and practices for understanding diversity and creating inclusion* (2nd ed.). Stylus.

New England Resource Center for Higher Education (NERCHE). (n.d.). Self-assessment rubric for the institutionalization of diversity, equity, and inclusion in higher education. https://www.utica.edu/academic/Assessment/new/diversity,%20equity,%20and%20inclusion.pdf.

Ritzer, G. (2021). The McDonaldization of society. In *In the Mind's Eye* (pp. 143–152). Routledge.

Rudnick, D. L. (2019). *Walking on egg shells: Colorblind ideology and race talk in teacher education, Multicultural Education Review, 11*(3), 216–233.

Wall, V., & Obear, K. (2008). Multicultural Organizational Development (MCOD): Exploring best practices to create socially just, inclusive campus communities. Paper presented at the AAC&U Conference: *Diversity, learning, and inclusive excellence: Accelerating and assessing progress.*

Witham, K., Malcom-Piqueux, L. E., Dowd, A. C., & Bensimon, E. M. (2015). *America's unmet promise: The imperative for equity in higher education.* Association of American Colleges & Universities.

Yosso, T., Ceja, M., Smith, W., & Solórzano, D. (2009). Critical race theory, racial microaggressions, and campus racial climate for Latina/o undergraduates. *Harvard Educational Review, 79*, 659–690.

CHAPTER 12

Reaching Back to Move Forward: Using Matrilineal Recipes to Create Kinship Within the Academy

DASMEN RICHARDS, TRAVON JEFFERSON, AND GRACE TUKURAH

Introduction

We offer up this chapter as a medium through which we may uplift and solidify counter-narratives of Black folk in higher education and the ways in which we create unique experiences for ourselves and others that keep us whole and support us. We also envision our words as an avenue to inspire those who look like us to also imagine how they can "do more than survive" (Love, 2019) in contexts that work against them.

It is important to us that through food, we can honor our legacies and families in historically White institutions (HWIs) and in academia more generally, which are institutions that were not initially designed to include folks like us. By honoring our matrilineal recipes, we are bringing to reality the dreams of our ancestors. We are therefore bringing the spirits of our ancestors with us to bear witness to and participate with us in our individual acts of resistance and our pursuit of joy as we accomplish our respective goals in academia.

Theoretical Groundings

This work is grounded in an endarkened feminist epistemological lens (Dillard, 2000) to weave together our narrative to amplify the significance of creating and extending maternal kinship ties through recipes. Particularly, Dillard (2000) states how this epistemological orientation forces the researcher to recognize that research is "social[ly] constructed and a cultural endeavor" (p. 662). Heeding this recognition, we are intentional in our choice of rooting endarkened feminist epistemologies in this labor of love to emphasize that the *personal* is indeed the driving force. Moreover, we believe that anchoring endarkened feminist epistemologies in our work will require a responsibility to deeply reflect and challenge us to speak to the "racial," but also the gender that is profound in the questions guiding our stories. Thus, we argue that there is a need to center storytelling in our work as it will honor and carry on the ancestral legacies that have been fostered in our lineages through oral traditions while providing us a unique opportunity to *do* research that can deepen relationships between not only us, but our elders and ancestors.

Methodology

In this chapter, we engage in memory work (Morrison, 1987) by employing duoethnography in which we, the authors, collaboratively share our narratives and thereby serve as sites of inquiry (Burleigh & Burm, 2022). Duoethnography as a method is dialogic in nature and juxtaposes the separate life stories of the researchers toward creating meaning and personal transformation (Norris, Sawyer, & Lund, 2016). Therefore, our sources of data come from our dialogues/interviews with one another and our journal reflections. As we recollect our stories and share them with one another, we engage in dialogue and questioning to unearth what has previously remained uninterrogated. The question we used to prompt our conversations is: *How do we engage in memory work to reflect on our matrilineal ancestral recipes to build kinship within our academic journeys?*

In asking this question, we focus on ways that we have created/extended kinship ties through recipes that have been passed down through matrilineal bloodlines. We describe our kinship ties as mechanisms that "buffer" or "absorb" stress and build community as we navigate our program and the academy more broadly (Murry et al., 2018, p. 11). Additionally, we identify someone as kin based on relational connectedness, commonalities, and mutual remembrance of one another. Continuing a rich historical tradition of African/Black women establishing fictive kinship networks for survival in West Africa and the United States, we create these kinship supports to build community and combat challenges associated with being Black doctoral students in a predominantly White institution. (Johnson, 2020; Murry et al., 2018). In this book chapter, we articulate how we use our matrilineal recipes to build kinship ties that act as extended networks of support beyond our homes to create a homeplace (hooks, 1990).

In the following section, "The Recipe," we draw from our experiences to foster a recipe that combines our matrilineal recipes. We include our words verbatim from recordings of our conversations with one another, where we tell stories of who we are and how we remember and honor our matriarchs through food. In addition, we weave in reflections from our journaling sessions. This intentional choice of formatting our work in this way amplifies each authors' recipes while weaving together our stories, which have helped us to cultivate spaces in academia, and in turn, extending kinship networks with fellow graduate school friends. We want to emphasize that our recipe is not a "one size fits all" model, but we write this chapter to serve as an inspiration to other graduate students to hone in on their cultural heritages, particularly matrilineal recipes, to help them extend and/or cultivate kinship networks with their graduate school peers.

The Recipe

Ingredients: A heaping tablespoon of self, "Who y'all be?"

T. Jefferson: I'm a third year grad student from Detroit, Michigan, Black man, educator, and philosopher. I'm from Detroit. My parents are from Detroit. My grandparents were born and raised in the city of Detroit. My great grandparents, depending on who we're talking about, most of them were born outside of Detroit and moved to Detroit when they were children during the Great Migration early to mid 1930s.

D. Richards: I'm a fifth-year doctoral candidate. I hail from Georgia. I was born in Riverdale, Georgia, but I spent most of my time in Fayetteville, Georgia, [and] my roots are deeply entrenched in the South. My mom is from Memphis, Tennessee, and my dad is from Charleston, South Carolina. So, lots of history there, but a lot of food history in particular, that has created a melting pot, to say the least, in our family, growing up eating things like hoppin' John's, red rice . . .

G. Tukurah: So, my family is from Nigeria. I was born and raised in Nigeria, and particularly northern Nigeria. My father and mother are from different places in Nigeria, but still the same general geographical location. I grew up bilingual, speaking Hausa and English. Hausa was the language I used mostly to communicate with my grandmothers, and English for school and friends.

I remember my brother telling me one time that my personality was sweeter when I spoke Hausa than when I spoke English, and I think that's partly because that was the language I used mostly to talk to my grandmothers. So, it makes sense that I would have a kinder, sweeter personality in that language than in English.

. . .

The first author is a Black woman doctoral student whose Southern roots plays a pivotal role in her deep, passionate love for food and how it serves as a tool for community building. The second author, a Black man doctoral student from Detroit, Michigan, has a profound connection to his matriarchal lineage. He holds his great grandmother, who migrated to Detroit in the late 1930s, in high esteem, and despite her passing, he preserves her memory through her recipes, which serve as a bridge to her spirit and legacy. The third author is a Black woman doctoral student from Nigeria who has lived in the

U.S. midwest for over a decade and remains tethered to home via traditional Nigerian cuisine yet sharing her culture through food to foster a multicultural community around her. As members of a racialized and minoritized demographic navigating academia in a predominantly White institution, this work amplifies and potentially validates our experiences. We share ways in which we have assembled separate and diverse pieces of our homes through our offerings of food and recipes to create a new homeplace (hooks, 1990) in academia.

One full cup of remembering and honoring our family: "How do your matrilineal recipes honor a specific familial tie or person?"

T. Jefferson: When I think about my matrilineal recipe, [and] honoring a specific person, I'm always thinking about my great grandmother, who was born in Florida in 1934 and moved to Detroit sometime before she was five. The Seven-Up pound cake, the recipe that I learned from her, honors her and honors the story behind her creative way of making the cake, because I don't know how or where she got the recipe from. She made it up, to be honest [laughs]. This was back when she lived in the projects in Detroit, in the Brewster project homes.

My family grew up poor. And so her recipe that she taught me was—I'm not going to say it was the poor version, but it was the version where you could tell it was like, "Hey, you don't have enough butter, so you gotta get a substitute here and there." So, she taught me the recipe, and to this day, I don't use every single ingredient she used. Like I said, I got money to buy enough butter, so imma buy it [laughs].

But for the most part, I keep the recipe as is, and it's to honestly honor her, honor her memory, and honor the fact that she came up with this recipe, and she's been making this recipe for I mean, as long as I've been alive and as long as her children have been alive, so that stretches well into the 1950s. So, yeah, okay, even though she's not here, the cake still lives on.

D. Richards: So, thinking about my great grandma [on my mother's side], [who] I'm honoring today, she is from Sledge, Mississippi, and she is the one that basically created a new beginning for our family in Memphis, Tennessee.

So that's where most of my maternal side lives, and they have spread across the United States, mainly [to] other southern parts of the United States, but also living in the midwest—Chicago . . . Minneapolis. So, we're everywhere, but I think what keeps us glued together is our recipes and thinking about the summers that I would visit my mom's side of the family in Memphis. I would look forward to it because I know I was going to get some good food. And then, having debates with friends now about spaghetti being an entree, or a side. [laughs] Um, it's known as an entree in my house—the Richards' house but thinking about growing up and going to Memphis in the summer. It was a side, so we would have grilled chicken with it—bbq chicken, fried fish [. . .]. And that was a cultural awakening for me when I had it for the first time. [. . .] I feel grateful and honored to have such rich histories through food.

A matrilineal recipe that I'm honoring today, and how that's kept me connected with my family, but also now in grad school, is my great grandma's red velvet cake. She baked a lot. She loved baking, and I feel like she extended that gift to my mom. I love my mom's red velvet cake. It's delicious. I brag about it all the time. And I also get offended when people say they don't like red velvet cake, because I'm like, "It's not supposed to taste like chocolate." And so I've had the opportunity of knowing what red velvet is supposed to taste like at an early age.

[. . .] and thinking about the rich color of red velvet, being reminiscent of the color of blood, right? So literally and figuratively, forms or perspective of blood or love through something as rich as a red velvet cake, and so I'm honoring her recipe today.

G. Tukurah: I grew up in the city, and both of my grandmothers lived rurally, but they would come and visit fairly often. We have a fairly close knit family on my father's side. It's a large family. My dad has 11 siblings, and I have tons of cousins, on my father's side. My mother's side is very small . . . 'til the day my grandmother died, we were her only grandchildren, which means that we were spoiled silly going to her house, or when she came to visit . . . she was great.

[laughs] [. . .] With my maternal grandma, we felt especially special. She was also a very entrepreneurial woman [. . .] the recipe that I chose to share comes from my mother's mom.

. . . red stew, which is a common red tomato stew, is common in Nigeria. Everyone has their way that they make it. And I remember this is something I'd help my mom often with in the kitchen. And most recipes in Nigeria are like freestyles . . . not two cups of this and three cups of that. You know, it's just, this is how it's done.

Eyeball things and, you know, feel the spirits lead you to add more, take away. But I particularly remember this recipe, of the technique in making this stew. My grandmother was the one who kind of let me know, "Well, this is how you know when it's right." And even though I had helped my mom so many times, I never really knew what to look for or knew when to go from this step to the next step, like, "how would I know when it was just right?" And I remember my grandmother just sharing that with me one time. We were outside, in an outdoor kitchen, smoke everywhere. And that memory just really stuck with me, because I was like, "Oh, this is it." It was a learning moment for me. When she died, I wrote my tribute for her. I included this story of her being the one to let me know or teach me how, how to make sure I was making red stew the right way. And because of that, I still think of her every single time that I am making red tomato stew.

. . .

As graduate students, we are constantly seeking ways to thrive in a space that is designed for us to minimally survive. Moreover, we found it to be powerful to name and center our great- and grandmothers in our conversation. Such an act allows us to constantly "know and remember" (Brown, 2013) our ancestors who shape who we are today. Additionally, it serves a purpose to honor and hold on to our legacies through the recipes that were passed down through our matrilineal bloodlines. During this portion of our conversation, what emerged was the uniqueness of our recipes within our families. Specifically, there was a poignant revelation that the way someone makes a certain recipe may not be the same across other families, which provokes a certain memory that is only identifiable in our bloodline(s), similar to a fingerprint. This meaningful discovery is significant in that these recipes are only made a particular way within our families and allows us to "call on the spirits to lead [us] through the recipe." By calling in our ancestors to guide us in our making of a particular dish, it solidifies the ways we honor and embrace our matrilineal bloodlines to carry us through our respective journeys in the academy.

Stir and bake until it is authentically you: "What's the importance of kinship networks to you during your grade school experience?"

T. Jefferson: In February, my great grandmother's brother passed away, he was 89. At the funeral, a lady I had never met before, and a few others were all sitting at the table eating at the repass. One lady next to her said, "Let's go ahead and introduce ourselves and say, how we know the person who died."

So, you know, it got to me, and I was like, "yeah, that's my great great uncle. He was the brother of my great grandmother." And that was all I said. And the lady was like, "The lady who makes the cakes?" And I was like, "yeah!"

And so, I, you know, this is February 2024. And I thought, "Oh, she passed away in 2019."

I wrote about that in my journal too, and it just made me think about the networks that I'm building, and how I'm building my kinship networks within grad school, thinking about how my great grandmother did it. Cause I didn't know that lady. [laughs] She's not even our family friend. I don't know who she is. [laughs] But she knew my great grandmother from just that one recipe. So, when I think about the importance of kinship networks and just building them. I think about that, I want people, my friends, my colleagues, my peers, to know me for, I guess, not necessarily the cake, but we're connected through something more than just [that] . . . and that made me start to think about, what do I want to be remembered for in the academy? Like, I don't really care too much about the publishing and presentations. I mainly care about the authentic friendships and relationships that I'm building.

And I do that through bringing y'all a cake[. . .]we can talk about the academy and journals all day, every day, but if I actually consider you a friend or someone that I do care about, I'm going to share that piece with you, and I will hope that is something that you remember me more for than that great abstract . . . so, that's how I'm trying to conceptualize it.

D. Richards: I know one of my love languages is acts of service. I am always inviting people over, and cooking food and being like, just show up—come as you are, because I want to show that I love and care for you through food and like you said, it allows you to bring about different conversations. Like last week, when Grace and I [met up for] dinner and conversation, it ended up leading to a conversation about academics. It started off with, "Oh, how did you make this broccoli?" And we talked about that for 20 minutes. It was a very riveting conversation, and we started talking about other things that were personal to ourselves. We got to know each other more deeply than we already did, solely through a dish, something as simple as we would think as broccoli, right? I think that's like the importance of kinship networks for me, getting through a time where grad school can be stressful. And you may have these feelings of duress, like, how can you bring people together so that we can feel whole again? And I think about that through food, right?

And calling in our elders or ancestors and using their recipes as a way to create the community that they have built in families, our kinship networks, and allowing my kinship network to be extended within my other friend groups in grad school. Thinking about my great grandma, she is known as the cook, like people who know her. It's like you said, similar. It's like your great grandma. They also were born around the same time. My great grandma was born in 1935 and so just seeing that as a connection, right? It's so beautiful. But she was known as the cook, like, "Oh, your grandma Bernice?! She can burn!" She was known as the caretaker of the family—the matriarch. I want to use that [title] because I want to honor her in that way, as the matriarch of our family. And so how do I continue her legacies through things such as a mac and cheese recipe that's near and dear to our hearts on my mom and dad's side? My grandfather could make some mac and cheese, but my great grandma could too. And so extending those recipes and sharing, passing those down to my mom and just remembering how conversations were had through a plate of food.

So, I want to create those same memories with my grad school friends, that allows us to escape from all of the things that we may be experiencing, as grad school students, right? Like the goods and the bads. But again, just reminding ourselves that we need sustenance and nourishment to continue to keep going in spaces that were not designed for us, and doing that in a way that is *whole, and full, and humanizing*.

G. Tukurah: When I was thinking about kinship, especially as an international student, I found that there are different ways in which I share food with people, depending on who the people are. But I'm also finding that when I share food, it's a way to sort of introduce myself and where I'm from, and inviting you to get to know me in that way.

I am a Nigerian in the USA, and people don't know the nuances about the different groups and the ethnic groups and the differences in foods. . . . and there are certain foods that are often associated with Nigeria. So, I find that if I'm going to a potluck or something, I'm bringing Jollof rice or something that says Nigeria in a way that people know. But I also realized that whenever I attend Nigerian gatherings, I find I'm trying to assert the part of Nigeria that I'm from by bringing food that represents Northern Nigeria because most of the Nigerian diaspora is from southern Nigeria. An example of a common Northern Nigerian food is Fura da nono, which is made from millet and yogurt, . . . it's very common to northern Nigeria. What was strange for me was the difficulty in finding the ingredients to make it here, because most of the Nigerian stores cater to the majority of Southern Nigeria's population [in the United States]. It felt weird, searching for something, for a piece of home . . ., that was not in the stores that catered to other people from my home. . . . so, it sent me down this rabbit hole of research because you know, I'm a researcher, and I found almost everything that I needed in the Indian grocery store, which was a revelation to me. But through all of that, finding out that this thing [fura] that I wanted to make, . . . is also enjoyed in Ghana, is also enjoyed in Senegal, it almost felt like I was finding siblings in other countries . . ., and it made me feel connected to them as well.

I am realizing more and more that a sense of self is important for me through the opportunity to introduce myself in that way, through that meal in particular. The first time I managed to make it [fura], I made an Instagram post and said something about how I felt the spirit of both my grandmothers present, because it was something that both of them would often make, even though I made mine slightly differently than they did.

. . . Also, there's a lady in the community. She was pregnant and was craving a particular soup from northern Nigeria. I made the soup for her several times, and she ended up naming her baby a variation of my name, and I attribute that to the cooking that I did for her.

. . . I love that I have been able to make connections through food, and able to feel that I was being seen and not feel lost among others.

. . .

Additional Notes: Conclusion

We have carved out space for ourselves in higher education through food and matrilineal recipes. We were able to see ourselves, but then also amplified the recipes and experiences of three Black women from Detroit, Mississippi, and Northern Nigeria. Through this conversation, we realized the recipes in this context cultivates a deep sense of self, helping us discover different parts of ourselves. Food is providing the space for that to happen, which we found powerful and beautiful. In the passing down of recipes, there is also a passing down of instructions for making something fulfilling out of basic ingredients. This conversation also demonstrates the importance of food in creating relationships and kinships because we are using it to connect with others and find comfort and solace within the academy, and at the same time, it is helping us to create a sense of self in these spaces, so we do not feel lost. Lastly and equally as imperative is the relatedness to how we are navigating these academic spaces that are again, not designed for Black people, but yet they still find ways to create connection through different gatherings and coming together through food. And that in itself, allows us to extend the kinship networks that we have already built within their families, but then also building further kinship networks with our graduate school friends.

References

Brown, R. N. (2013). *Hear our truths: The creative potential of Black girlhood.* University of Illinois Press.

Burleigh, D., & Burm, S. (2022). Doing duoethnography: Addressing essential methodological questions. *International Journal of Qualitative Methods, 21*, 16094069221140876. https://doi.org/10.1177/16094069221140876.

Dillard, C. B. (2000). The substance of things hoped for, the evidence of things not seen: Examining an endarkened feminist epistemology in educational research and leadership. *International journal of qualitative studies in education, 13*(6), 661–681. https://doi.org/10.1080/09518390050211565.

hooks, b. (1990). *Yearning: Race, gender, and cultural politics.* South End Press.

Johnson, J. M. (2020). *Wicked flesh: Black women, intimacy, and freedom in the Atlantic world.* University of Pennsylvania Press.

Love, B. L. (2019). *We want to do more than survive: Abolitionist teaching and the pursuit of educational freedom.* Beacon Press.

Morrison, T. (1987). *Beloved.* Vintage.

Murry, V. M., Butler-Barnes, S. T., Mayo-Gamble, T. L., & Inniss-Thompson, M. N. (2018). Excavating new constructs for family stress theories in the context of everyday life experiences of Black American families. *Journal of Family Theory & Review, 10*(2), 384–405. https://doi.org/10.1111/jftr.12256.

Norris, J., Sawyer, R. D., & Lund, D. (Eds.). (2016). *Duoethnography: Dialogic methods for social, health, and educational research.* Routledge.

CHAPTER 13

Thinking Beyond the Chocolate Chips: A [Comfortable] Baking Journey Toward Scholarly Possibility

ANGELA KRAEMER-HOLLAND

Ingredients: Chocolate Chip Cookies (adapted from Nestlé Toll House)

2 1/4 cups all-purpose flour
1 teaspoon baking soda
1 teaspoon salt
1 cup (2 sticks) butter, softened
3/4 cup granulated sugar
3/4 cup packed brown sugar
1 teaspoon vanilla extract
2 large eggs
2 cups (12-oz. pkg.) Semi-Sweet Chocolate Morsels
1 cup chopped nuts (optional)

Get the Ingredients

(A herstory-recipe of practice + directions + output)

I've operated on what I consider to be a teacher's schedule since I could walk and talk—by starting my day when it's still dark outside (don't ask how teaching evening graduate courses is going). I have always relished waking in darkness; as a child, waking early meant I could watch my mom bake. Chocolate chip cookies (still my favorite), brownies, snickerdoodles, pies, cakes, tarts; true upper Midwest affinities for and celebrations of chewy, buttery, sugary goodness. My dad worked as a first-shift production supervisor at Oscar Mayer—at one time or another, employment here served as a carnivorous-uniting family rite-of-passage—and my mom worked in the home. So, the still-dark early morning was our time. During these times, I learned to appreciate the order of baking: dry ingredients here, wet ingredients there, soft-ish butter (don't melt it!), eggs (one at a time!), sugar, and high-quality vanilla; and hawkishly watching the oven, monitoring and awaiting the cookies' rise, afraid to crack the oven door too early in our hopes for luxurious resulting confections. As I aged, I would marvel at the culinary creativity of the uninhibited contestants and hosts on cooking shows I watched occasionally—how did they just *know* what to add, and how much, and at *just* the right time without explicit instructions? To think outside the [culinary] lines seemed—and still seems—extraordinary, even unfathomable to me.

I've always been a bit of a rule follower; a directions reader before jumping right in, because risks abound with/in the alternative unknown. Baking recipes, and culinary directions more generally, reflected comfortable boundaries in which to operate; the space beyond these confines represented deeply unfamiliar terrain that required an uninhibited confidence I was, and still am, unsure that I possess. Throughout educational, occupational, and personal difficulties, I would bake almost weekly: My own little oasis of order in a world besieged by chaos (of which my mind wasn't usually spared, either). Oddly, this baking practice fell away during the most pronounced years of the COVID-19 pandemic; as I became more engrossed in augmenting my occupational capital on the academic job market (see Koro-Ljungberg & Cannella, 2017). When I recently took a position in, and moved to, Kansas, I experienced a world-unsettling professional and personal transition after living in Chicago for 12 years. It was during my first year in Kansas that I turned, once again, to weekly baking.

Preheat the Oven to 375 Degrees
(Create the comfy, cozy conditions.)

Although baking serves as a solace and familial connection, it also encapsulates my engrained comfort in directions, order, and product-driven notions of success. This chapter draws upon the metaphor of baking to illustrate my retreat toward the warming stagnant and secure, often so preoccupied with product, status quo, and self-interest—practices undergirding the encroaching neoliberal academy (Fielding, 2017; Koro-Ljungberg & Cannella, 2017). Despite baking and scholarly experience, I still struggle to imagine and enact possibility beyond the recipes, directions, and boundaries—stifling me from (re)imagining and (re)forming my baking and scholarly selves; regardless of the cozy and comfortable, or unfamiliar and invigorating conditions. Drawing upon the metaphors of recipe-and-directions-driven baking and the comforting staple of my baking herstory—the chocolate chip cookie—this chapter chronicles my baking and scholarly progression in/through the comfortable and performative (notably through instrumental academic accolades) (Fielding, 2017), toward the increasingly vulnerable and possible. Although this chapter charts the process-to-product arrival at the denouement of the chocolate chip cookie, the comforting cookie end-goal represents a kitchen-oriented crossroads, an illustration of uneven oscillations between the secure and the unknown and unbound as an early career qualitative scholar in the neoliberal academy.

Combine Flour, Baking Soda, and Salt* in a Small Bowl. Set Aside
*(*Just keep it sweet?)*

After years of baking with my mom and by myself, I learned that many baking recipes included salt as part of the "dry ingredients" mixture, an admonished ingredient in my household. When I was proficient enough to read, I'd point out the absence of our forgotten briny condiment-friend to my mom—my initial baking partner—who'd vigorously shake her head, reminding me she doesn't include salt in her baking *or* her cooking (and neither should I, by extension), a cautionary assertion stemming from familial heart disease and high blood pressure. This stern warning contoured the rest of my baking and cooking future: under no circumstances should one add salt—even if the recipe calls for it. I felt torn between my recipe and directions-following ethos and my desire for external baking validation. I didn't know what my cookies would taste like with saline, tangy salt; and I didn't want to ruin what I already knew to be successful (as affirmed through others' smiles and enthusiastic chewing while reaching for second or third helpings). It wasn't until adulthood that I grappled with the significance of this baking exclusion; only illuminated through the risk I took to follow directions and *in*clude it, complicating an already limiting choice between directives or validation.

White people have a long history of scholarly appropriation and knowledge exploitation for the sake of scholarly accolades and narrow publication metrics (Esposito & Evans-Winters, 2021), illustrative symptoms of the neoliberal academy (Fielding, 2017; Koro-Ljungberg & Cannella, 2017). The "neoliberal academic machine" (O'Shea et al., 2023, p. 16) and neoliberalism as an ontology have taught us to assess our self-worth based on productivity, efficiency, and external performativity (Ball, 2012), Whiteness-hooked ideals that entrench the existing inequitable academic structures (Hartlep & Hayes, 2016). The insidiousness of these neoliberal values rests in their seemingly unequivocal framing, allowing us to normalize these values, to let them infiltrate ourselves, within and beyond the academy. I've often relied on output and neatly bound rules for external validation, without grappling with the accompanying permissible, normalized exclusion—in the kitchen, in the classroom, in the academy. Subconsciously beholden to and enacting the practices I have come to criticize, this validation-seeking, rule following, shadowed version of myself would "remain unaccountable" (Anzaldúa, 2015, p. 2), until I could courageously "nudg[e]"—or thrust—myself "out of positions" (Lather, 1993, p. 684) that were suffocating my baking and academic being(s), to include salt (or something else), to concede that neither recipe-driven nor product-hitched approaches were worthwhile.

Mix Butter, Granulated Sugar, Brown Sugar, and Vanilla Extract in a Large Mixing Bowl Until Creamy

(Plan and prepare for cohesiveness and control.)

I realized I forgot to plug in the mixer. Yes, I am baking cookies while writing this chapter—it's necessary for research purposes. But much like inquiry and scholarly be(com)ing, my baking rhythm ebbs and flows, too; appearing in fits and starts.

Although some equate a "biscuit" with a "cookie," these are not the same baked delicacy, despite sharing a few similar ingredients. Biscuits are hard, crumbly, snappy; cookies are soft, chewy, luxurious—an important distinction reflective of the importance I place on words, descriptions, and order. Not only are classifications important when baking cookies, but so are the conditions *prior* to baking—expertly combining initially isolated ingredients to create the cookie's foundation. For example, cold butter stifles the creaming process with sugar and adds density to the cookie, but melted butter inhibits the cookie rise and taste. However, room temperature, slightly softened butter holds air and lightness; *just* enough texture with room to give into something else. When placed in the conditions of a hot oven, the air bubbles from the *softened* butter and the subsequent mixing (called creaming) of butter and sugar will expand the cookies to their *proper* height and rise. And so, baking requires deliberate planning and preparation to cultivate the *right* conditions to bake the *right* cookie. Taking time to cream butter and sugar before mixing in each egg ensures batter cohesiveness, uniformity, structure—and sweetness.

Disruptions to these just-right conditions and classifications are—and have been—difficult for me to imagine, let alone to enact. However, biscuits, cookies, baked goods, and scholars alike can refuse [their] fixed identities, spaces, or eras that might be ascribed to, or confine them (Brogden, 2015). For scholars rejecting such constraints, this process can cultivate a messy interrogation of self, (re)forming and be(com)ing toward a more critically situated self; that disrupts the instrumental onto-epistemologies of the neoliberal academy (Koro-Ljungberg & Cannella, 2017). Nevertheless, *adopting* a critical stance and *enacting* that stance is an important distinction—the latter which I struggled to materialize as an adjunct, still firmly cushioned by the academy's guardrails and the pursuit of instrumental success. Tell me what to do, and how to do it—to publish (or perish?), secure employment, craft delicious cookies—endeavoring to control as much of the conditions as I could by welding output and direction(s) to generate the *just-right* amount of security, validation, deliciousness.

Add Eggs, One at a Time, Mixing Well After Each Addition
(Creamy sweetness of validation can't stand on its own.)

However, creamy and sugary sweetness can't stand on its own. Eggs represent vital components for baking, performing multilayered functionalities—one of which involves binding together previously isolated ingredients—to help create a structured, stable cookie. They incorporate additional air and levity, fostering cookies' rise, and they emulsify to smooth and volumize cookie batter, necessary elements for a cohesive and secure cookie. Nevertheless, eggs can dwindle in their agency under uncertain or constricting conditions. Prone to overmixing, eggs and flour are to be mixed [in] separately at different stages of the pre-baking process, the former one at a time. Without careful ordering of these steps, cookies can look and taste unpleasant—dense, tough, deflated, unappetizing eyesores inviting scrutiny of the taste-testing, validation-granting audience. Although the order and precision of these steps is important, recipes rarely list the amount of mixing time for butter and sugar, each egg, and the flour mixture. Consequently, understanding the *right* time frame for each of these mixing steps depends on a nuanced coalescence of the baker's perception of uniform ingredient distribution, instinct, and practice that has amounted to delicious cookies (or "successful" output).

I've found that the sweetness of external validation doesn't appear from nowhere; my fusing of output and directions-driven, rule-following ethos thrives most often with/in clear, unwavering structure and stability. While I sometimes chafed against academic authority as a postsecondary student, after be(com)ing an instructor in the academy I often dreaded student critiques, questions, and pushback, exposing my not-so-subtle oppressive clinging to some semblance of control over pedagogical conditions and overt examples of scholarly efficacy. Driven by subconscious insecurity about my place in the academy and whether I "fit in" (Ball, 2012; Lincoln, 2019; Pasque & Salazar Pérez, 2015), the thought of admitting uncertainty, imbalance, or instability amounted to unscripted pedagogical risks that, I believed, would inevitably erode my credibility and externally visible "success" as an alleged "expert." While we're frequent subjects of critique from several circles within and beyond academia, public intellectuals are still humans embedded in the neoliberal academy and consequently subject to suppression, oppression, and neoliberal [institutional] battle fatigue (Bhattacharya & Boveda, 2020). We're taught to think of our pauses, silences, and uncertainties as seemingly unproductive, as pedagogical impediments, or obstacles to productivity; positioning us as persistently captured by the need for control, structure, and certainty (Ball, 2012; Fielding, 2017). However, it's these moments that foster possibility—however uncertain or vulnerable—moments that similarly encourage us to (re)unite our perception, practice, and instinct to transcend the banal desires for contextual control.

Gradually Mix in Flour Mixture

(Too much White = Baking-scholarly turmoil.)

Like eggs, flour creates cookie structure and stability, too. However, too much of its chalky whiteness can unearth disastrous [baking] consequences. When I mix in the flour mixture, I know—from both the recipe directions and contextual baking experience (perception, practice, instinct)—to carefully mix in flour a little at a time; otherwise, the flour swells, strengthens, billows up and over the bowl from the mixer's spinning and goes everywhere, creating a white-covered mess and destabilizing the ingredient collective. Combining the flour mixture too early—without other ingredients present—creates dense, unevenly baked cookies with exaggerated and hardened exteriors that fail to embrace the other ingredients, vulnerabilities, and other possibilities. Consequently, as part of this gradual mixing-in process, the mixer's spinning progresses through calculated stops and starts, watchful of the flour mixture's power to envelop other ingredients, other tools, and the baking environment.

Like for many others, the last few years represented a self and social reckoning with oppressive conditions, entities, and practices I initially embodied as unequivocal and illustrative of the way things are . . . working within, rather than against. Although I transitioned from student-to-scholar driven by a critical *approach*, whether I fully enacted this orientation academically, pedagogically, and more broadly was questionable, exposing the repressive neo/colonial-liberal shadowed self I sought to ignore. Repressed versions of ourselves intersect with—and sometimes grate against—broader social, political, and public D/discourses (Bhattacharya, 2015; Bhattacharya & Boveda, 2020). This grating/intersection fosters in/external tensions from (re)engaging with these "shadowed" selves and from un-learning the latent and comfortable ways of knowing/being/doing associated with them (Anzaldúa, 2015; Bhattacharya & Boveda, 2020). Tending to our multilayered shadowed selves means confronting our privilege(s), positionalities, and entrenched perspectives (Ellis, 1999; Jackson & Mazzei, 2008), an uneven, uncomfortable, and messy process. Although I've begun (re)visiting this shadowed version of myself, I am unsure of how much it's swelled, billowed over, and enveloped my subconscious, to a point from which I can't retreat, risk-take, or (re)imagine.

Stir in Chocolate Chips and Nuts (If Using)

(Don't miss the possibility!)

Just before molding the cookies onto the baking sheet, I do have the option to add other ingredients, to create another kind of cookie. Although I would sometimes bake chocolate chip cookies with walnuts, raisins, peanut butter chips, I'd find myself eventually pining for the reliable original. These versions all tasted fine at the time, but I felt that I needed a clear recipe for how to incorporate a new ingredient or change; any deviations from my tried-and-true chocolate chip cookie would be a risk I was unsure fellow taste-testers would appreciate in the cookie, the final product—signaling I was still tempted by external validation. These kinds of risks seemed too costly to make beyond the reliable and externally successful baking boundaries. I couldn't—and can't—shake how I still appreciate the just-right baking conditions that foster the "perfectly" baked chocolate chip cookie (often as determined by another); just as I do when I write something, and it's published—product proof of othered validation that I did something "well." The seemingly opposing distinction between the passive recipe-following baker and the ingenious sweets creator parallels my perpetual oscillation in/between the critical inquirer or the neo/colonial data double (Cheek, 2019); an uneven and untidy reckoning with shadowed and still-be(com)ing baking and scholarly selves. This time, I revert to the reliable original, not out of desire, but out of circumstance—I didn't think to purchase an additional, unspecified ingredient—a missed opportunity to ask and imagine the "what else?" (Osgood et al., 2020, p. 607).

Drop By Rounded Tablespoon Onto Ungreased Baking Sheets; Bake for 9 to 11 Minutes . . .

(Wait; hope for reassurance . . .)

I invested in a cookie scoop when I was an adult; because, over time, I grew tired of using just any spoon, creating oblong-looking cookies, jutting out every which way, attempting to break free from the rest of the batter. I hoped for a bit more uniformity and order to my cookies. However, once a batch enters the oven, the baking's somewhat left to chance. Did I miss grams of flour? Was the butter too melted? Were some dough-spheres less than spherical? (Do the answers to these questions matter?) Because I never invested in a baking scale (I pulled back from jumping into the too-instrumental baking deep end), I relinquished a bit of control upon placing each cookie batch into the heated oven, yet still hoping for the best—that I created the ideal [baking] conditions for thriving [cookies].

There's an (un)known rumor (or belief?) that adjunct professors have a finite academic "shelf life." If one hasn't created the scholarly conditions to self-market toward full-time employment after a few years, the proverbial windows closed. I contemplated this refrain when on the academic job market; questioning whether weeks of outside research, job talk, and teaching demonstration preparation was worth it—whether I controlled [any of] the conditions for my scholarly success. And so, I took the "publish or perish" aphorism quite literally (another life-or-death metaphor), as an attempt to control academic conditions, while still relishing in product-driven validation—a stark aphorism—a reminder that our academic worth hangs on time, productivity, patience, and willingness to play by the rules of the game (Pasque & Salazar Pérez, 2015). Churning out (mostly) paywall-fortified publications, large conference presentations, and always thinking about what to write next (let me get back to editing this book chapter . . .) allowed me to ignore the discomfort, uncertainty, and instability of waiting. I would hawkishly surveille my email for word of an interview or manuscript acceptance; much like I stood ready to open the oven door at 9, 10, and 11 minutes–watching, waiting, hoping for reassurance.

. . . Or Until Golden Brown

(. . . Or until it "fits.")

My move from Chicago to Kansas in 2022—a bound-place I'd never visited, let alone lived—turned my settled scholarly and personal selves upside down; cultivating a be(com)ing that similarly cultivated new sense-making endeavors. Assuming I filled a warm-body vacancy for a pre-imagined position (an assumption built on only unrelated occupational practice), I was flabbergasted by the invitation to *create* my role, to *create* my scholarly identity—without instructions. What would it mean to (re)create, (re)design myself? To (re)imagine my work—who could I be(come) through trying on scholarly identities, (re)ordering ingredients, including unlisted ones, or even *substituting* them—without a recipe, without directions? Would the reliable lose its allure, its comfort, its efficacy as a product? Or would the doer become with the deed (St. Pierre et al., 2016): similarly liberated, unfettered, (re)formed by the artistry of imagining beyond boundaries of cookie sheets, oven heat, product validation, and prescriptive instructions?

I recently took a more than/human turn in my work, seeing how or if it "fit"—me, me in the [neoliberal] academy, maybe both;

despite my risk-taking reluctance—especially when on scholarly display (Osgood et al., 2020). This turn inspired a 2024 conference presentation on be(com)ing that included music videos, paintings, car motors, and visual landscapes—a stark departure from my comfortable, language-dependent inquiry (see Kraemer-Holland, 2024). I hoped for no attendees, pining for submergence in the conference program deep enough to be overlooked. Exposing vulnerabilities, was—is—of another, riskier scholarly self (Bhattacharya, 2015; Pasque & Salazar Pérez, 2015); one who thrust me out of bound positions and orientations (Lather, 1993), and one who surfaced the affective connections that illuminated how the neoliberal, comfortable-but-damaging shadows of product validation had entrapped me from (re)imagining not-yets, the possibilities of fitting, not fitting, and be(com)ing in between.

Cool on a Cookie Sheet or Wire Rack

(From cookie sheet-confines to the supportively spacious.)

Vulnerability, the unknown, and the unstable: These spaces and sentiments of risk and possibility amplify our human-tethered "birthright" of "perpetual insecur[ity]" (Taylor, 2023, pp. 4–5), feelings that often inspire sprints in the other direction—toward self-defense and safety (Abram, 2010). Consequently, we fortify ourselves for perceived security, ignoring opportunities for connection emergent through shared experiences with/in the unknown or the unstructured. What's on the other side of vulnerability, instability, the possible and not-yet? Once the cookies have cooled, how could they still "test the veracity of new insight" (Bhattacharya & Boveda, 2020, p. 174) by inspiring the (re)forming and (re)imagining of other possible cookies? Could I "sort through previously lived stories" (Bhattacharya & Boveda, 2020, p. 174) and shadowed selves without judgment, without reverting to damaging, confining familiarity, toward a more limitless be(com)ing scholarly self? What matters—taste, appearance, or something else? How it looks—how it's perceived—or how it moves, how it makes me *feel*?

A Taste/Test Beyond the Cookie

After decades of baking this recipe, I've realized that every batch of cookies is different—like courses, students I learn with, conference presentations, publications, and scholarly be(com)ing possibilities. And the baking conditions, institutions, edu-political contexts oscillate, too. Some ovens are newer or more resilient than others (prompting a change to temperature or baking time). Sometimes I overpour the vanilla, change the order of ingredients (or even *substitute* them!), the standing mixer works too long, or cookie sheets warp and bend from the oven's heat—conditions that span beyond the black-and-white print of recipe instructions. These factors coalesce to impact the product, the outcome, the cookie itself; the altered conditions that (re)form the cookie, but a cookie emerges—moving, swelling, browning, cooling—regardless of the supportive or confining [baking] conditions.

I used to tell undergraduate students that teaching doesn't exist in a binary—teaching exists on a continuum—there are *different* ways to teach. Cookies and early scholars are similar—not only are there different cookies, ways to bake them, ingredients to add or substitute or (re)order; but there are also different ways to take scholarly risks, different ways to be(come) with/in the academy—in all circumstances, a multitude of possibilities. Cookies may taste differently than a previous batch but are often eaten or disposed of (sadly) in the end—their fate relatively sealed. Not so for us, for me; although particular conditions shape *some* of my be(com)ing with/in the academy, they cannot determine the totality of scholarly possibilities and futures. Regardless of where I am in my baking or scholarly journey, I can tweak the quality of ingredients, experiment with what exists, slowly massage/compress/dissolve boundaries before (re)creating the cookie, the scholarship, on unfamiliar, boundless un-terms. At the crossroads of the more than/human and my shadowed and still-be(com)ing selves, I'm peering over the edge of certainty, structure, and control; curious about what's on the other side of directions-bound baking, the not-yet-but-imagined futures beyond the chocolate chips—the risks, be(com)ing, and possibility—regardless of the baking or scholarly conditions.

References

Abram, D. (2010). *Becoming animal: An earthly cosmology*. Vintage Books.

Anzaldúa, G. E. (2015). *Light in the dark/Luz en lo oscuro: Rewriting identity, spirituality, reality* (A. Keating, Ed.). Duke University Press.

Ball, S. J. (2012). Performativity, commodification and commitment: An I-Spy guide to the neoliberal university. *British Journal of Educational Studies, 60*(1), 17–28. https://doi.org/10.1080/00071005.2011.650940.

Bhattacharya, K. (2015). The vulnerable academic: Personal narratives and strategic de/colonizing of academic structures. *Qualitative Inquiry, 22*(5), 309–321. https://doi.org/10.1177/1077800415615619.

Bhattacharya, K., & Boveda, M. (2020). Enacting Anzaldúan spiritual activism: Intersecting personal and collective shadows in public intellectualism. In T. C. Wells, D. L. Carlson, & M. Koro (Eds.). *Intra-public intellectualism: Critical qualitative inquiry in the academy* (pp. 171–192). Myers Education Press.

Brogden, L. C. (2015). An autoethnographic visitor: Liminal interrogations of lessons from the steps of the union. *International Review of Qualitative Research, 8*(4), 479–492. https://www.jstor.org/stable/26372168.

Cheek, J. (2019). Resisting the commodified researcher self: Interrogating the data doubles we create for ourselves when buying and selling our research products in the research marketplace. In N. K. Denzin & M. D. Giardina (Eds.), *Qualitative inquiry at a crossroads: Political, performative, and methodological reflections* (pp. 141–156). Routledge.

Ellis, C. (1999). Heartful autoethnography. *Qualitative Health Research, 9*(5), 669–683. https://doi.org/10.1177/104973299129122153.

Esposito, J., & Evans-Winters, V. E. (2021). *Introduction to intersectional qualitative research.* Sage Publications.

Fielding, N. G. (2017). Challenging others' challenges: Critical qualitative inquiry and the production of knowledge. *Qualitative Inquiry, 23*(1), 17–26. https://doi.org/10.1177/1077800416657104.

Hartlep, N. D., & Hayes, C. (Eds.) (2016). *Unhooking from whiteness: Resisting the esprit de corps*. Brill.

Jackson, A. Y., & Mazzei, L. A. (2008). Experience and "I" in autoethnography: A deconstruction. *International Review of Qualitative Research, 1*(3), 299–318. https://www.jstor.org/stable/10.1525/irqr.2008.1.3.299.

Koro-Ljungberg, M., & Cannella, G. S. (2017). Critical qualitative inquiry: Histories, methodologies, and possibilities. *International Review of Qualitative Research, 10*(4), 327–339. https://doi.org/10.1525/irqr.2017.10.4.327.

Kraemer-Holland, A. (2024, May 16). *With a click of my heels: Be/coming [a] Kansan through the everything else.* International Congress of Qualitative Inquiry, Urbana-Champaign, IL.

Lather, P. (1993). Fertile obsession: Validity after poststructuralism. *The Sociological Quarterly, 34*(4), 673–693. https://doi.org/10.1111/j.1533-8525.1993.tb00112.x.

Lincoln, Y. S. (2019). Sanity on the chopping block, or how to save yourself in an insane world. In Y. S. Lincoln, G. S. Cannella, M. F. Huckaby, V. Kinloch, and J. L. Miller (Eds.), *Employing critical qualitative inquiry to mount nonviolent resistance* (pp. 57–70). Myers Education Press.

O'Shea, M., Duffy, S., & Gilbert, E. (2023). Subjectivities, academic work and mothering practice: Navigating obscure and unspoken disciplines. *Gender, Work & Organization*, 1–22. https://doi.org/10.1111/gwao.13105.

Osgood, J., Taylor, C. A., Andersen, C. E., Benozzo, A., Carey, N., Elmenhorst, C., Fairchild, N., Koro-Ljungberg, M., Moxnes, A., Otterstad, A. M., Rantala, T., & Tobias-Green, K. (2020). Conferencing otherwise: A feminist new materialist writing experiment. *Cultural Studies↔Critical Methodologies, 20*(6), 596–609. https://doi.org/10.1177/1532708620912801.

Pasque, P. A., & Salazar Pérez, M. (2015). Centering critical inquiry: Methodologies that facilitate critical qualitative research. In G. S. Cannella, M. Salazar Pérez, and P. Pasque (Eds.), *Critical qualitative inquiry: Foundations and futures* (pp. 139–170). Taylor & Francis.

St. Pierre, E. A., Jackson, A. Y., & Mazzei, L. A. (2016). New empiricisms and new materialisms: Conditions for new inquiry. *Cultural Studies↔Critical Methodologies, 16*(2), 99–110. https://doi.org/10.1177/1532708616638694.

Taylor, A. (2023). *The age of insecurity: Coming together as things fall apart.* House of Anansi Press.

CHAPTER 14

Lessons for Hopeful and Hungry Academics: Conviviality, Community, and Rootedness Inspired Through the Sharing of Food and Kitchen Stories

JOSHUA HUNTER AND CHERYL HUNTER

Universitas, of which we derive the word university, translates to mean "the whole," or "community," grounding the modern definition of university as a community of and for learning. Faculty often enter academia to become part of a community of scholars within their academic fields; however, the "whole" of the university can and should extend beyond academics. For the authors, food (and specifically the process of cooking with scholarly mentors and colleagues), stirred their academic journey and provided the means for sharing amongst a diversity of cultures while rooting them in a local community.

We begin our chapter with short excerpts (*in italics*) recalling early mentoring experiences with senior faculty. These experiences of conviviality seeded our first memories of the academy. Memories of time spent cooking together with our faculty mentors set a tone of good fellowship that carried forward in how we approached our academic development. The second section of our chapter is a shared narrative description (*in italics*) of how a food cooperative developed amongst our fellow graduate students. This represents our second lesson of communion—how cooking food together solidified a communal experience in our academic lives. The final section of our chapter reflects the authors' growing awareness of rootedness and attempts at becoming emplaced as academics seemingly always on the move. We explore rootedness as metaphor for how food has shaped our lives and how it has extended our scholarship and academic work into spaces where gardens, food pantries, farmers' markets, story, and shared experiences have connected us to place in our process of dwelling.

Conviviality Seeded

We begin with two side-by-side italicized narratives of our early and formative experiences of being welcomed into the fellowship of scholarly endeavor through the conviviality of cooking and sharing meals. *Tea and Biscuits* and *Pasta al Dante* are personal narratives used to illuminate the lesson of conviviality that emerged within those experiences. Spending time in the kitchen with faculty mentors imprinted upon us not only the value of sharing family cultural food traditions but revealed how the act of cooking together was one of the best academic expressions of a convivial space, a place where the sharing of our personal histories came naturally, and we felt a part of something bigger than academics.

Tea and Biscuits

Entering her kitchen was a window into who she was, just like all kitchens are a reflection of their holders and homes, immediately personal. I had never been invited into a faculty's home, let alone for a meal. I felt both privileged and nervous. Sunlight poured into the kitchen, past window birdfeeders and windchimes outside, and thru suncatchers to finally land on the tremendous sleeping dog that had first greeted me with his cold black nose at the front door. The second sensation upon entering was the enveloping smell of bread that felt deeply welcoming. Tea had been brewed and drop biscuits were ready for the prepared butter and jams that I imagined came from her garden just past the kitchen windows. Somehow southern biscuits can be light and fluffy pillows of flour yet trickling with butter. The first bite reveals these are a family recipe, made by a grandmother who didn't speak English but taught her everything she knows about cooking. I wasn't expecting to share my own story of a grandmother that made me cinnamon-sugar toast every Saturday morning and taught me to play Kings-on -the-Corner at her kitchen table. I couldn't help but juxtapose the stories we all ended up sharing with ideas about how we learn, who holds expertise, what knowledge we value. By the end of our lunch, we'd laughed over shared stories of family, what brought us to our individual interests in school, and the difference between jam, jelly, and preserves.

I entered this experience prepared to review elements of course readings. I had no prior experience engaging with a teacher in such an environment, around a place that was intimately familiar to me, immediately drawing out memory of sights, smells, and feelings of family. This was a threshold moment of what experiential learning could be and what a community of learners could feel like.

Pasta al Dante

The first time I was invited to dinner, I felt a bit spellbound from the first moment I crossed the threshold. A postage stamp scrap of a galley kitchen, a broom balanced across the counters, fresh pasta drying hanging from the limbo stick, pots gurgling, a fantastic mess of a kitchen. A fresh set of China dishes for each course, a higgledy piggledy assortment, each tracing a line of familial descent. Ornate, essential, and storied, becoming towering stacks in the wee hours. Salad. Always at the end. Fresh greens, citrus-oranges, sure, but always grapefruit. Vinaigrette of juice, olive oil, salt, and pepper.

I often arrived early and helped in the cramped kitchen. Rolling pasta was utterly unknown to me and this occupied much of my time. Though I could also be called upon to chop peppers and onions, cut sausages, or toss the al dente pasta with a little parmesan, pasta water, oil, and salt to hang out till the sauce was finished. Amidst the cookpots we'd chat about food, classes, experiences, how my professor learned to cook at the knee of his Italian grandmother. I grew up in a family where food and story were intertwined and this felt familiar, though, through these early years at the university, I became aware of the intersection of food and scholarship mingling with a convivial gathering together.

One evening stands out. I was taking a graduate class on Dante. Being a senior, I was unsure of my academic chops. All the others were graduate students and one, an older woman, was reading his works in Italian. Truth be told, I felt a bit out of my depth. Nearing the end of term, we each had to recite one of the cantos from the Divine Comedy. I choose the first chapter in Purgatorio for I loved the idea of the ascent from the Inferno, surviving the cataclysm, the depths of sorrow, and then breathing free again, seeing the stars gathering and the rolling sea. The pasta was fresh and served with picante sausage, peppers, and tomatoes. We ate roasted chicken thighs and fennel with a simple pan sauce full of herbs and acidic traces of lemon. As usual salad was cleansing at the end. We toasted each other and the semester with prosecco, beer, and wine, conversation arcing widely. We told stories of places we had traveled, our families, how we understood the essence of truth and meaning, our thoughts on the world and its strange paradoxes, chaos, and at times utter nonsensical nature. As it turns out, Dante was doing something similar the whole time.

...

What we found as young academics was an invitation not only into the world of scholarly discourse and conversation, but an invitation into others' kitchens, fellowship around food and cooking, and sharing time and space with faculty mentors and other students. The space created and shared by our faculty, in their kitchens, impacted our own academic trajectories in a way that we only now have come to realize. Conviviality denoted a welcoming into fellowship. Conviviality revolved around the sharing of food and story.

Fears of fitting in academically were dispelled by the merriment of sharing food and story and connecting across all our disparate backgrounds. We both came to learn, each through different kitchen experiences, how the academy could be less about exactitudes, taxonomies, and categorization and more about interpretations, kindness, and curiosity. We started discovering that within the deep history of the university was a whole world of embodied and convivial awareness. This is where we both came to know what it meant to be a scholar.

For us, this was the origin story of our first blush as academics. It also stood in direct contrast with our classroom and institutional experiences in the academy, which did not connect to the deeply personal. These are standout moments because they were not the norm; we did not feel deeply connected to all our instructors, often felt disconnected from the content we were trying to digest, and would feel impostor syndrome during classroom discussions.

These first experiences outside the walls of the academy and within the kitchens of our mentors seeded what we carry forward as conviviality with our own students. Conviviality is more than students feeling welcomed into the academy; it is developing a sense of belonging to the entire community. Graduate students are often schooling far from home. We remember how lonely the walls of classrooms can be and how our early mentors invited us not just into their homes, but into their kitchens. They didn't just cook for us, they cooked *with* us. Their conviviality didn't provide just sustenance to hungry students. They shared with us who they were as people, not just as the academic we initially viewed them as. They opened a space for us to be part of their story, as they were living it, within the academy.

Reflecting upon those convivial kitchen moments may even explain why we subsequently spent so much time in our academic careers studying experiential and embodied awareness. While around the kitchen table we may have talked of classes and research, our conversations were much more universal, more ecumenical in topics and discourse. Our professors would pose innumerable queries that tracked across a wide field of ideas, concepts, and sensibilities. This shepherding of our conversations kept our attention focused on a wide and wholistic frame of reference, connecting our lives and experiences to our academic life, to each other and to the larger world.

Our growing awareness of how our scholarly lives intersected with a life beyond the academy became an essential part of our academic and social identities as we wrapped up our dissertations and slowly made our way into the larger current of the universitas. While it's easy to get caught up in the daily grind of academia, in abstractions and research, all of this musing, teaching, and writing happens somewhere very particular and unique on the globe. Keeping the lessons learned from our mentors we worked to consistently develop an awareness of the places we found ourselves, in the concrete experiencing of place. After all, these places are the shared storehouse of our ecological and cultural commons. Place and culture are two sides of the same coin, interconnected and dependent upon one each other.

Humans are embodied, multisensory beings. We come to know things by way of our embodied experiences with creatures, plants, and with things in the world. We have often asked ourselves as academics, how can we begin to pay greater attention to our sensory experiences, to our embodied co-construction of knowledge and meaning, to our rootedness when we found ourselves often feeling itinerant?

One starting point is akin to what anthropologist Paul Stoller called sensuous scholarship, and this fits into an important but oft-neglected discourse of embodied and experiential awareness required of the academic. This requires us to fully engage with people, place, and phenomenon in wholistic and sensual ways. Imagine scholars who are rooted to places and the endemic cultural and biological histories through the full spectrum of their senses. Tuning into our senses gives us a broader awareness and sensibility to what is going on around us, certainly as emplaced human beings, but also as community emplaced academics. What is the universitas for if not for engaging the wider world and enlivening our communities?

We found that embodied and experiential learning was the best way for us to marry our academic pursuits with our keen interest in where we lived. This was tricky for us as we moved several times before alighting in a spot where we finally settled down. Yet, in each place, we intentionally sought opportunities for engaging in local garden and food-related experiences such as building school learning gardens, working with food pantries, being guest chefs at our local food co-op, and slowly developing places where we could learn from as well as teach and mentor others in the craft of regenerative agriculture, local food pathways, and experiential learning.

Acts of Communion

In this next section, we share a joint narrative of how an initial graduate student potluck, where we were asked to bring a food from our own culture to share, subsequently developed into a ritual sharing of food traditions as part of a food cooperative. The food cooperative became a pivotal component of our early cultural experience in the academe as graduate students. The idea of cooking together and sharing of food started off as a way to get to know each other, sharing our own Midwest and Southern cooking roots with our fellow students from all around the country and world, and them in turn sharing theirs.

These initial acts of sharing food and cooking together evolved into a monthly food cooperative. We started regularly coming together to cook large batches of meals that we collectively processed, resulting in taking home a bounty to fill our freezers. The food we cooked together literally fed our family with two small children living off graduate stipends and assistance programs. Our daughters ate Moroccan rice, chicken tandoori, cabbage rolls, and perogies as mid-week meals. While it sustained us physically, the lessons of communal sharing and learning still resonate as we regularly cook for our own students. At the time with both of us working on doctoral degrees, we gravitated to a group of students with families, as we had two very young children. The cooking together and sharing of food started off as a way to get to know each other, sharing our Southern cooking roots with our fellow students from all around the country and world, and them in turn sharing theirs.

From potluck to food cooperative

Our first communal experience as doctoral students and our first glimpse of the fine folks we would get to know was at a welcome potluck for grad students. It was one of those late summer evenings where the heat and humidity of the day lingered in a still, blue haze across the hills and the only movement seemed to come from reverberations of cicadas. A long table displayed a crazy diversity of foods. Some we had never eaten and some, such as pasta with tomato sauce, other students had never tried before. We sat outside in a student's backyard in lawn chairs, drank beer, and ate together, beginning our graduate school experience with the sharing of food and stories. Here we found the universitas again and a kinship with a wide assortment of curious friends keen to embody and discover this new place.

And so, we explored new and local foods together. We experimented with flavors and spices and ingredients from far flung places. We grew gardens. We brewed beer. We baked bread. We had bonfires and celebratory feasts that shared cultural backgrounds. Mexican, German, Danish, Irish, Italian, South Asian. And we learned. About regenerative agriculture and permaculture, about local foods and local farmers. We learned to can fruits and veggies, pickles and jams. We learned to plant tomatoes, trellis beans, dig potatoes, and prune apple trees. We learned about moles and za'atar, baguettes and roasting vegetables, the mind-boggling magic of yeast and fermentation. A great coming together of experiences, knowledge, backgrounds, and stories. And the fruits of all this oftentimes played out in larger gatherings of families and friends.

On one particular May Day, we gathered at our old, rambling house to raise a May pole. We had brewed a special ale for the day, The Greenman Cometh, and everyone brought favorite dishes from home. Southern dishes of beans and greens and pimento cheese spread, delicate salads with wild edible flowers, Irish soda bread, Italian pastas and northern European potatoes and cheeses, Indian curries and Mexican enchiladas. Cakes and sweet treats full of honey and cream and berries like Cranachan. Celebration food. The semester had wrapped up and all of us were now looking towards living it up during those fleeting summer days of the student. We danced the maypole, played music, and later in the evening built a huge bonfire to jump across. This gaggle of people were all connected by the threads of the universitas in one way or the other and this solidified our community, our extended family through embodied experience and sharing deeply beyond campus.

. . .

Upon reflection, these experiences represent our second lesson of communion—how cooking food together firmly situated communal experience as a central feature in our academic lives. The food sharing was a cooperative for students and by students and included students in a range of different disciplinary areas. We found again that the sharing of food and cooking together enlivened our personal, familial, collective, and egalitarian connections and served to balance the competitive, individualistic, and hierarchical experiences often found in graduate education. We now understand how the food cooperative provided us a necessary contrast to other elements of our academic lives—those being the more traditional competitive and individualistic experiences in the academe.

Oftentimes graduate work felt lonesome, highly solitary, and outright competitive. Hierarchy, individualism, and competition seem to be hardwired into the structure of universities, but they often undermine the purpose of the universitas, the community. The cooperative sharing of food cultures and traditions and the growing and production of food fostered a communal experience that stood in contrast to the competitive and individualistic inclinations of the academe. In this way, food for us became both sustaining of community and a form of resistance to the broader norms of doctoral work.

The communal cooking and sharing of food as a cooperative experience was impactful for there was no hierarchy among the relationships or academic self-gain in the process. No CVs were enhanced. No grants were sought. Yet, it resounded with the intentions of the universitas and scholarship, a reaching out into the wider world with intentionality. Food connected us and gave us an awareness and sensibility beyond the content and context of our doctoral work. It allowed us to extend ourselves and ultimately our scholarship into spaces we did not expect. Exploring food cultures and cooking together not only fostered deep relationships with one another and our extended families but also tethered us to the place on the maps we found ourselves.

The emergent food cooperative with our fellow students stood out for its contrast to the university student experience as we had lived it. Rather than encouraging individualism, the food cooperative was a communal result of an expressive and wholistic engagement with others. Rather than judgmental and competitive, the cooperative was curious and collaborative. Rather than dwelling in abstractions we found ourselves experiencing place in embodied and primary ways, experiencing the wider world and grounding our awareness by dwelling in place. This is how we imagine the universitas—as a communion of people, not solely bound by the four walls of a classroom, but in the comings and goings of people sharing food, stories, and experiences.

Rootedness and Emplaced Dwelling

What does it mean to be rooted as an academic? How can we go about finding deep resonance with locality and place? Where can we find the interconnections between our scholarship, teaching, service, and outreach? There's certainly a tradition for this within the participant focus of ethnographic work, but we're keen to explore this more wholistically, radiating out from our scholarship to encompass a broader sense of rootedness, moving beyond what is purely academic into what is emotive, aesthetic and expressive.

Rootedness comes into focus when we begin to journey not out, but deep down *into* the place itself. Food is intrinsically bound to place and the histories, experiences, and stories therein. Therefore, we conclude our chapter by exploring the importance that *place* itself plays in our lives as academics attempting to dwell deeply in the many places we have lived. We understand rootedness and dwelling as being both convivial and communal and that our rootedness allows us to be more engaged and aware, helping us develop scholarship through immersive, participatory, and community-oriented work.

We often describe our academic life as a journey, our academic journey. Truth be told, though, as students dig into their course of study, they may forego a deeper journey into the place in which they live. We found this growing awareness of place is still a journey, just not one of many miles logged or mental abstractions. Rather, it is one of many years and biocultural stories, a deep digging into shared awareness, histories, and experiences tied to one unique spot on the globe and found among the varied food stories that intersect.

Our lives as academics are often one of movement and examining things in abstractive ways that too often assume a broad universality even though we live in a place full of nuance and particularities. Yet for all our abstractions we are ultimately tied to a little patch of ground and this shared place is supremely important. Ultimately, sharing a place may be the one thing we can all agree upon. To dwell and to dwell well upon this place asks important questions of our roles and responsibilities as academics, what we owe to each other, to the place itself, and to the land and its living beings, to a grand universitas.

Rootedness and dwelling in a place are largely structures of feeling, constituted more of expressive and emotive senses than the purely cognitive. We know that knowledge without personal connection leads to a shallow awareness, yet knowledge coupled with emotive resonance can lead to profound levels of engagement. We see this in students of all ages, and we found this to be the case when building learning gardens both in PK-12 schools and at the university.

The growing, harvesting, and cooking of food strikes a powerful chord for people of all backgrounds. Memories are oftentimes stirred by the smell of soil and rain, the feeling of sun-warmed tomatoes, the taste of just-picked raspberries, the sound of bumblebees, and the sight and texture of so much green. So, a great deal of our work is getting ourselves and others to sensuously engage with our surroundings and much of this comes in the way of outreach and community engagement through place-based learning gardens. We see this form of awareness and connection as keystone to what it means to be a scholar and an engaged participant of the universitas.

Our experience, like many in the academe has been itinerant, moving several times before finally settling in our present locale. Our process of becoming emplaced in a new location occurred through the medium of local food cultures, learning gardens, food cooperatives and food banks, farmers' markets, and learning new food cultures. Ultimately, our lives as academics found an unexpected expression in our community awareness and engagement through food. Most notably this has taken root in developing place-based learning gardens that provide the space for community and convivial learning about the natural world and our interdependence with nature through garden education.

Here we end our story by summarizing the lessons we learned through our academic life as the ingredients to how we try to dwell deeply in the place of universitas.

Emplaced Dwelling in the Academy

Begin with equal parts conviviality, community, and rootedness.

1. Do not dwell in the place alone, even if you only plan to dwell temporarily. Dwell with others. Be curious together of where your food comes from, how it is produced, and how your food history and choices impact where you live.
2. Delve into a deeper journey into the place in which you live. Learn the topography and stories of the place across the year, outside, and in all kinds of weather and seasons.
3. Plant a garden to share, harvest and cook out of the garden, listen to all the family histories. Understand that the big story of a place is made up of little, often unknown smaller stories.
4. Work in this place with your hands. Build, create, contribute to the physical landscape where you can see how you are an integral part of the community. Whether you are there 2 weeks or 20 years, ask yourself if the place is better off having had you as part of the community.
5. Remember when you were a new member and extend fellowship. Keep in mind that our membership in communities extends far beyond what is human and be kind and gentle with your touch upon the land.

CHAPTER 15

More Than (Just) Something to Eat: Reflections on How Food Invites Shared Learning and Renewed Commitments to Justice

SARAH B. SHEAR AND ANDREA M. HAWKMAN

"Food, in the end, in our own tradition, is something holy. It's not about nutrients and calories. It's about sharing. It's about honesty. It's about identity."

— Louise Fresco

Introduction: An Invitation to a Shared Table

The winding road that brought us to this chapter is an interesting one that continues to unfold before us. It started years ago with a study of Disney films, which then led us to a study of preservice teachers' engagement with critical race film literacy. It was within this most recent collaboration, which started in 2018, that we homed in on a particular challenge preservice teachers were having to identify and analyze the complex intersections of Whiteness, Jewish identities, and anti-Semitism both in and outside the United States. The preservice teachers who participated in that project all commented that their knowledge of Jewish people was limited only to lessons they'd received about the Holocaust. While those lessons are in no way insignificant, they do a disservice to students supporting students to understand the histories of Jewish people, the complexities of race and racism towards and within Jewish communities, Zionism, and the current crisis in Palestine, for example. As we continued to talk about where to go next, we continued to wrestle with how to support preservice teachers to develop the depth of knowledge—or at least how to begin the lifelong learning towards that knowledge—they need to understand the world in which we find ourselves and the support their students will also need. In those conversations we also began to confront our own need to learn more about these issues.

In order to move forward, we realized we needed to turn inward. At the time, we found ourselves circling around questions related to our identities, genealogies, and personal–professional understandings and relationships to/with Whiteness, Judaism, anti-Semitism, anti-Arab and anti-Palestinian racisms, and Zionism. As we will further describe in our reflections below, Sarah identifies as a cisgender, White woman with diasporic-settler heritage. Having ancestors who came to the United States either for wealth and land (Scottish, English, Welsh) or seeking freedom from persecution (Ashkenazi Jews from Poland and Russia), she takes responsibility for the settler structures her ancestors either helped create or willingly assimilated to as part of her work to examine settler colonialism in social studies curriculum. Andrea identifies as a lesbian, cisgender, White woman with Irish/English/Catholic ancestry from a working-class background. Her scholarship examines the ways that race(ism) and Whiteness shape social studies teaching and learning. Our efforts to begin to answer these questions took us headlong into critical family history research and shared readings beginning with Eric Goldstein's *The Price of Whiteness* (2008).

It was during one book club discussion, which we recorded on St. Patrick's Day, that another detour in the journey occurred—the detour into corned beef . . .

Andrea: *So, if we're in Ireland, beef in general is an elite meat. The farmer, the yeoman, the regular Joe in Ireland is not eating beef every day. They're eating pork, if they're eating meat at all. That's* *my family's story; we did not come from the Irish elite—that's definitely not where we got our connection with corned beef from.*

So then, if we're looking at class in the United States and Irish identity we're seeing Irish immigrants living in neighborhoods and urban areas alongside Jewish immigrants buying food from Jewish delis, Kosher delis. It's obvious then that the meat that's available is this corned beef, which is most likely cheaper than you know.

Sarah: *At the time, we [Jewish immigrants] were mostly in New York . . . We're living in the same neighborhoods. And most Jewish immigrants were likely kosher. They wouldn't have eaten pork.*

Andrea: *And so of course, this is where it came, but the story of it coming from a Kosher Deli. That piece of the puzzle was not delivered, was not told.*

Having been friends for years, we found that some of our most beloved foods have rich, complex histories that intersect with our individual and collective lives and work. Food, especially the sharing of meals, offers spaces to ask questions, share stories, ruminate on the past, and dream about the future. So, while we continue to read together and collect family histories, we also continue to talk and to eat. *One of the questions that's bubbled to the top is in what ways can conversations about/over food be meaningful in unpacking histories of race/ism, identity, and pedagogy?* We recently were able to spend time together in Seattle to work on these projects and share meals and conversation. It is from those shared meals and conversations that this chapter was born. We invite readers to join us at our shared table—to join us as we reflect on our learning thus far, to ponder the questions we are trying to answer, and to consider how food offers nourishment and renewal in our commitments to justice work.

In the sections that follow, we both offer an opening narrative reflection on our experiences eating and thinking together followed by a reply from each one of us. This organizational pattern is similar to the ways that our conversations flowed while together—one of us would share a point of reflection or observation that was connected to a story of personal history or pedagogical practice, then the other would respond in ways that highlighted connections, extensions, or questions that emerged from the table. We conclude the chapter with a set of additional wonderings, questions, and actions we are moving forward with as we continue in our friendship and work as teacher educators.

Lunch at a "Jewish" Deli

Sarah's Reflection

There was something oddly familiar and familial about walking into Dingfelder's, a well-worn Jewish deli in the Capitol Hill neighborhood of Seattle. Perhaps it was the hit of the smells—the salty smoke of cured meats, the pungent vinegars of kraut, or the veil of sugar lingering in the air as baked goods went in and out of the ovens. But something felt and smelled like home despite the fact that I'd never stepped into this space until Andrea and my lunch outing. I knew immediately that we needed an order of latkes, the crunchy richness of shredded and fried potatoes and onions—topped, of course, with either sour cream or applesauce. We could spend hours hotly debating which topping is better, but let's just agree that both are perfectly delectable.

There are a few delicious dishes to consider during our time at Dingfelder's, but I will continue for the moment to talk about the latkes. I couldn't help but tell Andrea about my Nana's brother, my Uncle Willy. He made the best latkes I've ever had. No one could match him even if they stood right next to him using the same recipe. His were simply magic.

I'm caught up in the nostalgia of the latkes when our sandwiches arrive, and I am hit with a wave of sadness, a loneliness for home. It's been hard living in Seattle thousands of miles away from my family. I try not to burst out crying the middle of the deli, and I get choked up telling Andrea stories of my Nana and her baking, and how she used to tell us as kids that we needed to lose some weight while simultaneously shoving a platter of fresh-from-the-oven strudel or rugelach towards us. There's something about the food and the stories that hits at the core of me—to the root of who I come from. I am the great granddaughter of Ashkenazi Jews who left Poland and Russia at the turn of the 20th century, and it was somewhere on the shores of Russia that my great grandfather, a tailor, changed his last name to Shear.

The conversation with Andrea, I feel, turns a bit somber as I share more of what I know about my dad's side of the family, and the dedication my great grandfather had to ensuring no one would ever know—and thus never remember—our original name. It's not written down anywhere. I take a few bites of my brisket sandwich. There's a loss, I try to awkwardly explain, for a name that I'll never know, like somehow something authentic about me was stolen. I've pored for years over family documents and photos, visited historical archives (to read the Lewis papers, my maternal great grandmother's family), and talked for hours with both my parents to try and understand who we come from and what motivations compelled them, for better or worse, to move to the lands we now commonly call the United States. Guilt and anger are wrapped up into how I feel during our lunch. It's not that I'm not proud of being a Shear, and I certainly understand the circumstances that my great grandfather found himself in that propelled him to make that decision, but being both Jewish and White are complicated, and there's a responsibility to be honest.

Our lunch conversation covers a lot of topics and raises a lot of questions about the intersections of Jewishness and Whiteness, and I can't help but recall some of our earlier work to support preservice teachers to better understand that being Jewish is bigger and more complex than any one historical moment like the Holocaust. I had family in Birkenau, and the horrors of that time are not lost on me. But I also can't not think about the current genocide of Palestinians in Gaza and the ongoing occupation of their homelands in the contemporary nation state of Israel. I've never been a Zionist, nor will I ever be. I can still be a Jew and understand how colonialism works. Thankfully, dessert has arrived. New York-style cheesecake. The sweet, creamy texture offers some momentary relief from the heaviness of the conversation. My great grandparents came to the United States believing this country would offer them freedom and opportunity, but for Jews coming to a settler nation itself built on White supremacy, that freedom and opportunity came at a cost. Stepping off the ship in New York in 1899, my great grandparents inadvertently became settlers themselves, adapting their Jewishness to become acceptable White Americans. It's my responsibility to understand how and why that happened—to understand and take responsibility for the privileges I inherited and to work towards a different future.

Andrea's Response

As a novice latke eater, I found the ones crafted at Dingfelder's to be delicious, but I most appreciated eating them while listening to Sarah share their significance in her family memories. Sarah's recounting of her Uncle Willy's latkes reminded me of the significance of another component of our meal, corned beef. Growing up in a family that claimed Irish heritage we frequently made corned beef and cabbage each March in recognition of St. Patrick's Day. It became such a beloved meal for me that it became a meal made for my birthday as well. The corned beef Reuben on rye that I had at Dingfelder's did not disappoint. Although this Jewish deli did not prepare the food in the same way that my Irish family would, this cross-cultural connection is one that sparked the beginning of this project between Sarah and me. In conversations we had while co-reading texts about Jewish and Irish immigration, our focus quickly shifted to the shared history of corned beef and how it plays a central role in understanding the immigrant experience for Jewish and Irish folks within the United States.

When our conversation shifted to focus on the intimate history of the Shear family name, I, personally, was thinking about the genesis of my family name—Hawkman. When my wife and I were preparing to get married we had several conversations about what our names should be. Should we retain our last names granted at birth? Adopt one name or the other? Hyphenate? It became quickly clear that the best choice for us, as we started this new queer family of our own, was to create a new name. Hawkman, our new family name, is a hybrid of the names my wife and I were given at birth. I am not hers, she is not mine—we are ours. Knowing that we were planning to have children, we wanted all of us to have the same last name, so that it was clear that we were claiming each other as family. So, as Sarah recounted the trauma of her family name and the legacies she carries with her as not knowing its genesis—my heart ached and it resonated with me. I understand the power of knowing where your name originates; we can point to the specific day in December when we went before a judge to change it. That said, this nation has a long history of forced or coerced name changes that do not accompany the same queer joy that does mine. I also recognize that for many people, particularly trans folks seeking to amend their name as an act of gender-affirming care, name changes accompany lengthy and expensive legal processes that require unnecessary paperwork and exposure to anti-trans bureaucracies that make the process harder than it should be. These decisions or actions can be heavy, challenging, and even traumatic. A name, as these conversations have affirmed, is deeply personal and laden with history and identity.

Dinner at an "Irish" Pub

Andrea's Reflection

Honestly, this meal at the "Irish" pub in Seattle was a microcosm of my education in U.S.-centric, White supremacist-controlled understandings of what it means to be Irish or to have Irish heritage. The meal, fish and chips, was listed as a traditional Irish dish—and yet the food was poorly prepared, lacked flavor, and other than the title of the dish had no resemblance to the preparation of this meal I had recently enjoyed while visiting Ireland just a few months ago. *Who puts Panko crumbs on Irish fish and chips?* I'm no expert on Irish food, but after just a week staying in Dublin I sampled enough examples of this pub staple to know that what this Seattle bar was serving just wasn't it.

When I was in Ireland, attending an academic conference, several local attendees asked me about my experiences in the United States and what led me to attend this specific conference. In one conversation, an Irish-local attendee asked, "Oh, the States love Ireland, don't they?" I laughed, sighed, and replied, "The U.S. loves its interpretation of Ireland. I'm not sure how much folks actually know about Ireland." This sentiment was understood by my new friend and also hit close to home for me. I recognized that my travels to Ireland were inspired by the early conversations Sarah and I had regarding Irish history in the United States. I was thinking specifically about Ireland's strident and vocal support of Palestine within the current Israel–Hamas conflict that was in stark contrast to U.S. Zionist efforts. The genesis of my travel to Ireland was similarly situated. Upon beginning to read alongside Sarah about Irish and Jewish history within the United States, I learned about the experiences of Frederick Douglass visiting Ireland. I quickly dove into a project exploring Frederick Douglass' time in Ireland, a journey he defined as transformative, shortly after the publication of his autobiography. This history of solidarity and justice was not represented in the ways I learned, both formally and informally, about what it means to be Irish or of Irish history.

Over food, and as Sarah shared more about her own genealogical legacies, I wrestled with gaps in my own genealogical understanding. *What did it mean for me to say I had Irish heritage? How was I honoring this legacy?* To this point, I had resisted engaging in deep genealogical work for several reasons. One being, I was uneasy with the ways that DNA-based websites track and maintain biological records of people. I knew I couldn't keep my family records out of those databases, but I was uncomfortable paying to add to this effort as it seemed like a large system of surveillance. I had heard stories of religious groups utilizing genealogy as a way to engage in shady behavior. Secondly, I had seen people utilize these databases in an effort to claim more diversity than their Whiteness justifies, particularly relating to genealogical connections to tribal nations—recognizing that affiliation with Indigenous communities is not as simple as traces of DNA as this obscures the colonizing violence of European American settlers. Additionally, as part of a queer family, biological ancestry does not tell a complete story for our past, present, and future so I avoided emphasizing biology altogether. When my kids ask if they are Irish (since my family is) the answer is always yes. Moreover, as a family formed outside of heteronormative expectations, situating our family heritage requires deeper contextual understanding of many ways that families tell stories of who they are. That said, through these conversations with Sarah and reflections thereafter, I have come to recognize that by not knowing with more clarity the legacies of my ancestors I have promoted a flattened version of the past that affirms the ubiquity of Whiteness and white supremacy. My avoidance of this knowledge has not served the past nor is it in alignment with my personal–political commitments. I was, in essence, acting as this horrible fish and chips plate—claiming a connection but not in ways that were responsible or accurate.

In sharing these stories over food and continuing to reflect on these interconnected exchanges and experiences, I began to reconsider the power of genealogical information. I am looking toward restorative and justice-minded genealogical work that can assist me in gaining a responsible sense of my family's past in an effort toward more robust accountability for the legacies of power and privilege that have brought me to this confluence of history, identity, education, and responsibility.

Sarah's Response

Let me begin by saying I am thankful to have a palate that dislikes fish, so no horrible Panko-covered fish and chips for me! I opted for the safety of a cheeseburger, which is definitely not a historically Irish dish. In recalling our conversation that night and Andrea's reflection above, I am struck by several wonderings and questions. First, I think Andrea raises important points about the issue of identity and who has the power to claim it, whether that identity be Irish or otherwise. I agree that DNA-related genealogy sites have attempted to make easy what is quite complex and have inadvertently invited people to claim identities and communities they know nothing about. My own mother's family, for example, was shocked when I informed them that we are Irish by way of France (on one side of the family) and Scotland (on the other). Does movement of people across time and space make them more or less part of a community than not? Is it more important to consider *who claims us* regardless of our geographic locations? These are compelling quandaries to ponder as we eat and talk.

Moreover, I am struck by the importance of recognizing that all our journeys towards deeper understanding of ancestry are multifaceted and take time. The avoidance of genealogy, as Andrea reflected, and the flattening of the past are poignant lessons for me to hear my friend share. My journey to ask explicit questions that name not only how I came to be here but also lay bare the motivations of my ancestors, for ill or not, sometimes feel easier to ask than they may feel to Andrea. I am learning from listening to her stories that for her as a queer person and a queer mother it is not as routine a family research endeavor as it is for me. In our conversations, and in hearing and reading Andrea reflect about both Whiteness and queerness, I am moved by the tensions she wrestles with and the responsibilities she has that are multifold—responsibilities to her own self-growth, to her children and partner, and to the commitments she's made to work in solidarity for better futures in education and society. Emergent strategist Andrea J. Ritchie wrote, "Love is what gets us to what is transformative, resilient, and helps us create new possibilities we cannot otherwise imagine" (2023, p. 233). All of these responsibilities Andrea carries, I believe, come from a deep feeling of love, and it is from this place that her work will continue to evolve.

Before Leaving the Table: Renewed Commitments, Moving Forward

As we talk, the waxing and waning of our vulnerabilities amidst our wonderings about family genealogies invite us to also embrace a momentary burst of laughter. How is it that in this random pub, in a random neighborhood of Seattle exists over our heads banners of collegiate flags (University of Missouri, Penn State, and University of Washington) that mark their own sort of genealogy?

We met when we were grad students at the University of Missouri—Mizzou—Sarah was on her way out as Andrea was just beginning. Sarah headed to Penn State Altoona for her first tenure track position, and it was during her time at Penn State that we conducted the research project with preservice teachers. Throughout the years engaged in this project (and its many iterations), Andrea moved into her own tenure track journey at Utah State before transitioning to Rowan University, and Sarah moved onto the University of Washington at Bothell. Across each of these moves, we continued to engage around critical media literacy, Whiteness studies, and teacher education and began our work in critical family history. Across projects and meetings we recognized that time was often spent talking, reading, writing, and thinking—whether on Zoom or in person—over food, coffee, or drinks.

There is an intimacy of connection food provides that offers a disarming of the walls we often surround ourselves with as people and as academics. Although we've been friends for over a decade having first met during grad school, we continue to regularly meet via Zoom and communicate frequently via text, but we rarely spend time in physical proximity to one another—Sarah lives in Washington State and Andrea lives in New Jersey. As noted above, this project at the intersections of history, identity, pedagogy, and food has been one we have tinkered on for quite some time; however, it was not until we were able to enjoy meals and extended time and conversation together that we gained deeper insight into each other's pasts, presents, and concerns for the future highlighted here. We were both struck by the ways that casual conversation about foods we love and loathe could lead so quickly toward deep excavations of self and family.

As we prepare to leave our shared table, we offer readers some questions for consideration as they talk and eat with others:

1. Can you recall a specific meal or food-related experience that sparked a conversation about race or identity for you?
2. How do the dishes from your childhood reflect the racial dynamics present in your upbringing?
3. Have you encountered instances where sharing food has helped break down racial barriers in your community?
4. What challenges have you faced in discussing race and identity through the context of food, especially in educational or social settings?
5. How do you navigate the complexities of race and identity when sharing meals with people from different cultural backgrounds?

We wonder what continued impact these food conversations will have on us personally and professionally. We continue to ask questions about our genealogical pasts, thinking with each question how the answers may support a renewed and strengthened commitment to the justice movements we've been part of both in and outside of education. In her own critical family history work, Christine Sleeter (2011) wrote,

> I believe that examining ourselves, our families, and the legacies we inherited can be useful in teacher education. However, telling the stories we grew up hearing is not enough, given that those stories have probably been filtered through the dominant national narrative. Having inherited stories that legitimate our place in that system by airbrushing out the context of race and class . . . Having done so, we can begin to ask ourselves some questions that might lead to acting. (pp. 430–431)

As such, taking up this work not only compels us to ask more complex questions about our own lives and families, our positions within the ongoing struggles and dreamings toward freedom and justice, but also how to take action(s) in our classrooms to model for our students how to begin the process of naming and fighting systems of oppression that have for too long defined who we are.

References

Goldstein, E. L. (2008). *The prices of whiteness: Jews, race, and American identity*. Princeton University Press.

Ritchie, A. J. (2023). *Practicing new worlds: Abolition and emergent strategies*. AK Press.

Sleeter, C. E. (2011). Becoming white: Reinterpreting a family story by putting race back into the picture. *Race Ethnicity and Education, 14*(4), 421–433. DOI:10.1080/13613324.2010.547850.

CHAPTER 16

Critical Lessons Learned While Making Cinnamon Rolls with My Son

BRIANNE PITTS

I Was Inadvertently Mentored by a Late Night Tray of Cinnamon Rolls

An Appetizer

After years in the elementary classroom, I'm an early career academic with a penchant for stickers and beatnik poetry, looking to break into the higher-education scene. I recently joined the tenure track at an upper-Midwestern predominately white institution (PWI). Hired during the COVID-19 pandemic as a second-career social studies teacher-educator, I arrived on campus as one of three untenured faculty in my department, masked, and isolated physically and mentally.

That first year, I found no straightforward recipe for success, and without balance, I was quickly consumed by a workaholic lifestyle. The freedom of scheduling and "Midwest nice" led to overcommitments in service and research. Finally, I had to rest when a semester-long illness accompanied a course overload and my children's begrudging march through puberty. Suffering from sudden bursts of hunger, wilts of exhaustion, and physical fatigue required introspection and a re-orientation of values. Slowing down and working to heal myself and reorient priorities, I turned to baking. This chapter will document the critical lessons learned while making cinnamon rolls with my teenage son. We'll marvel at our innovations and notable failures, experiencing emotional and physical highs and lows. Embark on this journey with us.

Preheat the oven to 350 degrees and prepare yourself a batch of sweet and savory nostalgia. Using family recipes as a conceptual metaphor for curriculum and the academy, I'll draw from ephemeral primary sources and first-person intergenerational-culinary accounts to question the history of recipes we've served as "receipts" of understanding (Merriam-Webster, 2024).

Shake up your favorite recipes and re-evaluate the long-held methods (and messages) we've passed. Let's wonder:

- Can we model flexible culinary skills and teach young chefs to substitute ingredients and match flavor profiles to their audience's culinary needs?
- As academics model heritage through learned methodologies, do we stop enough in-the-making (like baking) to question the ingredients our recipes were founded on?
- What receipts (or recipes) of familial and academic heritage(s) serve as a roadmap for future generations gastronomic (and educational) liberation?

I wonder about all this while making cinnamon rolls with my son.

Consider this food story an academic fairytale, told through a series of generational vignettes (as conceptual metaphors) or ingredients (as receipts) of history. These elements mirror my baking (or teaching/researching) process. Some methods are generalizable, such as, "Hey, a recipe for cinnamon rolls." Others might feel far out to you, but familiar to others (i.e., cardamom?) Each time we bake, it's a singular experience, and the spoils are meant to be shared.

Bring Your Ingredients

What if we could refashion our favorite recipes, leaving nostalgia behind, releasing our faded memories as quickly as moldy fruit disintegrates back into the earth?

> I think that history is the story of the past, using all the available facts. That nostalgia is a fantasy about the past using no facts, and

> somewhere in between is memory, which is kind of this blend of history and a little bit of emotion . . . I mean, history is kind of about what you need to know . . . but nostalgia is what you want to hear. (Smith, 2022)

So, dear culinary leaders, I invite you to stumble along with my metacognitive, multimodal (yet moves-like-molasses) research process. Come break or make bread with me and taste my ancestral line. Let's refashion some old recipes, cutting them up, quilting them back together—pasting back only the parts that still serve our collective humanity. Refusing the use of hateful historical markers, pedagogies, or ingredients. We can no longer engage just at a distance, colonizing spaces we still seek to liberate.

Too often, I fear we hear of others' successes, and then fall short of action. As example, I don't compost, but I know I could mulch my leftovers and return them to usable earth. I recognize this missed opportunity as a fallible habit I've inherited and lazily carried on. What other habits do I still need to understand? Where do I lazily carry on injustices for the sake of ease?

It'd be easy to adopt my middle school children's mentality: "If I don't do it, someone else will, so I can just wait for help." When I first entered the university and the kitchen, I waited—but no help arrived. We, collectively, are the adults in the room. We must take responsibility for the recipes and messages we push forward. It is no longer acceptable to pass on practices we've inherited without revision—especially if they have ingredients poisonous to others. For example, we bring gluten-free birthday snacks for students with allergies. Similarly, teachers too can differentiate for students' needs, jettisoning lessons and beliefs causing traumas.

The Main Course (of Action?)

"You dislike cooking."

It wasn't nostalgia in his observation; instead, my husband's statement confirmed what I'd always known, but I had hoped he and the children couldn't taste. I really don't like to cook. I have never been driven to invest time in the kitchen. Though cooking dinner didn't always feel like such a chore, no matter my input, the outcome was almost always bland, oddly seasoned, or deemed "creative"—to put it nicely.

Methods

In the last 10 years, as I've stretched my culinary skills. I've sorted, scanned, and baked familial recipes alongside (articles and research projects). I've highlighted and annotated ingredients and read about competing epistemologies as I whipped up banana bread with the kids. I gleaned strategies for instruction (and baking) frameworks for future investigation. These leaves (or left behind) recipes born from generations of academic literature. Mourning (this morning), as I document my ancestors' past baking/cooking and dining history, I draw connections between parallel formats for learning. Like my grandmother's script—I consider my mentors in the field who've passed—how carefully can I read their hand? How closely do my methods resemble theirs as I attempt to honor their memory (Do my rolls taste like Gramps'? Does my writing honor my advisor Carl's?)?

The food stories I love most involve the passing on of knowledge and shared connections to joy and shared sustenance from what we've created together. My gramps' apple-cardamom rolls (Dad's Dad, "super papa" to my kids) and Grandma Jackie's cream cheese frosting (from her favorite carrot cake—see recipes at chapter's end) on top. By baking in this fashion, I've combined the teachings of my maternal and paternal lines.

My academic recipes similarly combine the teachings of my forefathers (as shared by Dr. Ashley Woodson as a family tree of scholarship). Through our ancestry, both academic and physical too, we carry on the methods and ontologies we've grown on. Combining mentors' modeling, we must learn how to let our scholarship R.I.S.E.

The recipes' ingredients are elements essential to the plot of our collective stories. Who we are, where we come from, and what we know, value, and observe. As a white woman educational researcher who focuses on Black histories, I look to self and family history to understand the debts we owe. In this, I've struggled to make space for rest, introspection, and reflection while working to bring honor to my ancestors' gifts *and* account for their debts owed in both the academy and kitchen. Collecting family artifacts alongside credits in my Ph.D. program, my homework often accompanied my children's breakfast—where I'd draw out my ideas as they ate. I couldn't always type it up, so I practiced being present wherever I was. At work in elementary classrooms, I launched a study inspired by what I found missing from the teachings we brought to the classroom.

"Why isn't there a white history month?" I heard her ask. A naive, and well-meaning, but often-biting educator for young learners. So enraged by my lack of ability to interrupt the harm, or respond adequately back to intervene, I launched a 3-year study to find the answers instead. My doctoral work examined pitfalls and possibilities of instruction from predominantly White educators during Black History Month (Pitts, 2020).

These cinnamon rolls that taught me something?

The hand-me-down pastry delights are from two generations past. Each time I bake them, I add another story; making these rolls feels like a walk down memory lane—like an artifact with seasoning used to contextualize their flavor. The enjoyment doesn't begin when eating the tasty treat. Instead, it comes from the hunt for receipts, the recognition of handwriting, family folklore, ephemera, and the *new* learning they inspire. Over the last 16 years, I've had the pleasure of making my great-grandmother Rose's cinnamon rolls with some of my very favorite people. The first time, I was a sous chef for my paternal grandfather Bob.

Just into my second-year teaching, he thought it would be the perfect time to teach a newly pregnant morning-sick educator on spring break (me 16 years back) to make his mother (my Scandinavian Great Grandmother) Rose's cinnamon rolls.

His task was lofty, as I had never made bread from scratch. We began standing in his kitchen shoulder to shoulder. It was a foreign and familiar place. The kitchen was a place I'd not spent a lot of time in as a child. I was often in other rooms with cousins, laughing or playing games. Now alone, cooking, with Grandpa. The only time I think that ever happened—he was constantly on the move, and so was I. But here we were.

Before my arrival, he'd laid eggs to rest at room temp and had bowls waiting and ready. As he pulled out the last ingredients, I marveled over images of our shared family on the fridge. Though we are all now adults, our likenesses were in their tweens; some cousins were still infants in this parallel universe of Polaroid snaps and yearbook photos. These smiling younger versions of my family (I'm one of 18 cousins) listened along as Grandpa talked through different bread-making recipes. We eventually decided on his favorite, a modified version of his mother's recipe. Jotting the recipe step by step, I wrote the ingredients and Gramps' recommendations on a yellow legal pad. We made the dough with lukewarm water. "*Test the water with your fingers; make sure it's not too hot.*" So, I poured the water and milk in but worried about whether the yeast survived. While we baked, I absent-mindedly smudged the paper with oil and butter. Nowadays, the spotted yellow parchment is more of a Mad Libs–style game than a sure way to bake. Each time we make it, we try to fill in portions of the recipe that are now transparent with age and grease.

Now, I bake alongside my nearly 15-year-old son (August, named after Grampa's father). These days, we read from a photocopy of the old recipe in my kitchen, where the fridge is adorned with different faces. It's been 8 years since my paternal grandfather Bob passed away. August never made the rolls with Gramps, but he is willing to bake with me on occasion, and that's when my joy overflows.

One evening last spring, we (my son and I) began baking cinnamon rolls together, laying out eggs so they would warm to room temperature. When we couldn't make out the cursive on the recipe, we interpreted what was there, used ingredients on hand, and experimented while following the same yellow, oil-spotted recipe (See more about filling in the blanks in family recipes at https://onborrowedthyme.com/connecting-with-my-ancestors-through-their-recipes/, 2023). We made a double batch. One iteration had more salt (a tablespoon by mistake), and another had wheat flour rather than white, as an attempt at Gramps' ½ and ½ suggestion. We cracked the eggs, doubled the yeast, added lukewarm water, and stirred. Kneaded and covered. Set in a plastic dish and let both rise in the sun for a few hours.

Later, we brought the loaves inside the house, punched them down, and put the kitchen towel–covered bowls back on the counter to rise again. When we finally remembered them, three times in size, we floured the kitchen table and rolled out the dough, cutting it in half.

August and I added the butter/sugar/spice mixture, cut up fruit (see recipes). We rushed to bake a batch, hoping to have the rolls ready before bed. Cutting them 1 and ½ inches across, cinnamon rolls sliced and in the oven at 350 degrees. Delicious? Nope. Our first batch of oversalted late-night cinnamon rolls came out hard as rocks. They were awful. They looked good and had the proper formatting (but something needed to be fixed somewhere along the way).

Exasperated, I left the rest of the dough to rise in the trays covered with a kitchen towel and would return in the morning. When I woke, they had twice increased in size. The little rolls were fluffy and aromatic after 20 minutes of baking, and their little sugar crystals sparkled. When the rolls came out crispy (thanks to egg wash), I made cream cheese frosting from my maternal grandma Jackie's Carrot Cake recipe (see recipes at the end of this chapter). The resulting collaboration was tasty and set a high bar for future bread rolls. What was the difference between these batches' overall success?

One effort was allowed to rise.

Rise is what well-prepared, *resting* yeast bread will do. The second batch of rolls Rose (capitalized for its significance in the recipe, and as my family name). We quasi-successfully followed my grandma Rose's methods through Gramps' instructions—but we made something altogether new. This second batch came out crooked and bursting with fruit. They were ugly, much sweeter, fruity-delicious (Gramps recommended thinly cutting up an apple before rolling up the cinnamon/butter/sugar mixture to stay moist), and apples spilled out from the roll's center, looking more like flowers (see recipe).

In the last year of teaching, months of doctor's visits, and even this cooking adventure—I'd rushed around trying so hard to please I'd forgotten to take a moment to reflect on the gifts (or ingredients) that made me and allow myself to rise. The lack of time to Rise. That was lesson one from the rolls.

Upon this realization, it struck me that "R.I.S.E." was also a strategy my business professional father (who only recently I got to bake the cinnamon rolls for) taught me—stressed out?—need to "manage your managers"? R.I.S.E. is what comes to mind with distressed students and me when anxiety takes over. My father taught me to Reflect or was it Relax (I could never do both at once), Insulate, Say "Ah" (in relief, or as an internal expletive), and Empathize. He told me that these strategies allowed him to say the hard things, share the difficult moments, and make it through. I'd not given myself the chance to R.I.S.E.

Like those first rolls, I'd taken in too much salt, tried to "make it" too quickly, and came out hardened inside. My early baking/and academic mistakes allowed me to reflect, revise, and (m)bake it differently the next time. I'll first consider my family's (academic and historical) recommendations.

Getting the rolls there—took some artistry. Gramps' experience allowed him to share some of his favorite bread-making recommendations. He suggested adding two packets of yeast to make lighter, fluffier bread. Like the recipe's recommendation—I suspect I need to double more of my *active ingredients*, in this case, *joy*, which helps grow everything around it.

The rolls, were they really that good? In experience and gifts of learning, yes. There are several things I learned while making these cinnamon rolls with my son. These ideas run parallel to my experience in the academy: (1) A recipe (like life) will never be linear; (2) It will always have twists and turns, so why not make a double batch?; (3) No matter how bad it turns out, the fun or learning gained was worth it; and, (4) The leftovers (in food or knowledge) were more than enough to share. This cinnamon roll recipe tethers me to my ancestral past and connects my son and my daughter to their future worlds—as part of the creative process. I may not be a chef of note at this point in my career. Still, I'm committed to letting ideas, and the joy from collective recipes R.I.S.E.

Inspired by this process, I share a recipe, as extended method from which to bake, amend, and rework. Through the making, the baker communicates or learns the ingredients that grew them. We might call the result a genealogy of memory. A process as old as baking, of creating one piece to feed many. A conglomerate built from history, emotion, and community. That feels important.

I still don't like to cook, but I will continue to hone the skill. I have fallen in love with my family's nostalgia and instead seek truth through investigation. By making recipes (or academic articles), taking notes, and sharing what I've learned, I'll encourage others to play with their family/academic recipes and add on. To wonder with histories and recognize the need to R.I.S.E. while leaving RECIPES behind for future generations.

Dialogue for Dessert

Meals bind us through familiar textures, smells, and flavors. Told as food stories, the genealogy of this author's recipes forms a collective family history (served here as cardamom-infused strawberry-rhubarb cinnamon rolls), sprinkled with nostalgia and frosted with cream cheese frosting.

As I recount this tale, and my initial failures to rise, I work to develop a healthier balance of ingredients for the next iteration. I'm learning to value my ancestral offerings as knowledge passed across multiple generations, but likely fallible (just as our forefathers' research provides us with literature for inspiration and critical analysis in the academy). In the re-making, the telling-again, I recognize the need to revision and assessment, striving to meet the needs of our time.

As future academic years progress, I will privilege not only investments of time and attention essential to teaching, service, and research but will recall at once where I come from . . . in the kitchen, academy, and home. I'll continue to weave in ingredients that tell a story in reverence through image, recipe, and reading recommendation. You've just read an anecdote that serves as unconventional reflexive journal. Each component helps us mark the time: a time to let things rest, and another to envision. Then, energized, we rise up and take action.

A recipe is nothing more than a lesson plan, a direction you can begin—a starting point to add to, just like an academic framework or a methods class. The recipes and lessons I'm best at are ones I've made repeatedly. I've revised or modified these pieces and gotten to the point where I don't need the paper copy because I understand the measure. I've practiced, put in the work, and developed strategies to let it prove to R.I.S.E. and to extend.

For me, revisiting the original recipe to find the primary source is important. Reference check it like you would the receipts we are left in from modern media. Some ingredients and recipes are best left in the past. The assessment of the work and the outcome is fallible without the human component—the reviewer's taste. The ingredients may be insignificant independently (just as any theory, framework, or scholarship may be alone), but collectively, they make magic.

I'm working to find beauty in the process of making. It's not enough to marvel at how the food tastes, but at the care that went into it. It is significant when we share a meal with someone. I hope that, in time and space, this becomes a co-constructed meal.

Cooking connects many of us to family and community. Breaking bread at the kitchen to the table, and savoring the flavor, while exploring individual interests. The time to bake, to cook for more than warmth and sustenance, is a significant privilege. I return to ask: Are these hand-me-downs or genealogies of thought?

My answer is still rising. Let's continue on as sociologists who learn from dinner time ethnographies. Sitting close, we can marvel together over the loopy recipe handwriting, offer modifications for accessibility/interest, and work together to meet a need or reach a goal. Each recipe we build together becomes a shared page of decisions and outcomes, of collective opportunities to rise.

Since baking with my grandpa, we've moved to a new state, and I'm a few years into college teaching. As an early elementary teacher turned teacher-educator, I still dabble in creative storytelling (MO state champion, 1998); only my audience has shifted in size and purpose. I learn from missteps in daily encounters in the classroom and academy, just as I do when my rolls fail to rise. I look to moments of livingness to remind me of the precious learning that comes from time to rest. I draw parallels in my early career academic growth.

The chance to write and reflect for joy. To learn through the messages our food stories send. I took this opportunity to share a story—and tell it strangely.

I hope some portion of this chapter will offer you a new or accessible metaphor. Others can use the same template (RECIPEs) to create wildly different outcomes: (R)eflect/Relax and mirror the response, (E)mpathize—sharing emotional connection, (C)larify—what was said, heard, and, (I)ntentions that were understood, (P)araphrase shared learning from the adventure (include both highs and lows), (E)xplore new avenues and lines of flight, (S)ynthesize by working through iterations—or charting the next steps.

Then, other educators and committed culinary academics can reframe possibilities for future action through their own new conceptions (or concoctions). This is a tale of cooking and academic inconsistency; how lacking experience can lead to wild innovations and dangerous (or unappetizing) failures. But I feel my cooking helps me see metaphors in other things.

I hope the seasonings caught your fancy and the ideas folded in were appealing enough to let the flavors linger. In the coming week, I'll encourage you to jot down a recipe or two (metaphorical or not) and share the joys of breaking bread and breaking long-held biases, too. Such confidence requires practice, some missteps, and if we let it R.I.S.E. we grow in community and share our knowledge outward; that's enough.

Recipes

Recipes for Making Bread. "Try them all, as these are favorites."

— Gramps R.

Swedish Cardamom Bread
(Sweet & Festive Breads, N.D.)

- Two packages of active dry yeast
  ("I almost always use two packets of yeast. It's quicker and produces a lighter bread." Gramps R., 2008).
- ¼ cup warm water
- 2¼ cup warm milk
- ¾ cup butter or margarine melted and cooled
- One egg
- ½ teaspoon salt
- One cup sugar

- 1½ teaspoon cardamom (Gramps says, "I use whole pea-sized ground")
- 7½ cups of all-purpose flour

Dissolve yeast in water and milk. Add butter, egg, salt, and cardamom, gradually mixing in the many cups of flour. Turn the dough onto a floured surface and knead until smooth (Grandpa cut the dough into three pieces). He'd add a few drops of yellow food coloring. This first batch was the cardamom braid dyed yellow to resemble a Challah.

Gramps would brush it with an egg bath, allow a bit of time to rise near the oven under a clean kitchen towel, and bake it at 350 until done. Then, he'd roll out the other two-thirds of the dough into a large rectangle with plans for creating cinnamon rolls/buns or braids then add an extraordinary mixture of delight. For a variation, stir in some brown sugar and butter and heavily sprinkle cinnamon, cardamom, and nutmeg.

Grampa Bob's variation favors apples and cinnamon sugar. Slice Granny Smith apples into tiny slices and lay them flat alongside the center of the rolled rectangle of dough 2 inches from the edge. Fold and roll. Add nuts or raisins. Make frosting if you wish.

Bri's iteration (with rhubarb, strawberries, and cream cheese frosting): Slice the fruits extra thin and spread them alongside the inside of the roll, as you would in a pie filling. Add a layer of cinnamon sugar and cardamom. (Cover when they start getting bubbly and making jelly/caramelized sugar.) Bake until done. Then, when cooled, add frosting.

Grandma Jackie's Cream Cheese Frosting:
Ingredients:
½ cup butter, softened
½ pound cream cheese, softened
4 cups confectioners' sugar
1 teaspoon vanilla extract
(optional 1 cup pecans)

Combine butter or margarine, cream cheese, confectioners' sugar, and 1 teaspoon of vanilla in a medium mixing bowl. Mix until smooth and creamy. Refrigerate when done, OR make in massive amounts, freeze, and stash smaller amounts in the freezer for later. I froze what we didn't use for future baking projects. What can you use it on? Banana bread with cream cheese frosting, cinnamon rolls, birthday cake—cream cheese frosting is like a mixed methodology appropriate for any breakfast bread or pastry dish (see recipes).

References

Merriam-Webster. (n.d.). *When a recipe was a 'receipt.'* Merriam-Webster. https://www.merriam-webster.com/.

Pitts, B. R. (2020). *Black history month in suburban schools: An examination of K-12 pedagogies* (27964129) [Doctoral dissertation, University of Wisconsin - Madison]. ProQuest Dissertations Publishing.

Smith, C. (2022). *How the word is passed: a reckoning with the history of slavery across America.* Bay Back Books, Little, Brown and Company.

CHAPTER 17

Pedagogies of Maíz: Living Ancestral Saberes and Cultivating Relational Teaching and Learning Practices

MARIAL QUEZADA

Introduction

According to Western science, more than 7,000 years ago peoples Indigenous to what is today known as Central México first cultivated maíz, a plant that relies on human intervention to help with its germination, creating co-dependency between corn and humans (Rodríguez, 2014). Today, many Indigenous peoples and their descendants across Abya Yala, a word the Guna people use to refer to the American continent (Keme & Coon, 2018), and Turtle Island, the ancestral name for what now is called North America, sustain relationships with maíz, planting, growing, harvesting, and cooking with it, passing on its stories and teachings, as well as gratitude for it (Rodríguez, 2014). Maíz teaches us about the history and continuity of Indigenous lands, its original peoples, and lifeways (Rodríguez, 2014). Maíz also teaches us about relationality, the interconnectedness of all beings and reciprocal relations (Wilson, 2008), offering valuable lessons applicable to teaching and learning.

In "Our Sacred Maíz Is Our Mother," through storytelling, the late Roberto Cintli Rodriguez (2014) demonstrates how maíz has always been much more than sustenance for people of Mesoamerica; "Corn was also what they were made of, where they came from, what they lived for, and how they counted time" (Rodriguez, 2014, p. 159). Through narratives highlighting these relationships with maíz, documented in oral and written forms such as rock paintings, creation stories, and songs and dances, Rodriguez traces the migration and the persistence of "maíz culture" over time and across the continent (Rodríguez, p. 161). Highlighting stories told by Mesoamerican elders, he points to how people who are Indigenous to so-called America have maintained sacred covenants as well as daily interactions with corn for millennia. Rodriguez contends, as does Bonfill Batalla (1996), that corn helps to tell a story of the continuity of culture and the survivance (Vizenor, 2008) of Mesoamerican peoples, despite multiple and overlapping colonialisms (Blackwell et al., 2017). This chapter builds on the work of Rodríguez (2014), focusing on maíz teachings within the context of education.

In the pages that follow, I trace my journey as a learner and teacher educator while restoring my relationship with maíz and its/my ancestral homelands in Central México and the knowledges that flow from them, which, in just one generation in my family, began to dramatically diminish. Centering on Indigenous intellectual traditions, I recognize stories as theories and data (Brayboy, 2005), and that stories in all their diverse forms are important tools for teaching (Archibald, 2008; Burgess, 2013) and play a vital role in Indigenous survivance (Morrill & Sabzalian, 2022; Vizenor, 2008). Engaging Archibald's (2008) storywork and Tachine & Nicolazzo's (2022) "storyweaving," I offer stories about what I've learned through pedagogical encounters with maíz. I draw from my memories and family stories of my abuelo "Wello," who cultivated in me a deep desire to remain connected with maíz, our relatives, and knowledges from the ancestral territories of the P'urhepecha people in present-day Michoacán. I also draw from my experiences and reflections while becoming a teacher educator and participating in a Coahuiltecan community-led teacher education program, Tānko Institute: Xinachtli Pedagogy for Educators.

Grounded in what maíz has taught me, my family, community, and ancestors for over millennia, I share how maíz shapes my philosophy and pedagogy as a teacher educator. Drawing on ancestral and "familia and comunidad-based saberes" (Urrieta, 2013), or knowledges, that that may have been "disrupted and replaced" by colonialism (McCarty & Lee, 2014, p. 103), land education (Tuck et al., 2014) and Indigenous elder, abuela/o, or grandparent epistemologies (Archibald, 2008; Gonzales, 2014; Muñoz, 2019; Rodríguez, 2014; Urrieta & Martinez, 2011), I highlight lessons I've learned from maíz and my abuelo, honoring them as my first teachers. Recognizing that these saberes have historically been unseen by/within the whitestream (Grande, 2015) academy, from K-12 to teacher education, it is my hope that this chapter inspires Latinx, Indigenous Latinx, and other non-Anglo educators to (re)consider what we have seen and learned about teaching and learning within our families, from our abuelo/as, elders, and our "more-than-human" teachers (Nxumalo, 2021).

The Gift of Maíz

My earliest memories of maíz are shucking corn as a young girl with my abuelo, "Wello," when he came to visit in the summer. We would sit together on the patio by my mom's garden in unceded Wampanoag and Massachusett lands peeling ears for what felt like hours. Watching his weathered hands and following his lead to remove the husks and silks, we would occasionally whisper back and forth in English and Spanish. Later, after grilling the corn, I would sit across from my Wello in awe as he would eat ear, after ear, after ear of corn while I tried to keep up with counting how many he had consumed. According to my father, my Wello could eat as many as 10 ears of corn in one sitting. Until he passed, my Wello, a strong and slim man from Jaramutaro, "el lugar de las cuevas," or "the place of caves," in P'urhepecha, known in Spanish, as La Piedad, Michoacán, maintained his appetite (for corn). My Wello loved maíz and he passed on his love to me.

My Wello grew up along the Rio Lerma, where present-day Jalisco meets Michoacán and Guanajuato harvesting maíz, camote, and other crops in the milpa and raising animals. He grew up eating tortillas, corundas, atole puscua, elote, among other traditional dishes made with corn prepared by the women in our lineage, who continue to pass on these foodways. Through the Bracero program, along with millions of men from predominantly Central and Southern Mexico, in the 1940s my Wello and Tio Jose were recruited by the U.S. government and encouraged to leave behind their families and homelands to work with short-term labor visas in the United States. After travelling over a thousand miles north, crossing the Rio Bravo/Grande and colonial U.S./Mexican border from Ciudad Juarez to El Paso, they were greeted with a shower of chemicals to clean "los indios sucios." Temporarily, my Wello would transition from cultivating crops in the milpa in Michoacán under the sun to laying the railroad tracks across the lands of so-called Texas, under a boss who threatened him with a gun. After carrying out months of "spirit-murdering" (Love, 2019) and back-breaking labor, like countless others poached from their homelands to build "the American dream," my Wello had to return to Michoacán. Years later, guided by my Tio Jose, my Wello made his way to so-called Connecticut to work in a steel factory. When he wasn't working with metal, he found a way to work with the land. Behind the home in which he lived with my Wella, father, and tía, he created a milpa where he grew corn, chiles, and more. According to my Wella, my Wello loved to grow, cook, and eat corn as much as he liked to gift it to friends and family, who would turn it into tamales or tortillas to share.

While my Wello did not have the chance to complete primary school nor the opportunity to learn how to write, my Wello embodied literacies of the land from which he/we come (Styres, 2018), saberes that most U.S. schools do not teach. Even after my Wello was extracted and separated from his/our ancestral homelands, he remained connected to the land through corn. My Wello's story tells of the survivance of his/our relationship with maíz, one that we maintain not to contribute to a capitalist colonial system that commodifies it, but rather to provide sustenance for our families and to ensure the continuance of our culture. My Wello taught me that maíz is a gift that teaches about who we are, from where we come, and offers guidance for where I/we are going.

Maíz as Metaphor

Three years ago, as I began a doctoral program in Cultural Studies in Education at the University of Texas at Austin, I also began working with Indigenous Cultures Institute (ICI), a nonprofit organization located in so-called central Texas founded by Dr. Mario Garza and Maria Rocha, members of the Miakan Garza Band of Coahuiltecans. I've since helped launch and develop ICI's teacher education program, the Tānko Institute: Xinachtli Pedagogy for Educators, and I currently serve as the Director of the Institute as well as its affiliated youth program. Coordinating these Indigenous community-led programs while completing graduate school helps me to recall, recognize, and remain rooted in the saberes that the lands, waters, and our communities have always offered us.

For two decades, members of Miakan Garza Band of Coahuiltecans along with Carlos Aceves and Lucia Carmona, co-founders of the Raices del Saber Xinachtli Community School, dreamt of, prayed for, and labored to develop the Tānko Institute (M. Rocha, personal communication, February 2024). The Tānko Institute consists of a 3-day annual summer institute and ongoing learning community for P-20 teachers and community educators guided and facilitated by elders. The Institute introduces educators to Indigenous pedagogy known as Xinachtli, which draws on Coahuiltecan, Maya, and Mexica philosophy and knowledge and has been developed by Nahuatlaca elder Carlos Aceves over the past 25 years. Tānko is a Coahuilteco word that means "to teach" and Xinachtli is a Nahuatl concept meaning "the moment a seed germinates," representing the pedagogy's view of children and learners as sprouting seeds full of infinite possibilities (Aceves, 2004). The Xinachtli pedagogy draws on learners' cultural heritages, existing knowledge bases, and the lessons from the natural world; it recognizes potential in each learner and that everything and everyone has gifts to offer and cultivate.

Through the training in the Xinachtli pedagogy, Maestro Carlos Aceves highlights the power of metaphors (Aceves, 2008). Metaphors, which have long been used as a tool for teaching by Indigenous peoples, offer a way to interpret, cope with, and create a renewed sense of understanding of our reality (Aceves, 2008). As told in many creation stories and as taught by my Wello, corn is a gift to humans that requires our intervention. Corn seeds must be removed from the ear of the corn before being planted in the ground. Corn embodies a "millennial interrelationship" (Bonfill Batalla, 1996, p. 12) between human and "more-than-human" life (Nxumalo, 2021). Similar to Xinachtli, the P'urhepecha word "andarani" refers to the moment maíz germinates (Tejeda Alvarado, 2019, p. 182). Viewing students as kernels of sprouting maíz highlights the duality of teaching and learning and reciprocity that naturally exists between us as educators and learners. It also underscores an approach to teaching that diverges from a banking model of education (Freire, 1970/2007) in which teaching is viewed a transactional transfer of knowledge from a teacher to student. As humans depend on maíz and maíz depends on humans, I depend on my students as they depend on me. This approach also understands that knowledge is created learning from and with each other, it is co-constructed, continuous, and takes place in community (Cajete, 1994). While we educators may help facilitate the growth of our students, as seeds, they inherently possess the ability to transform, and in turn help us to do the same.

(Re)Learning to Grow Maíz

On the final day of the first-ever Tanko Institute: Xinachtli Pedagogy for Educators and marking the end to the first year of my doctoral program, Maestro Carlos Aceves gifted me heirloom corn. "Do you know how to plant it?" he asked. "I can learn," I responded, thinking of my Wello. In my younger years, it didn't occur to me to ask my Wello what he knew about planting and harvesting maíz. Now the first in my family to pursue a Ph.D., presented with the opportunity to grow maíz, I reflected on the saberes my Wello held, which my many years of academic training has never offered. Naming elder and abuelo/a epistemologies recognizes that knowledge grows with lived experiences and values our grandparents, who often serve as some of our first and foremost educators (Gonzales, 2014; Muñoz, 2019; Urrieta & Martinez, 2011). This perspective is at odds with the academy, which locates knowledge in "experts," researchers, teachers, professors who have studied an academic discipline. While elder epistemologies continue to be undervalued, delegitimized, and subtracted by Western institutions, Indigenous peoples have long understood elders as knowledge keepers and teachers (Gonzales, 2014).

My siblings and I didn't grow up sembrando y cultivando maíz like my Wello. We grew up consuming ears of corn and tortillas made of genetically modified maíz purchased from supermarkets, disconnected from the growing process. During college, thanks to friends and family in the so-called U.S. Southwest, I was introduced to a variety of Indigenous corn dishes including Hopi piki bread from the four corners region, blue corn frybread from the Navajo-owned food truck on the way back from Zuni, blue corn mush made by my Mama Moone outside their hogan near Shiprock, giant tamales made by Mama Coriz for Kewa Pueblo feast days or selling, and hearty handmade tortillas made by Fan and Gamber on the Pima rez. These encounters with maíz and the memories of my Wello motivated me to (re)learn my family's maíz foodways. Eventually, I began cooking with maíz and masaharina (nixtamalized corn flour) and sharing baked goods made of maíz. On the final day of the Tanko Institute that first year, when I gifted Maestro Carlos blue corn cookies, he gifted me seeds that set me on the journey of (re)learning how to grow maíz and cultivating a relational teaching philosophy and practice that is rooted in my ancestral saberes.

Our elders or grandparents are not only holders of Indigenous knowledges, they also actively pass the knowledge on, covertly, overtly, and strategically (Gonzales, 2014; Muñoz, 2018; Urrieta & Martinez, 2011). They don't just "keep traditions, they teach traditions" (Gonzales, 2014, p. 44). Mexican elders, even when having encountered multiple forms of colonialism, the imposition of language, religion, and values maintain Indigenous practices in their daily lives, which they teach in various ways (Bonfil Batalla, 1996; Gonzales, 2014). Elders and grandparents play an important role as educators in maintaining and passing on "familia and comunidad-based saberes" and Indigenous ways of knowing, outside of colonial institutions (Urrieta, 2013).

In "Decolonize Your Diet: Plant-based Mexican American Recipes for Health and Healing," Luz Calvo and Catrióna Rueda Esquibel (2015) highlight the importance of speaking with and learning from our elders: "Talk to elders in your community about the foods they ate growing up: What foods did they eat then that are no longer available? How was food prepared? What herbs and plants did they use for medicine? How did they conduct their ceremonies?" (p. 38). Reclaiming and living these knowledges can restore our health as well as our relationships with our communities, including the land. Becoming conscious of how colonialism shapeshifts and shapes the saberes that are passed on (or not) within our families, by growing maíz, I am relearning and revaluing the saberes of my Wello, my family, and my ancestors, so that I may encourage my students to consider the same.

Cultivating Relational Teaching and Learning Practices

On a recent visit to Jaramutaro, driving from Guadalajara, approaching the municipality, there are no signs of maíz, only seas of agave. While milpas are increasingly less visible, maíz manifests in the city murals and in the dishes eaten by the community and served in the homes of my family. Entering the ranch on the outskirts of the city across from the river and at the foot of Cerro Cuajuarto, in P'urhepecha meaning "el cerro de arena," or the "hill of sand," the streets are lined with rows of agave while the sign overhead reads "Cultivadores de Maíz." If you venture on foot down the dirt roads, tucked behind the homes, you will find the corn stalks that still remain standing, united, amidst a blanket of blue-green. Inside the home of one of my primas we sat and listened as she shared that the harvest yields less and less corn each year. She reminisced about memories of the river when it was overflowing and when they used to eat by its shores. These days, she said, as the river grows drier and the maíz harvest weaker, the agave along with the cartels seem to spread like wildfire. The commercialization of agave, exportation, and consumption of tequila have had a profound impact on the region. Family stories and storied maps document the expansion of blue agave and the threats that shifting waves of colonialism pose not only the continuation of maíz, but to life and lifeways that depend on it (Mejía Guadarrama, 2023).

Indigenous lands, which are home to 80% of our planet's biodiversity, face ongoing dispossession, extraction, and exploitation

(McCoy et al., 2020), contributing to the destruction of our planet and climate change. Indigenous lands moreover are home to nearly 70% of the planet's linguistic diversity and their emplaced knowledges (Gorenflo et al., 2021). Indigenous educators, scholars, and activists, including the elders teaching the Xinachtli pedagogy, highlight connections between the devastation of Indigenous lands, our planet, and the U.S. public school system, which is designed to prepare students to participate in the capitalist society (McCoy et al. 2020). To address this, Indigenous scholars highlight the importance of land education, which centers on Indigenous ontologies (ways of being) and epistemologies (knowledges), "including Indigenous understandings of land, Indigenous language in relation to land, and Indigenous critiques of settler colonialism" to disrupt capitalist notions of land as property (Tuck et al. 2014, p. 13). Moreover, they insist on revitalizing education models based on "Indigenous systems of relationality" (McCoy et al., p. 4). These models, they contend, will instead prepare young people to tend to the land, community, and each other, moving us away from a system based on independence and competition towards one of collective responsibility. They will move us from a system based on rationality and progress towards one of wellbeing and growth, and from a system based on separation from nature towards one of interdependence and connectedness (McCoy et al., 2020). These scholars insist that we must work together to reimagine and reconstruct approaches to education that will strengthen the wellbeing of *all* people and our planet, helping to move from a society based on "extraction, competition, and waste, to one based on mutual respect, support and sustainability" (McCoy et al., 2020, p.6).

Students at the Raíces del Saber Xinachtli community school learn to grow corn, harvest it, study it, cook with it, and prepare and share food made of maíz with their families. Visiting Raices with Tānko Institute educators last year, we observed one maestro lead a science and math lesson with the fourth graders on atole. Students were asked to research atole recipes, record, and share back what they found. They were instructed to discuss among themselves any knowledge they had of other recipes or experiences preparing or drinking it. After listening to the students share what they found from their desktop research and their existing knowledge, the maestro asked if any of the students have heard of or had blue corn mush. They then told a story about Navajo blue corn mush, highlighting foodways and practices shared by Indigenous peoples across the continent and the differences between it and atole. That evening, the students were encouraged to go home to seek stories from their families to bring back and share with the class.

Conclusion

Knowledge rooted in the land, families, and ancestors of Latinx, Indigenous Latinx, and other non-Anglo students (and teachers) has historically been unseen by/within the academy, from K-12 to teacher education. It is my hope that this chapter plants and waters seeds for learners and educators to remember, acknowledge, and share the lessons gleaned from our first and foremost relations and teachers, including the "more-than-human" (Nxumalo, 2021), such as corn, as we cultivate our approaches to teaching and learning. Maíz is a gift that for millennia has nourished my family, community, and ancestors as we have nourished it. Maíz is much more than food, maiz is metaphor, a vessel of ancestral saberes, and a teacher of reciprocal relationships. Rather than striving to produce and consume the latest teaching method, or filling "a gap" in teacher education research, how can we as educators build on what has always nurtured us? How do we respectfully recognize and learn from and with millennial Indigenous teaching and learning traditions? How do we cultivate teaching and learning practices based in Indigenous systems of relationality?

On the final day of the Tānko Institute this year, during a workshop organized with Luna Vela from the Neighborhood Molino, participants shared maiz stories from their childhood, encountered different varieties of maíz, the nixtamlization process, and how to make masa and tortillas. Some of us had the opportunity to use a metate to grind the corn into masa. For me, this was a first and deeply moving experience through which I reconnected with maíz in an at once ancient and new way. At the end the workshop, Luna gifted me leftover masa made from maiz azul.

The next day, I spent hours reflecting on the institute and (re) learning how to make an ancestral food made with maíz known as corundas. Where my family comes in Michoacán, corundas are triangular-shaped tamales wrapped in green corn leaves. I had been wanting to make corundas for a while, and after being gifted masa the day prior, I accepted what I was presented. While the maíz I had been trying to grow in a maceta, now for a third year, was likely not going to give ears of corn, it had leaves to offer.

(Re)learning to grow corn while becoming a teacher educator, I have learned that no siempre "se cosecha lo que se siembra," you don't always "reap what you sow," or in other words, every seed we plant may not grow. When I planted maíz for the first time, the stalks barely grew. The second year, the sun scorched some of the crop and I harvested just a handful of malnourished mazorcas. This third year, making corundas, I was reminded that growing maíz is much more than a "successful" harvest, it's full of little lessons, including unexpected ones, along the way.

References

Aceves, C. (2004). The Xinachtli Project: Transforming Whiteness through mythic pedagogy. *Counterpoints, 273*, 257–277.

Aceves, C. (2008). Undoing Whiteness in the classroom: Critical educultural teaching approaches for social justice activism, *Counterpoints, 321*, 237–253.

Archibald J.-A. (2008). *Indigenous storywork: Educating the heart mind body and spirit*. UBC Press.

Blackwell, M., Boj Lopez, F., & Urrieta, L. (2017). Special issue: Critical Latinx indigeneities. *Latino Studies, 15*(2), 126–137. https://doi.org/10.1057/s41276-017-0064-0

Bonfil Batalla, G. (1996). *México profundo: Una civilización negada*. Grijalbo.

Brayboy, B. M. J. (2005). Toward a tribal critical race theory in education. *The Urban Review, 37*(5), 425–446. https://doi.org/10.1007/s11256-005-0018-y.

Burgess P. (2013). Building the beloved community: A life practice. *Hulili: Multidisciplinary Research on Hawaiian Well-being, 9*, 11–34.

Çajete, G. (1994). *Look to the mountain: An ecology of Indian education*. Kivaki Press.

Calvo, L., & Rueda Esquibel, C. (2015). *Decolonize your diet: plant-based Mexican-American recipes for health and healing*. Arsenal Pulp Press.

Freire, P. (1970/2007). *Pedagogy of the oppressed*. (M. B. Ramos, Trans.). Continuum.

Gonzales, S. M. (2014). *Abuelita* epistemologies: Counteracting subtractive schools in American education. *Journal of Latinos and Education, 14*(1), 40–54. https://doi.org/10.1080/15348431.2014.944703.

Gorenflo, L., Romaine, S., Mittermeier, R., & Walker-Painemilla, K. (2012). Co-occurrence of linguistic and biological diversity in biodiversity hotspots and high biodiversity wilderness areas. *Proceedings of the National Academy of Sciences of the United States of America, 109*, 8032–8037. 10.1073/pnas.1117511109.

Grande, S. (2015). *Red pedagogy: Native American social and political thought* (Tenth anniversary). Rowman and Littlefield.

Keme, E., & Coon, A.W. (2018). For Abiayala to live, the Americas must die: Toward a transhemispheric indigeneity. *Native American and Indigenous Studies, 5*, 42–68.

Love, B. L. (2019). *We want to do more than survive: Abolitionist teaching and pursuing educational freedom*. Beacon Press.

McCarty, T., & Lee, T. (2014). Critical culturally sustaining/revitalizing pedagogy and indigenous education sovereignty. *Harvard Educational Review, 84*(1), 101–124. https://doi.org/10.17763/haer.84.1.q83746nl5pj34216.

McCoy, M., Elliot-Groves, E., Sabzalian, L., and Bang, M. (2020). Restoring indigenous systems of elationality. Center for Humans & Nature: Expanding Our Natural & Civic Imagination. https://humansandnature.org/restoring-indigenous-systems-of-relationality/.

Mejía Guadarrama, L. (2023, October, 21). *La expansión del cultivo del agave azul en el municipio de La Piedad, Michoacán*. https://storymaps.arcgis.com/stories/8f5d679e50a74fd1b2206cdde12e2ee9.

Morrill, A., & Sabzalian, L. (2022). Survivance-based inquiries in and beyond the academy. In A. R. Tachine & Z. Nicolazzo (Eds.), *Weaving an otherwise: Reframing qualitative research through relational lenses* (pp. 29–43). Stylus Publishing.

Muñoz, M. (2019). River as border, river as lifeblood: Troubling the irreconcilable discrepancies of colonial occupation from/with/on/of the Frontera. In L. T. Smith, E. Tuck, & W.K. Yang (Eds.), *Indigenous and Decolonizing Studies in Education* (pp. 62–81). Routledge.

Nxumalo, F. (2021). Decolonial water pedagogies: Invitations to Black, indigenous, and Black indigenous world-making. *Occasional Paper Series*. 2021. 10.58295/23753668.1390.

Rodríguez, R. C. (2014). *Our sacred maíz is our mother: Indigeneity and belonging in the Americas*. University of Arizona Press.

Styres, S. (2018). Literacies of land: Decolonizing narratives, storying, and literature. In L.T. Smith et al. (Eds.) *Indigenous and decolonizing studies in education* (pp. 24–37). Routledge.

Tachine, A. R., & Nicolazzo, Z. (2023). *Weaving an otherwise: In-relations methodological practice*. Taylor and Francis. https://doi.org/10.4324/9781003448648

Tejeda Alvarado, F. (2019). *El Lienzo de Jucutacato. Códice Postcortesiano*. H. Camara de Diputados. http://biblioteca.diputados.gob.mx/janium/bv/ce/lxiv/liejuc_codpost.pdf.

Urrieta, L., Jr. (2013). Familia and comunidad-based saberes: Learning in an indigenous heritage community. *Anthropology & Education Quarterly, 44*(3), 320–335. https://doi.org/10.1111/aeq.12028.

Urrieta, L., Jr., & Martínez, S. (2011). Diasporic community knowledge and school absenteeism: Mexican immigrant pueblo parents' and grandparents' postcolonial ways of educating. *Interventions: International Journal of Postcolonial Studies, 13*, 256–277. 10.1080/1369801X.2011.573225.

Vizenor, G. (1999). *Manifest manners: Narratives on Postindian survivance.* University of Nebraska Press.

Wilson, S. (2008). *Research is ceremony: Indigenous research methods.* Fernwood Publishing.

CHAPTER 18

A Cross-Cultural Gastronomy: Feminist Narratives on Boundaries and Bridges

MILA ZHU

Taste of Transgression: A 12-Course Culinary Journey
July 1, 2024, at 7:30 PM
Jordan's Sweet Home in Texas

Amuse-Bouche: Intersectionality Infusion
Beetroot Carpaccio with Feta Mousse and Walnut Dust
Fresh Apple-Ginger Juice

Appetizer: Fluidity
Duo of Soufflés - Blue Cheese and Raspberry
Pomegranate Mint Spritzer

Soup: The Not-So-Melting Pot
Spicy Tom Yum with Mixed Seafood and Exotic Mushrooms
Lemongrass Coconut Water

Fish Course: Migration and Movement
Migrant Fish Stew
Citrus Cilantro Cooler

Salad: Rhizomatic Roots
Wild Herb and Edible Flower Salad with Pomegranate Dressing
Lavender Lemonade

Pasta: Weaving the Web of Society
Hand-cut Tagliatelle with Interwoven Flavors
Basil Watermelon Juice

Intermezzo: Essence of Equality
Lemon and Lavender Sorbet

Main Course: Deconstructed Identities
Deconstructed Ratatouille
Paired with Pinot Noir

Cheese Course: The Complexity of Mothering
Assorted Global Cheeses with Honeycomb
Pear and Sage Juice

Pre-Dessert: Sweet Equity
Miniature Dessert Sampler
Mixed Berry and Hibiscus Tea

Dessert: Anarchy of Flavors
Chaos Cake
Espresso Martini Mocktail

Digestif: Transcending Boundaries
A Flight of Herbal Infusions
Aromatic Herb Tisane

We cordially invite you to join us for an evening of exquisite flavors and profound conversations, where each course promises to challenge the palate and engage the mind.

This is So Quintessentially Kitty

I slip the invitation back into my backpack, poised to ring the bell at Jordan's sweet—strike that—scorching hot Texas home. Today marks another orbit around the sun for me, and what better way to celebrate than a reunion with this formidable trio of women. Here's a fun throwback—nine years ago, just before I defended my dissertation, I was navigating the freshly inked waters of divorce with a 9-month-old in tow. Aadhya eloquently described my situation as—her words, not mine—"jobless, degree-pending, miserably divorced with baby in arm." Seriously, someone ought to award that girl a medal for possessing the most hazardous tongue in human history. In a moment of vulnerability (which I'll deny if ever directly questioned), I rallied my three musketeers. Originally, this was purely self-serving: should anything happen to me, my baby would have not just godmothers but fierce—no, baddie—godmothers. Like many academic plans, though, it went awry. Instead of forming an emergency team, our meetings became something deeper: navigating life's storms with comforting food.

"Happy Birthday. I see you're one more year wiser now," Jordan teased as she swung open the door, the white dress she wore dancing in the breeze.

Jordan, blending Hong Kong and British heritage, has perfected her art with a DMA in Piano Performance. A married mother, she balances lofty personal goals with family duties. Her diverse background enriches her teaching, connecting cultures through music's universal language.

"Older, yes; wiser, debatable," I quipped, stepping in with the menu-themed invitation. "Seriously, how long would it take to prepare all this? We jet her in and put her straight to work—it's almost criminal."

Jordan's grin widened as she led me further inside. "She's organized with a flow chart for tonight; everything's under control."

"She," Kitty, has moved to Paris for a communication degree. From Tokyo, her vibrant spirit thrives amid her studies. Contrasting her male-dominated upbringing, she delves into Eurocentric philosophy, enriching her culinary and personal explorations. Choosing to remain unmarried and child free, Kitty fiercely maintains her independence, weaving her experiences into her creative and academic pursuits.

And there was the flow chart.

Once inside, I was immediately greeted by the whiteboard Jordan uses for her home-based music studio. I had genuinely thought *flow chart* was just one of Jordan's metaphorical flourishes. But no, there it was, in all its meticulously planned glory:

Kitty's Gastronomic Master Plan

1. Pre-Arrival Preparation (D-2)
   - Shopping: Sourcing fresh and exotic ingredients.
   - Pre-cooking: Slow-cooking broths, marinating proteins.
   - Sauces: Preparing advance dressings and sauces.
2. Day Before Arrival
   - Desserts and Breads: Baking and setting aside.
   - Vegetable Prep: Chopping and storing in labeled containers.
3. Day of Event
   - Morning Setup: Arranging kitchen stations for each course.
   - Afternoon Cook: Final preparations and cooking most dishes.
   - Evening Execution: Reheating, plating, and serving.
4. Post-Dinner
   - Cleanup: Organized with help from Jordan and Aadhya.
   - Relaxation: Enjoying leftovers and winding down with herbal teas.

"Right . . . that's staggering." I marveled at the flow chart, cross-checking it with the menu in hand. It just had to be Kitty.

"Hey, you, wrong place. This is an adult-only zone. We're serving wines tonight. Not age-appropriate," Aadhya quipped as she swept in from stage left, our longstanding inside joke. Years ago, when I first joined the faculty, Aadhya's excitement led her to accompany me for HR paperwork. All went smoothly until a mix-up at the campus police station, where a student worker demanded my class schedule, mistaking me for a freshman.

"I can't believe they thought you were a fresher," Aadhya teases without fail, "Should've sent you back to play school."

Here's to the forever-play-school Asian gene.

Aadhya, meaning "the first power," symbolizes resilience. Honored as Teacher of the Year, she navigates life as a first-generation Indian immigrant with degrees in Math and Math Education. Despite fertility challenges, she draws strength from her community, her students, and our unshakeable friendship.

"Happy Birthday!" Kitty exclaimed as she burst from the kitchen, waving one of my long-term cringe-inducers—Deleuze and Guattari. Today's provocative selection? *A Thousand Plateaus* (Deleuze & Guattari, 1987). Yes, that labyrinth of rhizomatic theory and bewildering jargon—fascinating to some, utterly baffling to others. Given the ubiquity of these authors at academic conferences, you'd think everyone would be dazzled by their poststructural antics. But here's a little secret at conferences: sometimes, we just pretend to grasp the concepts and ask questions that might not even be relevant, just to cover our bafflement.

Just imagine the following meme-worthy narrative that aims at capturing the sometimes-perplexing dynamics of session presentations:

> **Presenter:** Here's a Spicy Tom Yum I prepared!
> **Audience Member 1:** I hate spicy food. Why is this even here?
> **Audience Member 2:** Have you considered making a salad instead?
> **Audience Member 3:** How does this relate to the beetroot carpaccio?
> **Audience Member 4:** I haven't tried it, but let me suggest a few modifications.

Anyway, I eyed the book warily. I genuinely hoped our dinner tonight wasn't an experiment in deterritorialization. I sincerely prayed the designed menu had nothing to do with embodying chaos theory.

As I mulled this over, Kitty swept her hand dramatically, announcing, "Let's embark on our culinary odyssey." She unveiled the Amuse-Bouche: Beetroot Carpaccio with Feta Mousse and Walnut Dust. "This dish," she detailed, "features thinly sliced beetroot, its earthy tones lifted by airy feta mousse and a sprinkle of crushed walnut for crunch." She paused, adding, "The secret lies in marinating the beetroot in olive oil, balsamic vinegar, and a hint of orange zest, just long enough to tenderize while preserving its crispness."

As we each took a delicate plate, Kitty offered glasses of Fresh Apple-Ginger Juice, explaining, "More than a palate cleanser, this blend enhances the beetroot with its sharp sweetness and a ginger kick to awaken the senses."

I raised my hand, schoolgirl style.

"Yes, Miss Mila," Kitty acknowledged with a mock-serious nod.

"I thought we had declared this an adult-only zone, complete with wine pairings? Hypothetically speaking," I added, "I'd suggest Prosecco—for its light and fruity notes that dance so well with the earthy beetroot and the salty feta."

"About that," Jordan chimed in, draping an arm over my shoulders in a comradely fashion, "you'll get your fair dose of Pinot Noir with the main course. As for now, Kitty and I took the liberty of making an executive decision to moderate your wine intake—to spare us the full spectacle of your alcohol-induced loquaciousness in, say, about 30 minutes."

Ah, so here's another tale for you. During the dreaded dissertation slog—every grad student's rite of passage—I hit a monstrous writer's block. You know the type: sitting in front of the computer for hours, producing nothing but sighs. My dissertation committee chair, ever the innovator, suggested a remedy: social drinking. The plan? Invite peers over, imbibe just enough to blur the edges, then send them packing and get typing. She swore it was the slight weariness mixed with a buzz that would loosen my obsession with perfection and spur progress. And would you believe it? That absurd methodology worked wonders.

Just a tiny lingering side effect—I've been quite the talker post-vino ever since.

I groaned. As a single mother and junior faculty, such indulgences are rare, especially free from the delightful demands of a 9-year-old.

"Ladies, ready for a taste of Fluidity?" Kitty guided us to our seats, poised to introduce the next course, "Tonight features a Duo of Soufflés—Blue Cheese and Raspberry, celebrating life's harmonious contrasts."

She presented each plate, the soufflés standing tall. "The magic is in the egg whites' whip and precise timing," Kitty confided. "The robust blue cheese in one balances the sharp sweetness of the raspberry in the other." Accompanying the dish was a Pomegranate Mint Spritzer, its zest slicing through the richness to cleanse the palate.

I mused aloud, "A Riesling might be an intriguing pair—its sweetness could offset the sharp and tart flavors here."

Catching Aadhya's playful glare, I quickly added, "Hypothetically, of course."

"It reminds me of Hua Cheng and Xie Lian," Aadhya noted. "My high schoolers are obsessed with *Heaven Official's Blessing*" (Mò, 2021-2023).

"My students as well," Jordan added.

"I prefer the original Chinese novel," I admitted, grimacing slightly. "The English dub just doesn't capture its essence—it loses a lot in translation." I continued, "Yet, *Heaven Official's Blessing* excels as a medium to explore gender fluidity, echoing Butler's (1990) ideas on gender performativity. It challenges traditional gender norms and fosters important discussions on nonbinary identities, which is vital for promoting inclusivity and understanding of LGBTQ+ identities in education."

As we finished our spritzers, Kitty transitioned us to the next course with a playful grin, "Let's stir the pot a bit, shall we?" She unveiled "The Not-So-Melting Pot," her twist on classic Spicy Tom Yum. "This is a fusion of traditional Thai spices and a bounty of seafood and exotic mushrooms, each bite bursting with flavor." She detailed the soup's base: a rich broth infused with lemongrass, galangal, and kaffir lime leaves, enhanced by plump shrimp, delicate scallops, and tender squid, finished with a kick of chili oil.

She pointed to our drinks, "And to complement the fiery Tom Yum, we have Lemongrass Coconut Water—its soothing sweetness will temper the heat."

"Any 'hypothetical' wine pairings?" Jordan teased.

I leaned in, "Gewürztraminer—its spicy profile would dance perfectly with the Tom Yum's heat."

She smirked.

As the zest of the Tom Yum lingered on our palates, Kitty seized the moment to transition us to the next culinary chapter. "Next," she announced, "we explore the theme of Migration and Movement with our Migrant Fish Stew."

Kitty served the aromatic stew, explaining, "This dish honors the diverse journeys of migrant communities, blending coastal recipes where each ingredient tells a story." Referencing Ray's (2016) work, she noted how it mirrored the cultural preservation efforts of ethnic restaurateurs.

She detailed the stew's composition: "We start with a Mediterranean base of tomatoes and saffron, layering in locally sourced salmon, cod, and mussels, each chosen to enrich our hearty broth. A splash of white wine heightens the seafood's sweetness, while parsley and cilantro unify the flavors."

Kitty then introduced a complementing drink, "To enhance this experience, I've paired it with a Citrus Cilantro Cooler, a suitable beverage that balances the stew's richness."

After a thoughtful pause, her smile playful, she teased, "Unless, of course, you have a better 'hypothetical' wine pairing in mind, birthday girl?"

"I do actually—but it's not that important. However, if you insist," I replied in one breath, feigning solemnity, "I'd suggest a Sauvignon Blanc. Its crispness would dance quite nicely with the light, aromatic broth of the stew."

The table erupted in gentle laughter.

As we set our spoons down, still savoring the last traces of the sea's bounty, Kitty was quick to introduce a lighter, more ethereal course. "From the depths of the ocean to the earth's surface," she began playfully, "let's explore the concept of Rhizomatic Roots with our Wild Herb and Edible Flower Salad."

I facepalmed. Then groaned. Then facepalmed again.

Unfazed, she served a visually stunning salad, vibrant with colors and textures. "This salad," Kitty explained, "features a mix of wild herbs—each picked for their unique flavors and health benefits—and edible flowers, which add a splash of color."

She drizzled a pomegranate dressing over the salad, the ruby-red droplets glistening like jewels among the greens and petals. "The dressing is a simple trio of pomegranate juice, extra virgin olive oil, and a touch of honey. It's designed to enhance, not overpower, the natural flavors of the herbs and flowers."

Kitty then poured a glass of Lavender Lemonade for each of us, its soothing purple hue promising refreshment. "And to accompany our salad, I've prepared a Lavender Lemonade. The floral notes of lavender echo the subtle complexities of our salad, creating a harmonious blend of flavors and aromas."

Aadhya eyed me, a hint of expectation this time.

"I don't have any grand insights," I confessed solemnly.

Aadhya gave me another sidelong glance.

"Well, if I were to venture a guess, I'd suggest a Rosé," I suggested, playing along with her playful scrutiny. "Its floral notes might just mirror the edible flowers in the salad beautifully. But since we're navigating the 'Rhizomatic Roots,' I must admit, my understanding of such complex layers might not be as deep as the roots themselves," I added, blissfully ignorant and proud.

As we savored our first bites, the herbs' crisp freshness melded beautifully with the dressing's sweet tang, while sips of lemonade soothed and refreshed us between mouthfuls.

Kitty seized the moment to transition to the next course. "With each dish, we add more layers to our evening," she declared, introducing the "Weaving the Web of Society" with our hand-cut Tagliatelle. "This pasta reflects society's complexity and interconnectedness," she explained, serving the perfectly twirled noodles. "Each strand, unique and vital, contributes to the collective strength and beauty."

She detailed the accompanying sauce: "A blend of sun-ripened tomatoes, aromatic basil, and a touch of garlic, enriched with cream and Parmesan to unify the flavors."

Complementing the pasta, she offered Basil Watermelon Juice. "This pairing," Kitty noted, "is crisp and invigorating. The basil resonates with the herbs in the dish, while watermelon adds a refreshing cleanse to the palate."

"This, I do have a suggestion for," I offered, "A Chianti would be ideal—Echoing the principles outlined by Johnson and Robinson (2016), a Chianti, with its noted acidity and body, proves an adept match for creamy pasta dishes, engaging the palate with a balanced attack on richness, much like a well-versed critic through a superficial argument."

As we took our first bites, the flavors of the tagliatelle danced together in perfect harmony, each ingredient enhancing the others. The basil watermelon juice was a bright and refreshing partner to the pasta, cutting through the richness and preparing us for the next course.

And just like that, Kitty was ready to cleanse our palates and refresh our senses with a thoughtful interlude.

"As we transition from our pasta to the depth of our main course," Kitty began, "let us pause and ponder the 'Essence of Equity' with our next dish—a Lemon and Lavender Sorbet." She revealed small, elegant bowls containing the pale, pastel sorbet. "This sorbet," she explained, "is crafted to embody the idea of equity through its balance of flavors. The sharpness of the lemon represents clarity and brightness, cutting through prejudices and preconceptions, while the lavender adds a soothing, gentle touch, promoting peace and empathy."

According to Spence (2017), such a balance in flavors not only pleases the palate but also communicates deeper societal values, reinforcing the role of gastronomy as a medium of expression. Sutton (2010) further elaborates on how sensory experiences with food can articulate and foster understanding of abstract concepts, such as equity in Kitty's narrative. As we took our first spoonfuls, the icy mixture melted on our tongues—the sharp citrus beautifully offset by the subtle, sweet lavender. Refreshed by the sorbet, we were now perfectly primed for the deeper explorations that the remaining courses promised.

With a thoughtful nod towards the theme of the evening, she introduced "Deconstructed Identities" through an innovative culinary creation. "As we delve into the complexities of identity," Kitty began, "I offer you a deconstructed ratatouille. This dish breaks down the traditional components to highlight each ingredient's unique qualities and flavors."

Before us were plates artistically arranged with individually roasted vegetables—zucchini, bell peppers, eggplant, and tomatoes, each enhancing its natural sweetness and texture. "In this deconstruction," Kitty explained, "each element stands alone but contributes to a harmonious whole, mirroring how individual identities are distinct yet integral to the community."

Kitty then served us each a glass of Pinot Noir. "This wine," she noted, "with its complex layers and subtle undertones, pairs beautifully with our dish. It complements the earthiness of the vegetables and the richness of the herbs, celebrating how diversity enriches our communities."

As we enjoyed each bite, the flavors blended perfectly, yet each vegetable retained its unique character. The Pinot Noir mirrored this balance, its delicate notes enhancing the meal without dominating, perfectly aligning with the evening's theme of nuanced identities.

Following the contemplative main course, Kitty introduced the next plate with a gentle pride, "As we reflect on the many layers of our identities, let's transition to a course that explores 'The Complexity of Mothering' through an array of global cheeses paired uniquely with honeycomb," Kitty said, carefully arranging the cheese platters in front of us.

"This assortment," Kitty elaborated, "features cheeses from around the world—each one telling a story of tradition, nurturing, and craft. From the sharpness of aged Cheddar to the creaminess of Brie, and the boldness of Roquefort, we explore how mothering, much like cheese-making, varies culturally but always aims to nourish and enrich life." According to Counihan (1999), just as each cheese reflects its own cultural backstory, so too does each style of mothering reflect its cultural context and the values it transmits.

Kitty pointed to the small chunks of honeycomb accompanying the cheeses. "The honeycomb represents the sweetness and labor of motherhood. Just as bees tirelessly work to create these structures, so too do mothers in shaping the lives of their children."

Blaffer Hrdy (1999) eloquently captures this sentiment, illustrating how maternal efforts are intricately woven into the fabric of our biology and culture, fundamentally structuring human society. I mused over the connection.

Oh, and just as a side note, if curiosity gets the better of you, I'd pair this course with a Port. Its deep richness and subtly sweet undertones are the perfect companions to the bold flavors of our global cheese ensemble.

To complement the cheese course, Kitty served Pear and Sage Juice. "This drink, blending refreshing pear with earthy sage, complements the cheeses' richness and symbolizes how nurturing roles rejuvenate our spirits, much like this juice refreshes your palate."

As discussions on mothering softened, Kitty smoothly transitioned to a lighter note. "In honor of fairness and balance in life, let's enjoy some Sweet Equity," she announced, presenting a variety of miniature desserts, each a tiny marvel of flavor and craftsmanship.

"This sampler," she explained, gesturing to the array of tiny treats on the platter, "includes a variety of desserts from different traditions and cultures, each crafted to ensure that every taste and preference is represented equally. From a decadent chocolate truffle to a zesty lemon tart, and a rich raspberry cheesecake, this course embodies the idea that diversity enhances and sweetens our collective experience."

As we each selected a few miniatures to sample, Kitty poured a vibrant Mixed Berry and Hibiscus Tea. "This tea," she noted, "with its bold berry flavors and a hint of floral hibiscus, is both refreshing and invigorating. It's meant to cleanse the palate and prepare you for the diversity of flavors in our sampler, just as equity prepares society for a richer, more varied existence."

Tasting each miniature dessert was a delightful experience, with the flavors bursting in our mouths, their richness cut by the tangy, sweet tea. "This course," Kitty concluded, "is a reminder that when everyone gets an equal seat at the table, the world becomes a sweeter place."

As the final notes of the pre-dessert discussions faded, Kitty prepared us for the grand finale of the evening with her signature flair.

"Now, let's embrace a touch of delightful disorder," Kitty announced, capturing everyone's attention as she introduced the dessert course. "Prepare for the Anarchy of Flavors with our Chaos Cake, a dessert that defies expectations and breaks all the rules."

She brought out the Chaos Cake, an intriguing combination that appeared as a mishmash of layers and textures. "This cake," Kitty explained, "is a playful medley of different elements—dark chocolate ganache, tangy raspberry coulis, and salted caramel, all enveloped in a light vanilla sponge. Each layer is unexpected yet deliberately planned, representing how even in seeming disarray, there can be a deeper order."

As we each received a slice, the rich aromas mingled in the air. Kitty then served the Espresso Martini Mocktails, a blend that looked every bit as potent as its alcoholic counterpart. "This mocktail," she said, "with its robust espresso base and a hint of vanilla, complements the boldness of the Chaos Cake. It's crafted to energize and invigorate, echoing the cake's spirited anarchy."

"This course," Kitty finally concluded with a satisfied smile, "challenges the norms of traditional desserts and invites us to find pleasure in the unpredictable and the unconventional." Drawing upon Bauman's (2000) exploration of modernity and chaos, she added, "Just as Bauman suggests that out of chaos comes freedom and creativity, this dessert embodies the joy of breaking free from conventional structures to celebrate the beauty of spontaneity and complexity."

As the last bites of the Chaos Cake were savored and the echoes of laughter from our discussions about culinary anarchy began to subside, Kitty smoothly transitioned us to a serene conclusion for our elaborate feast.

"To gently guide us back from the thrilling edge of anarchy, I propose we end our evening with 'Transcending Boundaries,' a flight of herbal infusions," Kitty announced, presenting each of us with a small, elegant tray featuring a selection of delicate glass cups, each steeped with a different herbal tisane.

"This flight," she explained while gracefully pointing to each infusion, "includes a range of herbs from around the world—lavender from France, chamomile from Egypt, mint from Morocco, and rooibos from South Africa. Each herb has been chosen not only for its soothing properties but also for its ability to evoke a sense of place and tradition."

As we sampled each tisane, Kitty shared a brief history of the herbs, intertwining their cultural significances with their botanical characteristics. "These infusions," she continued, "represent how diverse elements can come together to form a more cohesive and harmonious whole. Just as these herbs cross geographical and cultural boundaries, so too can we, in our discussions, our friendships, and our community engagements."

Kitty complemented the herbal flight with her own Aromatic Herb Tisane, skillfully blending individual flavors into a harmonious whole. As she poured the steaming tisane, she said, "This is my own concoction, crafted to unify the diverse infusions into one seamless experience. It represents our collective journey tonight—richly diverse, intricately complex, yet ultimately cohesive in its purpose."

As we sipped the warm, fragrant tea, the room filled with a tranquil ambiance, reflecting the soothing effects of the herbs. This final course was not only a moment of relaxation but also a profound reminder of the evening's exploration of identity, community, and the beautiful complexities of human interaction.

"With this final sip," Kitty reflected, her voice imbued with a quiet intensity, "we transcend more than the boundaries of our individual tastes; we surpass the confines of our own perceptions and spirits. Here's to a world where such transcendence is feasible and fervently celebrated—a toast to the boundless possibilities of understanding and connection."

Epilogue

Alright, I can't just leave you wondering.

For the Pre-Dessert, dubbed "Sweet Equity," if I were pushed for a pairing, I'd lean towards a Moscato d'Asti—its gentle sweetness harmonizes beautifully with a smorgasbord of desserts. Though, truth be told, the Mixed Berry and Hibiscus Tea is quite the revelation on its own.

As for the "Dessert: Anarchy of Flavors," should curiosity prevail, a Ruby Port is your ally. Its rich, vigorous essence embraces the chaotic symphony of flavors within the Chaos Cake like a lost friend.

Here's to another trip around the sun. Cheers to more delightful mayhem and delicious pairings in the year to come.

References

Bauman, Z. (2000). *Liquid modernity*. Polity Press.

Blaffer Hrdy, S. (1999). *Mother nature: A history of mothers, infants, and natural selection*. Pantheon Books.

Butler, J. (1990). *Gender trouble: Feminism and the subversion of identity*. Routledge.

Counihan, C. (1999). *The anthropology of food and body: Gender, meaning, and power*. Routledge.

Deleuze, G., & Guattari, F. (1987). *A thousand plateaus: Capitalism and schizophrenia* (B. Massumi, Trans.). University of Minnesota Press. (Original work published 1980).

Johnson, H., & Robinson, J. (2016). *The world atlas of wine* (8th ed.). Mitchell Beazley.

Mò, X. (2021–2023). *Heaven official's blessing: Tiān guān cì fú* (Vol. 1–8). Seven Seas Entertainment.

Ray, K. (2016). *The ethnic restaurateur*. Bloomsbury.

Spence, C. (2017). *Gastrophysics: The new science of eating*. Penguin Books.

Sutton, D. E. (2010). *Food and the senses*. University of California Press.

ABOUT THE AUTHORS

Editors

T. Jameson Brewer, Ph.D. is an associate professor of social foundations of education at the University of North Georgia. His teaching experience spans from the middle school, high school, undergraduate, master's, and doctoral levels. Broadly conceptualized, his research focuses on the impact of privatization of public education by way of school vouchers, charter schools, alternative teacher certification, and homeschooling. Additionally, he researches the impacts of Christian nationalism on public schools and democracy. Find more at www.tjamesonbrewer.com

Cleveland Hayes, Ph.D. is the Associate Dean of Academic Affairs, and professor of Education Foundations in the Urban Teacher Education Department at the School of Education at Indiana University-Indianapolis. Dr. Hayes teaches elementary foundations of education, elementary science methods, Critical Race Theory, and qualitative research methods. Dr. Hayes considers himself an interdisciplinary researcher. He is on the executive board of the American Education Studies Association (AESA) and the Vice President of Division G–Social Context of Education for the American Education Research Association.

Contributors

Dr. Andrea Arce-Trigatti holds a Ph.D. in Education from the University of Tennessee, Knoxville. As an interdisciplinary scholar, her research centers on program evaluation, faculty development, education policy, and critical thinking and collaborative learning strategies as applied to various contexts, including engineering education and higher administration. She is a founding member of the award-winning Renaissance Foundry Research Group and has helped to develop and investigate pedagogical techniques utilized to enhance critical and creative thinking at interdisciplinary interfaces.

Brandon Beck is a doctoral candidate at Clemson University in the Teaching and Learning program. As an educator, historian, and qualitative researcher, he focuses on Black education history, social studies education, and critical social theory. His research employs qualitative methods and oral histories to examine Black education and challenge historical norms related to school desegregation. Beck aims to archive and promote Black experiences to advance the field of Social Studies Education.

Dr. Maria José Botelho is Professor of Language, Literacy, & Culture at the University of Massachusetts Amherst. Dr. Botelho's research centers on critical multicultural analysis of children's literature; critical literacies and multiliteracies pedagogies; and ethnographic/critical literacy practices as professional learning. Her current book project puts to work ethnographic/critical literacies practices to help educators reimagine K-8 literacy teaching. Dr. Botelho teaches courses on critical literacies, ethnography, writing for publication, children's and young adult literature, and preK-16 literacies.

Dr. Kala Burrell-Craft is an Associate Professor in the School of Education, Social Sciences, and the Arts at the University of Maryland Eastern Shore where she serves in the Educational Leadership program. Dr. Burrell-Craft uses critical theories to research topics related to identity development, educational spaces (urban and rural), antiracist teacher preparation, and social justice.

Dr. Madina Djuraeva is a transnational multilingual scholar from Bukhara, Uzbekistan. An Assistant Professor at the University of Nebraska at Omaha, her current teaching and research interests include translingual voices, global competence, service learning, and peace in the multilingual learner and teacher education. She has published in the Applied Linguistics journal, International Journal of Bilingual Education and Bilingualism, and World Englishes.

R. Jamaal Downey is a dad, son, brother, social commentator, and the passionate cook for his family of seven. His personal story and academic interests converge around identity; language, ideology and consciousness; pedagogy, and epistemology. Dr. Downey is currently an Assistant Research Scientist in engineering and studies Whiteness.

Mia Furman is an undergraduate majoring in Economics. After graduating from Cookeville High School at 16, she continued her education, currently studying in the College of Business at Tennessee Tech University. She has completed courses in environmental economics, macroeconomics, microeconomics, and statistics. Her research interests include food policy and technology and food economics. She plans to study Food Technology at Wroclaw School of Agriculture.

Grace Poon Ghaffari, Ph.D. is a motherscholar practitioner, daughter of Chinese immigrants, and embodied healer. Currently, she is an Assistant Professor of Counselor Education at San Jose State University. Rooted in de/colonial and abolitionist ways of being, Grace's research and praxis explores healing and harm among student survivors of sexual and relationship violence, as interconnected and shaped by systems of oppression.

Dr. Anissa Guerin is a native of Hammond, Louisiana. She earned her Doctor of Philosophy degree in Educational Leadership and Research with a concentration in Higher Education Administration from Louisiana State University. As an Assistant Professor and Doctoral Program Coordinator at Texas A&M University-Commerce, her research centers on minority women and girls in STEM, diversity and equity issues in higher education, and the mental well-being of Black women leaders in academia.

Andrea M. Hawkman, Ph.D. is a queer motherscholar and Associate Professor of Social Studies Education at Rowan University. She teaches undergraduate and graduate courses in social studies education, diversity in education, and educational foundations. A former high school social studies teacher, Hawkman's research focuses on Whiteness and queer studies in education, critical media studies, and social studies teacher education. She enjoys camping, baking, and listening to music with her family.

Joshua Hunter, Ph.D. is an Associate Professor at the University of North Dakota where he teaches courses in qualitative research methods and ethnography and directs the Outdoor Leadership and Environmental Education program. His outdoor life, research, and writing spans a wide variety of topics and experiences in outdoor, place-based, and nature-based learning, ranging from wilderness experiences and environmental interpretation to early childhood nature-based play. He is co-creator of Gro.UND Learning Gardens with his partner, Cheryl Hunter, on the campus of UND. These days he spends much of his time outside with students, building and sharing the gardens with others and thinking about apple trees.

Cheryl Hunter, Ph.D. is a field-based education researcher and Professor at the University of North Dakota. She teaches courses in qualitative methods and design, curriculum and instruction, gender, education and the environment, and experiential education in nonformal education settings. She approaches field-based education research as inherently community based, participatory, action oriented, and working for social justice. She co-created the Gro.UND learning garden project with her partner, Josh Hunter.

Travon Jefferson is a doctoral student in the Curriculum, In- struction, and Teacher Education program at Michigan State University. His research currently centers implementation and impact of Black Education Studies in teacher preparation and urban teacher development and identity.

Laura Jewett, Ph.D. is Professor of Curriculum Theory and Curriculum Studies at The University of Texas Rio Grande Valley. She earned a Ph.D. in Curriculum Studies from Louisiana State University. Research interests focus on the triptych of consciousness, culture, and curriculum and ethnographic desire in qualitative research.

Angela Kraemer-Holland, EdD, is an Assistant Professor of Curriculum and Instruction at Kansas State University. As a former Chicago high school teacher and teacher educator with a background in Curriculum Studies, Angela draws inspiration from these professional experiences to inform her lines of critical qualitative inquiry that explore neoliberalism in education, teacher socialization and subjectivity, and education policy-as-discourse.

Bonnie Samantha Maldonado (she/ella series) is a Doctoral Candidate in Africana Studies at the University of Pennsylvania. Her research seeks to understand how food and food making practices offer glimpses into understanding Blackness, gender, sexuality, embodiment, worldmaking, and freedom in the Dominican Republic and diaspora. Bonnie interrogates how Black Dominicans use food as object, embodied knowledge, and epistemology to care for one another transnationally and transtemporally.

Dr. Ferial Pearson is a Kenyan Indian queer disabled Muslim immigrant, an Associate Professor at the University of Nebraska at Omaha, and a multiple national award-winning educator for 24 years who has taught at the high school and university level. She and her teenage students founded the globally recognized Secret Kindness Agents Project. Her research interests include peace, justice, and kindness education, as well as intersectionality in critical, trauma-informed, and culturally sustainable pedagogies.

Kekailoa Perry (Dad), JD is an Associate Professor of Educational Foundations at the University of Hawaiʻi at Mānoa, College of Education. He is an imu practitioner, activist, and scholar. Kekailoa teaches courses in Hawaiian Studies, Educational Foundations, Indigenous Refusal, and Guerrilla Intellectualism. ʻOhana Perry is a family of authors collaborating on the chapter.

Keri Perry (Mom), MBA is a Ph.D. student at the University of Hawaiʻi at Mānoa College of Education. She has over 27 years of experience in the financial industry and has been working over the past five years at education institutions focused on Indigenous education. Her main hobbies involve cooking and feeding her ʻohana. ʻOhana Perry is a family of authors collaborating on the chapter.

Makualiʻi Perry (Son), BA is a graduate of the University of Hawaiʻi and educator at Loko Ea fishpond. Makualiʻi continues the family tradition of imu cooking and currently develops culture- and land-based curriculum for all levels of education (preschool through college) centering on the restoration of the Loko Ea traditional Hawaiian fishpond on the island of O'ahu. 'Ohana Perry is a family of authors collaborating on the chapter.

Brianne Pitts, Ph.D. is a former elementary school teacher who teaches social studies methods and coordinates the elementary education program at Western Michigan University. Brianne's research centers K-12 Black history education, critical literacies, Whiteness in education, and generational traumas. Her 13 years of classroom experience strengthens her commitment to student-centered, liberatory instruction, and her belief we must do this work together.

Marial Quezada is earning her Doctorate in Curriculum and Instruction at the University of Texas at Austin, focusing on Cultural Studies in Education and Indigenous Studies. She also serves as the Tānko Institute Director for the Indigenous Cultures Institute, coordinating their teacher education program and youth program. As a doctoral student, she teaches undergraduate students that are becoming educators, like herself. She practices, studies, and writes about relational pedagogies, including land-based and community-centered learning and teaching.

Dasmen Richards is a Ph.D. candidate in the K-12 Educational Administration and Leadership program at Michigan State University. Her research centers Black girls and Black girlhoods to spark the imaginative possibilities of educational spaces.

Kristin Robair is a native of New Orleans, Louisiana. Ms. Robair received a Bachelor of Arts Degree in English Education and Mass Communication from Southeastern Louisiana University, a Master of Public Administration Degree from Southern University and A&M College, an Education Specialist Degree from Louisiana State University, and is currently a doctoral candidate in Educational Leadership and Research with a concentration in Higher Education Administration from Louisiana State University. In East Baton Rouge Public School System, Ms. Robair is a District Literacy Coordinator and an adjunct instructor at Southern University A&M College. Her research interests are literacy (adolescent and interdisciplinary, public policy, pop culture), urban education, student learning and development, and college and career preparation and mentoring.

Dr. Sandra Rodríguez-Arroyo is a Professor of ESL/Bilingual Education teacher education at the *University of Nebraska at Omaha.* Her teaching and research interests include preparing teachers to work with multilingual learners (MLs), translanguaging perspectives, asset-based service-learning experiences with diverse learners and families, faculty mentoring, recruitment and retention of BIPOC teachers, and Latina faculty testimonios.

Dr. Dennis L. Rudnick, an Assistant Professor of Education at Metropolitan State University of Denver, has over 25 years' experience as an educator, researcher, administrator, facilitator, program developer, consultant, and public speaker on multicultural, civil rights, and social justice issues. Dr. Rudnick's research focuses on the relationships among identity, ideology, socialization, knowledge construction, and their impacts on white anti-oppressive teacher identity development. He is the editor of *Resisting Divide-and-Conquer Strategies in Education: Pathways and Possibilities.*

Dr. Sarah B. Shear is an Associate Professor of Social Studies and Multicultural Education at the University of Washington-Bothell. Her award-winning scholarship examines settler colonialism in K-12 social studies curriculum, teacher education, popular media, and qualitative research methods. As a member of the Turtle Island Social Studies Collective, Dr. Shear is committed to collective action to combat oppression in education. She enjoys baking and taking road trips with her two fur kids, Nico and Odin.

Dorota Silber-Furman, Ph.D. is an Assistant Professor in the College of Education at Tennessee Tech University (TTU). She is a member of the National Association for Multicultural Education and a board member of its Tennessee chapter. Dorota graduated from the University of Wroclaw with a Bachelor of Arts in Romance Languages. She also earned a Bachelor of Science in Multidisciplinary Studies, and a Master's Degree in Curriculum and Instruction. She holds a Doctor of Philosophy in Education degree from TTU.

Mark Stern, Ph.D. is an Associate Professor in the Department of Educational Studies and Academic Director of the Office of Undergraduate Studies Scholars Program at Colgate University. His work has focused on the political and cultural economies of contemporary American society. His basement always has at least three fermentation experiments, sometimes more.

Dr. Jovan T. Thomas is a native of Thibodaux, Louisiana. Dr. Thomas received a Bachelor of Science degree in Public Health from Dillard University, a Master of Social Work degree from Southern University New Orleans, an Education Specialist degree from Louisiana State University, and he earned his Doctor of Philosophy degree in Educational Leadership and Research with a concentration in Higher Education Administration from Louisiana State University. At Southern University and A&M College, Dr. Thomas is the Interim Dean for University College and an adjunct instructor. Dr. Thomas's research interest are student access and achievement, equity and diversity, student learning and development, and mentoring.

Grace Tukurah was born and raised in North Central Nigeria and is currently a Ph.D. candidate in Science Education and Education Policy at Michigan State University. She enjoys spending time with her family and enjoys spending time outdoors, especially when the weather is warm. When she is not researching science knowledge produced by Black girls and women, she is likely cooking, taking care of her plants, or enjoying a movie.

Dr. Laura Walls received her Ph.D. in applied linguistics from UCLA. She is an associate professor at the University of Nebraska at Omaha where she teaches courses in Spanish as a heritage language, composition, bilingualism, and sociolinguistics. Her scholarship focuses on heritage language acquisition and pedagogy. Other research interests include sociolinguistics, experiential learning, discourse analysis, and language ideologies.

Mila Zhu, Ph.D. is an Assistant Professor and EDUC Program Coordinator at Southeastern Oklahoma State University, where she also serves as the Founding Director of the Center for Asian Resources and Intercultural Studies. Dr. Zhu's research interests span curriculum theorizing, philosophical foundations, and teacher education. Currently, she has a particular focus on Esports and Ludology in education.

INDEX